Entrepreneurship and Openness

INDUSTRIAL DYNAMICS, ENTREPRENEURSHIP AND INNOVATION

This series aims to discover important new insights in the relationship between the three cornerstones of economic development: industrial dynamics, entrepreneurship and innovation. In particular, the series will focus on the critical linkages between these three foundations. For example, the entry and exit of firms with differentiated growth processes can influence industrial development, but at the same time can also reflect the current industrial context shaping the entrepreneurial activities of single firms or individuals. A similar interaction linking industrial dynamics to entrepreneurship and innovation can also be identified. For instance, the particular technological regimes of industries may influence innovative activities, but the technological trajectory and type of innovative activity can, in turn, have a positive or negative influence on industry development. Innovation and entrepreneurship are also closely linked, since many types of entrepreneurial activities are barely distinguishable from similar innovative endeavors. Hence, the series addresses the linkages among the three fields in order to gain new findings concerning the nature of economic change. Theoretical, empirical as well as policy-oriented contributions are welcome.

Titles in the series include:

Innovation in Low-Tech Firms and Industries
Edited by Hartmut Hirsch-Kreinsen and David Jacobsen

Entrepreneurship and Openness
Theory and Evidence
Edited by David B. Audretsch, Robert E. Litan and Robert J. Strom

Entrepreneurship and Openness

Theory and Evidence

Edited by

David B. Audretsch

Max Planck Institute of Economics, Jena, Germany and Indiana University, USA

Robert E. Litan

Ewing Marion Kauffman Foundation and Brookings Institution, USA

and

Robert J. Strom

Ewing Marion Kauffman Foundation, USA

INDUSTRIAL DYNAMICS, ENTREPRENEURSHIP AND INNOVATION

Edward Elgar

Cheltenham, UK • Northampton, MA, USA

Published by
Edward Elgar Publishing Limited
The Lypiatts
15 Lansdown Road
Cheltenham
Glos GL50 2JA
UK

Edward Elgar Publishing, Inc.
William Pratt House
9 Dewey Court
Northampton
Massachusetts 01060
USA

A catalogue record for this book
is available from the British Library

Library of Congress Control Number 2009921526

ISBN 978 1 84720 779 1

Printed and bound by MPG Books Group, UK

KAUFFMAN

The Foundation of Entrepreneurship

The Ewing Marion Kauffman Foundation is a private nonpartisan foundation that works to harness the power of entrepreneurship and innovation to grow economies and improve human welfare. Through its research and other initiatives, the Kauffman Foundation works to prepare students to be innovators, entrepreneurs and skilled workers in the 21st century economy through initiatives designed to improve learning in math, engineering, science and technology. Founded by late entrepreneur and philanthropist Ewing Marion Kauffman, the Foundation is based in Kansas, City, Mo. More information is available at www.kauffman.org

MAX-PLANCK-GESELLSCHAFT

The Max Planck Institute of Economics conducts research on a broad set of problems relating to change in modern economies, including experimental economics and entrepreneurial studies. Located in Jena, Germany, the Institute is part of the Max Planck Society for the Advancement of Science, Germany's largest research organization. The Max Planck Society employs some 4,200 researchers in some 80 Institutes in both the sciences and the humanities. Information about the Max Planck Institute of Economics is available at www.econ.mpg.de

Contents

Contributors

David B. Audretsch, Ameritech Chair of Economic Development; Director, Institute for Development Strategies, Indiana University; Director, Entrepreneurship, Growth and Public Policy Group, Max Planck Institute of Economics (Germany); Research Fellow, Centre for Economic Policy Research (London); Senior Fellow, Kauffman Foundation

David Audretsch's research focuses on the links between entrepreneurship, government policy, innovation, economic development and globalization. His research has been published in over 100 scholarly articles in the leading academic journals and he has published 30 books. He is the co-founder and co-editor of *Small Business Economics: An International Journal*. He is the recipient of the 2001 International Award for Entrepreneurship and Small Business Research by the Swedish Foundation for Small Business Research.

William J. Baumol, New York University, Harold Price Professor of Entrepreneurship, Academic Director, Berkley Center for Entrepreneurial Studies in the Stern School of Business; Senior Economist, Professor of Economics Emeritus, Princeton University

William Baumol is the past president of the American Economic Association, the Association of Environmental and Resource Economists, the Eastern Economic Association and the Atlantic Economic Society. His honors and awards include 11 honorary degrees and many memberships. William Baumol is the author of more than 35 books and over 500 articles published in professional journals. He has written extensively about labor market and other economic factors that affect the economy. Among his better-known contributions are the theory of contestable markets, the Baumol–Tobin model of transactions demand for money and Baumol's cost disease, which discusses the rising costs associated with service industries.

Amar Bhidé, Glaubinger Professor of Business, Columbia University

Amar Bhidé has been studying entrepreneurship for about twenty years. He is a member of the Center on Capitalism and Society and spearheaded the launch of its eponymous journal, *Capitalism and Society* (published by the Berkeley Electronic Press) which he now edits (with Professor Edmund Phelps). He is also a member of the Council on Foreign Relations and a

Fellow of the Royal Society of Arts (RSA). Bhidé has several publications in the areas of entrepreneurship, strategy, contracting and firm governance; these include eight *Harvard Business Review* articles, papers on corporate governance in the *Journal of Financial Economics* and the *Journal of Applied Corporate Finance* and numerous articles in the *Wall Street Journal*, *The New York Times* and *The LA Times*.

Michael R. Darby, NBER; University of California, Los Angeles; American Enterprise Institute

Michael Darby currently serves as the Warren C. Cordner Professor of Money and Financial Markets at UCLA Anderson School of Management and in the Department of Economics at the University of California, Los Angeles, and as Director of the John M. Olin Center for Policy at UCLA Anderson. Concurrently he holds appointments as Chairman of The Dumbarton Group, Research Associate with the National Bureau of Economic Research and Adjunct Scholar with the American Enterprise Institute. Darby is the author of eleven books and monographs and numerous other professional publications. He and Lynne Zucker are currently publishing on productivity in basic science and its commercialization with a special focus on nanotechnology.

Edward L. Glaeser, Fred and Eleanor Glimp Professor of Economics, Harvard University; NBER

Edward Glaeser is the Director of the Taubman Center for State and Local Government and Director of the Rappaport Institute of Greater Boston. He teaches urban and social economics and microeconomic theory. He has published dozens of papers on cities, economic growth, and law and economics. In particular, his work has focused on the determinants of city growth and the role of cities as centers of idea transmission.

Robert E. Litan, Vice President, Research and Policy, Ewing Marion Kauffman Foundation and Senior Fellow, Economic Studies, Brookings Institution

Robert Litan has authored or co-authored over 20 books, edited another 14, and authored or co-authored over 200 articles in journals, magazines and newspapers on a broad range of public policy issues. He has lectured in banking law, consulted, and testified as an expert witness in a variety of legal and regulatory proceedings involving domestic (banking, antitrust) and international (primarily trade) issues. He has also consulted for the Department of Justice on antitrust matters and co-authored two Congressionally-mandated studies for the Treasury Department; in 1998–99 he was the main author of the Report of the President's Commission to Study Capital Budgeting.

Catherine L. Mann, Professor of International Economics and Finance, Brandeis University, Senior Fellow, Peterson Institute for International Economics

Catherine L. Mann's current work focuses on the economic and policy issues of global information, communications and technology, particularly with reference to the US economy, the labor market and international trade. She is author or co-author of two books that focus on the policy foundations for effective use of technology for domestic development and external competitiveness. She also studies broader issues of US trade, the sustainability of the current account and the exchange value of the dollar.

Edmund Phelps, Department of Economics, Columbia University

Edmund Phelps is the winner of the 2006 Nobel Prize in Economics. He is the McVickar Professor of Political Economy at Columbia University and the Director of Columbia's Center on Capitalism and Society. Phelps is known for showing how low inflation today leads to expectations of low inflation in the future, thereby influencing future policy decision making by corporate and government leaders. He also pioneered the analysis of the importance of human capital, or workers themselves, for the diffusion of new technology and growth in the business and corporate world.

Robert J. Strom, Director, Entrepreneurship, Research and Policy Kauffman Foundation

Robert Strom is a past president of the National Association of Economic Educators and Vice President of the National Council on Economic Education. He has published and lectured extensively in economics and entrepreneurship. He is a co-editor, with William Baumol and Eytan Sheshinski, of *Entrepreneurship, Innovation, and the Growth Mechanism of the Free-Enterprise Economies*, Princeton University Press, 2007. His work at the Kauffman Foundation includes support for funded research on questions of importance to entrepreneurship.

Gylfi Zoega, Professor, Department of Economics, University of Iceland

Gylfi Zoega is a Professor of Economics at the University of Iceland and a part-time Professor at Birkbeck College, University of London. He graduated from Columbia University in 1993 and worked as lecturer, senior lecturer and reader at Birkbeck College. In 2003, he became a Professor at the University of Iceland, and in 2006, a part-time Professor at Birkbeck College. Zoega's work falls within macroeconomics and labor economics. Within macroeconomics he has published papers on economic growth, in particular the relationship between natural resource abundance, institutions and growth, as well as unemployment theory. In labor economics, he has focused on human capital theory and issues having to do with hiring and firing, as well as wage setting in an intertemporal context.

Lynne G. Zucker, University of California, Los Angeles
Lynne Zucker is Professor of Sociology and Public Policy and Director of the Center for International Science, Technology, and Cultural Policy at the School of Public Affairs at the University of California, Los Angeles. She is also a Research Associate at the National Bureau of Economic Research and a Fellow at the California Council on Science and Technology. Her training is in organizational sociology, institutional theory, economic sociology and social psychology. Zucker's current research, being done in collaboration with Michael Darby, is on basic science and high-technology industries, particularly those using nanotechnology and/or biotechnology. Her current major interests are on the processes and impact of knowledge transmission from basic science to commercial use, especially their impact on the economic performance of firms, on the creation of new organizational populations (some of which become new industries), and on productivity growth.

Introduction

David B. Audretsch, Robert E. Litan and Robert J. Strom

The single most important measure of an economy's success over the long run is its record on growth, for it is only through the production of more goods and services with a given labor force that residents will be able to enjoy continued improvements in their standard of living. Rapid growth, in turn, requires not only high rates of saving and investment, but most importantly, continued innovation: new products and services, and new ways and methods of producing and delivering them.

But inventions alone do not generate innovation. Only when inventions are commercialized – bought by willing buyers – are they diffused throughout an entire economy, thereby raising output. Entrepreneurs, those who launch new enterprises, have proven to be vital to this commercialization process, at least in the United States. Whereas existing firms with well-established products and customer bases may concentrate on incremental improvements of what they already offer, entrepreneurs who have no stake in the status quo may be willing to take bigger risks with untested, or even 'radical' ideas. It should not be surprising, therefore, that some of the more important 'radical' inventions of the past two centuries have been brought to the marketplace by one or more entrepreneurs rather than by existing firms. Prominent examples include the telegraph, telephone, radio and television; railroads, airplanes and automobiles; computers and the software that runs on them; and air conditioning (Baumol, 2002).

Entrepreneurial activity can thrive, however, only in 'open' settings in which consumers and firms are free to transact with one another. Without such freedom, few would rationally take the risk of launching an enterprise that can only succeed by persuading customers to freely enter into new transactions by purchasing new goods or services, or if the entrepreneur is selling something that is already found in the marketplace, to switch from existing suppliers to a new one. By the same reasoning, the more customers who have the ability to make these choices, the greater the potential rewards that entrepreneurial success can bring, which in turn should encourage more entrepreneurial risk taking. Openness and entrepreneurship, therefore, should be mutually self-reinforcing.

In fact, economies around the world have become much more open in the post-World War II era. Governments have lowered or erased legal barriers to trade and the movement of capital and people, both within and across national boundaries. Continued advances in communications and transportation also have sharply reduced the costs of search and transacting. Not coincidentally, living standards for billions of people, in developed and less-developed economies alike, have risen dramatically.

The rapid changes that openness has facilitated also can be threatening. Firms that are not equipped to respond to shifts in customer tastes or to adopt new modes of production, and workers who have difficulty adapting to new job requirements, can find themselves worse off in the highly competitive environment of an open economy. Some may be displaced for lengthy periods of time. Many who promptly find alternative lines of business to pursue or jobs to take may take a cut in income. Others who are not immediately affected by the competition may still fear the worst. For all of these individuals, openness is likely to be viewed more as a curse than a blessing.

Through most of the post-World War II period, in much of the world, the beneficiaries of growth and change, including those who have expected to benefit, have outnumbered or have exerted more political influence then those who have been hurt or feared a loss in economic position. How else can one explain the successive multilateral trade agreements that have lowered the barriers to commerce between countries?

But attitudes toward openness – especially to flows of goods, services and people across national borders – have been shifting in recent years. The chaos of the anti-globalization demonstrations of the late 1990s and the early 2000s may have receded, but significant segments of developed country populations have become anxious about the perceived threat to their jobs and wages posed by the willingness of able workers in less-developed countries to work for much lower wages. So far, this anxiety has made governments more hesitant to pursue new trade agreements. Whether it will induce governments also to backtrack from earlier deals and/or encourage them to regulate domestic economic activity in ways that slow the pace of change within their countries remains to be seen.

Given this apparent shift in attitudes toward openness, the Kauffman Foundation and the Max Planck Institute believed it appropriate to bring together a group of leading scholars in July 2007 to reconsider various ways in which openness is connected to entrepreneurship, innovation and economic growth. This volume contains the papers presented at this conference.

To be sure, the skeptics thus far have focused their critiques on 'external' openness – or the ease of transacting with parties from other countries. For this reason, the next three chapters following this introduction concentrate on the linkages between this type of openness and entrepreneurship. Less noticed, but potentially just as important, is the linkage between 'internal' openness – that is, culture or the ease of transacting and/or moving within countries – and entrepreneurial activity. The last three chapters of this volume focus on these aspects of openness and entrepreneurship. Taken together, the various chapters paint a complex, though clearly positive, portrait of the ways in which open economies lead to more entrepreneurial activity, which augments growth.

The positive relationship between growth in international trade and economic growth has been well established. Over the past two centuries, world economic output (GDP) has increased by a factor of 40, while the share of exports in world GDP – a measure of the importance of trade – has multiplied by a factor of 13. Together, these two statistics imply that world trade has increased in volume during the past two centuries by 54 000 per cent!

In Chapter 1, William Baumol of New York University explores how entrepreneurship has been critical to the growth of trade, and why it will continue to be important in the years ahead. We have just noted in this introduction the contribution of entrepreneurs toward the continued innovations in transportation and communications that are very much responsible for the growth of trade. To these innovations Baumol adds another, less obvious but no less important advance: the introduction and now widespread use of the giant shipping container, which has dramatically lowered the costs of moving items between and within countries. He further highlights the role that trade and the entrepreneurs who made it possible played in the economic development of the Netherlands, a tiny country without natural resources but which nonetheless enjoyed the most rapid growth in Europe and indeed the world over a span of four hundred years, from roughly the year 1400 to the year 1820.

It is not only goods and services that cross national boundaries and thereby enhance economic welfare, but also technology. Baumol notes the transformative impact that the importation of railroad technology from Great Britain had on the United States in the 18th century. More recently, he observes that while the United States and Japan currently each account for about 30 per cent of the world's patents, even these shares are so small that both countries must continue to import advanced technologies developed elsewhere in order to remain economic leaders.

Yet as we have just noted, trade creates losers as well as winners, especially when skills and technologies exist in many countries to make or deliver the same products. Baumol argues that in such a circumstance, workers in these countries compete with one another, and thus low wages in one location can exert downward pressure on wages in other, richer societies.

More broadly and controversially, however, Baumol further argues that the outsourcing of some production from high-income to low-income countries can raise productivity and wages in low-income countries and thereby cause the price of other products they export (and which are not beneficiaries of outsourcing) to rise. This price increase may result in greater consumer costs than the consumer benefits from the outsourcing. As Baumol sums it up:

> It still will *usually* remain true that trade will yield benefits to both trading countries, and that the country with the enhanced productivity will increase its gains from trade. But the law of comparative advantage, itself, *says nothing about how the total gains from trade will be shared between the countries at issue* (emphasis added).

Entrepreneurship, however, offers a way out of this dilemma. Open trade has been opposed throughout much of US history, in part, out of a fear of 'cheap foreign labor'. The United States nonetheless has profited from its dealings with the rest of the world by continuing to innovate, thus producing unique products that are desired at home and elsewhere in the world. Given the central role that entrepreneurs have played in this innovation process, Baumol argues that entrepreneurs are key to ensuring that open trade in the future translates into gains rather than pains for the United States.

Given the linkages between entrepreneurs and the global economy, it is natural to ask how innovations (many of them commercialized by entrepreneurs) diffuse throughout the global economy. In Chapter 2, Catherine Mann of Brandeis University and the Petersen Institute for International Economics uses data on venture-backed deals in the information technology (IT) sector to examine how the US venture capital industry itself is globalizing.

Mann begins by briefly summarizing the two classic discussions of the innovation cycle, the 1967 product cycle model developed by Raymond Vernon and the 1976 paradigm of foreign direct investment developed by John H. Dunning. Vernon posited that rich countries, with the most sophisticated tastes, drive innovation. Once new products are introduced in these economies, they are standardized and exported, and eventually manufactured abroad in lower-wage economies and shipped back to the originating country. Vernon did not focus on ownership links between firms in home and foreign economies. In Dunning's paradigm, firms weigh three factors when deciding to produce abroad: the benefits of the foreign location (such as lower wage costs, transportation costs and communications facilities), the firm's own advantages, and the relative costs and benefits of various forms of contracting out (such as through licensing). Dunning originally analyzed patterns of innovation between firms in the home country and foreign economies.

Mann offers her 'globalization of venture capital model' as a synthesis of the Vernon and Dunning models. In particular, in Mann's model, venture funds an innovative product, whether produced at home or abroad. The conventional wisdom has been that venture firms require geographic proximity to the companies they invest in and thus invest only close to home. That venture is going global may reflect either or both of two considerations: the opening of once-closed foreign markets to foreign direct investment, or greater demand abroad for venture financing.

For insight on what may be driving the globalization of venture finance, Mann uses a database compiled by Thomson Financial on venture-backed deals by US venture firms in IT from 1980 to 2005. Mann focuses on IT because of rapid innovation in that sector and the high share of IT in venture capital investment over the past two decades.

First, how important are foreign firms as portfolio investments for venture firms? In absolute dollars, such investments peaked in 2000 at $13 billion, and since then have fallen back to roughly $3 billion annually.

Second, what countries do venture firms seem especially interested in? The top two destinations have been the United Kingdom and Canada, both developed economies. Only three of the top fifteen destination countries can be characterized as low-wage economies: Brazil, China and India. This broad geographical pattern is inconsistent with the view that venture firms investing abroad seek out portfolio companies that have the advantage of lower wages, either at the start-up stage or in later rounds of financing. However, when Mann disaggregates the data by type of IT company, she finds that venture financing of portfolio firms in China in particular has been concentrated in the hardware segment, which is consistent with the low-wage thesis.

Third, Mann investigates the extent to which patterns of demand have affected foreign direct investment by venture firms. In particular, she notes that whereas demand in industrial countries has been strong for the past decade in all segments of the IT sector – software, IT services, hardware and communications – spending in developing countries on IT has been much greater on IT hardware and communications than software. Might this have influenced the type of foreign firms in which venture firms have invested? Mann presents data that is consistent with this 'demand pull' hypothesis.

Fourth, Mann notes that venture firm investments in U.S. IT companies has followed a predictable pattern, initially concentrating on operating systems and specialized tools controlling the 'inside' of the computer, and then moving to support effective use of the computer through more innovative applications software. Mann doesn't find this pattern being replicated in venture investments in foreign portfolio companies. There the investment has remained concentrated on operating systems and specialized tools, but has not gravitated toward business applications. Mann suggests a reason: that applications in foreign markets require localized knowledge that is not well suited for financing by US-based venture firms. The exception is venture investment in foreign firms specializing in entertainment, gaming and scientific software, where the markets are more global.

Finally, Mann reports that venture firms have been moving away from financing start-ups in India and China, and instead concentrating on acquisitions and firms engaged in later-stage development. Foreign start-up investment is concentrated on more developed economies – Sweden, Israel and the United Kingdom, in particular.

Whereas Baumol examines whether 'offshoring' helps or hurts the economies of firms engaging in the practice and Mann looks to the foreign activities of US-based venture firms, Amar Bhidé of Columbia Business School in Chapter 3 examines why venture-backed U.S. firms have engaged in offshoring – outsourcing some of their functions to foreign firms. His findings are based on surveys of roughly 100 chief executive officers of such venture-backed companies.

Bhidé reports that the firms in his survey used offshoring only to a limited extent. They generally were reluctant to develop their core products or services in far-off locations, even if labor costs there were much lower than at home. Other factors which limited offshoring included the firms' managerial inexperience in such matters, the limited supply of capable workers in offshore sites coupled with the strong demand for them from larger companies engaged in offshoring, difficulties in communications across multiple time zones (despite the Internet) and cultural differences.

Nonetheless, among those venture-backed entrepreneurs who engaged in some kind of offshoring, why did they do it? Some of Bhidé's interviewees suggested that they had 'no choice' – because no domestic supplier of a critical input or component was available, or because the idea or product behind their business initially was developed abroad. Others who offshored by choice cited the advantage that overseas sourcing provided because their founding team had experience with such practices, or because they were encouraged to do so by their investors. Although the general impression is that firms offshore because of cost, the respondents to Bhidé's survey offered more nuanced explanations: costs did matter for some, but others stressed that offshoring enabled them to circumvent tight local labor markets or speed their product development.

One function that most venture capital (VC)-backed companies had not offshored was research and development, at least thus far. The respondents cited the need to keep their R&D staff close to home and thus close to customers. Some companies reported that it was difficult to partition R&D activities, with some pursued on-shore, others at a distant location. Others who kept their R&D functions at home also pointed to cultural differences that would pose coordination and management problems if all or a portion of their research and development were offshored.

Respondents singled out the development of cutting-edge software, which typically requires small groups of highly motivated, highly skilled programmers. Given the high stakes involved, companies deciding not to offshore software development reported that the relatively small savings in labor costs weren't worth the benefits of finding and using such talented individuals at home. The CEO respondents were more comfortable, however, offshoring more routine functions, such as data entry and call centers and some routine manufacturing activities, a finding that accords with popular perceptions about offshoring.

Another factor that mitigated the desire of CEOs to offshore was a concern that valuable intellectual property could leak abroad, to the long-run detriment of their companies. This concern was voiced more strongly about China than about India, however. A related concern about offshoring was the weak enforceability of contracts in foreign locales, again especially with respect to activities in China.

Bhidé devotes special attention to attitudes toward offshoring of CEOs of companies engaged in the development of pharmaceuticals and medical devices. Here, too, the popular perception is that such companies want to offshore clinical trials to low-wage countries to save on testing costs. But the pharmaceuticals developers in Bhidé's survey were more circumspect. Some reported concern that the large 'contract research organizations' (CROs) that engaged in such testing would not give sufficient attention to start-up companies. Others reported that patients for testing were more available in Europe, not in low-income countries such as India. Manufacturers of medical devices, however, had more favorable attitudes toward offshoring, but only for clinical trials and not for other R&D functions.

Bhidé concludes by contrasting the responses of the VC-backed companies with much larger enterprises, those on the Fortune 100. The larger companies were more active in offshoring, and Bhidé offers several reasons for this. Large companies have more financial resources, more experienced global managers and greater experience conducting business abroad than the start-ups. Also, larger companies have more routine activities that are suitable for offshoring.

As we suggested at the outset of this chapter, the ultimate aim for all economies is rapid growth, which in turn is driven by continued innovation or what some economists call 'dynamism'. But what determines dynamism, and is openness one of those driving forces? What role, if any, do national culture and values play in a country's record for innovation? Edmund Phelps and Gylfi Zoega address these questions in Chapter 4.

The authors begin by suggesting that measures of job satisfaction are better indicators of dynamism than one traditional measure, labor productivity. Individuals who are happy with their jobs are likely to be employed in endeavors that are mentally stimulating and creative, which are factors essential for innovation. What, therefore, can explain job satisfaction or overall happiness?

Economists often presume that happiness is highly correlated with income. Yet time series survey evidence does not support such a linkage: levels of reported happiness do not appear to rise over time, despite rising incomes. Phelps and Zoega conduct a different test: to see whether a positive relationship exists between the two variables on a cross-sectional basis, using job satisfaction responses in 2000 from the *World Values Survey* for 22 OECD countries. In fact, they find that happiness and per capita GDP are positively related, and in statistically significant fashion, but only up to a per capita GDP level of 70 per cent of the US level. Beyond that point, they find that reported happiness and GDP per capita are not statistically linked.

Phelps and Zoega use the same cross-sectional data to document that several other variables are positively related to reported happiness: an index of economic freedom (measuring among other things, the cost of establishing and closing a business, public spending and taxes), external openness (the ratio of the sum of imports and exports to GDP) and average hours of work. The trade variable, in particular, suggests a positive relationship between openness and the authors' measure of dynamism (reported happiness). A series of other variables, such as the unemployment rate and inflation, are not statistically significant.

The authors postulate that culture and values are important determinants of each of the variables found to be related to happiness, drawing on earlier work of Phelps, who found cultural characteristics to explain recent European economic performance (unemployment, labor force participation and productivity growth). To test this proposition, the authors again look to the responses to various questions in the *World Values Survey* as proxies for culture and values. These responses display marked differences between the English-speaking countries of the OECD and the Continental

European countries. In the former group, people report greater emphasis on achieving on the job, showing initiative, having an interesting job and having a favorable view of competition than in the latter countries. The Nordic countries fall in between the English-speaking and Continental countries in their views on competition. Japanese respondents place greater emphasis on job security than those in other countries, but otherwise the Japanese are similar to Continental Europeans on all other dimensions. The authors also consider questions and responses that measure the degree of trust people have for one another (a measure of social capital), attitudes toward the government's civil service and the strength of people's religious views.

Do these cultural variables help explain any of the happiness-related variables the authors previously identify? Broadly speaking, the answer is yes. Trust positively affects GDP per capita. Confidence in the civil service is positively related to GDP per capita, economic freedom and openness to trade. Good work ethics are positively related to economic freedom and hours of work, but negatively related to openness. And work initiative is positively related to openness. The authors do not indicate, however, which way the causation runs in their statistical work: that is, it is not clear whether culture affects the various happiness-related variables, or whether the variables drive culture.

In sum, Phelps and Zoega demonstrate that it is not just income that generates happiness, and thus presumably innovation and dynamism. Other variables, including measures of economic freedom and openness, as well as culture, all appear to play an important role. Furthermore, there are clear differences in culture between English-speaking countries, on the one hand, and Continental European countries, on the other – and these differences seem to help explain differences in economic performance between the two.

The chapters up to this point are concerned with the role that openness plays in the economic performance of entire countries, at one extreme, or in the performance of entrepreneurial firms, at the other. Chapter 5, authored by Edward Glaeser of Harvard University, turns the spotlight on the forces that influence the economic performance of particular regions or cities, paying particular attention to the role of entrepreneurship.

Glaeser measures entrepreneurship by two admittedly less than ideal indicators – the self-employment rate and average firm size. He reports considerable variation in the self-employment rate across all these groups, although there is less variation across metropolitan areas than across industries or income groups. Notably, all but eight of the metro areas for which Glaeser reports data have self-employment rates that lie between 3.2 per cent and 7.8 per cent, a relatively narrow range. Interestingly,

Silicon Valley has one of the lowest self-employment rates of any of the metro areas, while cities in Florida rank at the top (rankings which should highlight the limitations of the self-employment rate as a measure of entrepreneurship).

Glaeser posits that average firm size should be inversely correlated with entrepreneurship: the smaller this average, presumably the more entrepreneurial firms there must be within any grouping. In addition, Glaeser reports significant negative correlations between average firm size and the self-employment rate, which helps confirm the usefulness of average firm size as an indicator of entrepreneurial activity.

Are either or both of these measures of entrepreneurship related to measures of metropolitan growth, such as employment growth by industry sector? Glaeser reports statistical evidence of such a linkage, finding that both entrepreneurship measures predict future employment growth. He then posits four possible variables that may drive local entrepreneurial activity: educational levels; the impact of being surrounded by other entrepreneurs or an 'entrepreneurial culture'; the availability of key inputs (proxied by local area venture capital, the number of firms capable of supplying local firms in a given industry and the concentration of employees in occupations useful to particular local industries); and measures of local customer demand. What does the available statistical evidence say about these alternative hypotheses?

Glaeser reports the results of regressions using both of his measures of entrepreneurship, together with a third entrepreneurship variable, the birth rate of new firms. He confirms that more highly educated individuals are more likely to be entrepreneurs, but this variable only explains a small share (7 per cent) of the variance in self-employment rates across metro areas. Self-employment rates are also correlated with age. Another set of regressions suggests a modest linkage between city size and entrepreneurial activity, but little connection between venture capital and self-employment. Glaeser's regressions relating to the importance of local entrepreneurial culture are mixed: self-employment rates increase among individuals living in metropolitan areas with higher concentrations of 'entrepreneurial industries', but this effect does not hold within industrial sectors.

Glaeser confirms that the presence of an appropriate workforce – individuals in occupations fitting the industrial mix – has an important effect on entrepreneurship, when it is measured by firm birth rates. He finds no such linkage, however, when entrepreneurship is measured by the self-employment rate. However, the self-employment rate is positively linked with a measure of local area input suppliers. None of the regressions show any relationship between the various entrepreneurship indicators and indicators of local customer demand.

Glaeser concludes by cautioning that his statistical work is only suggestive of the importance of entrepreneurship to metro area growth and the factors that seem to drive entrepreneurship at the local level. The most powerful results indicate that labor supply – in particular, educated workers – drive entrepreneurship. Local areas that wish to have entrepreneurial growth should focus, therefore, on basic policies that can attract and retain such individuals.

While college-educated people seem to be essential for any region's economic success, are any other factors relevant? In the final chapter of the volume, Lynne Zucker and Michael Darby of UCLA suggest that one such additional, important determinant is the presence of individuals they call 'star scientists' – individuals who not only excel at scientific research but also have demonstrated entrepreneurial skills.

Zucker and Darby begin their analysis by drawing upon previous scholarship demonstrating that basic science developed at universities has been key to the successful commercialization of scientific discoveries. This occurs through the entrepreneurial endeavors of the professors themselves, through the licensing of inventions developed by university faculty to established companies, and through the employment of 'star scientists' by commercial enterprises. In short, of the three channels by which university inventions find their way to the marketplace, the mobility of the discovering scientist accounts for two (through entrepreneurship or employment).

To gain further understanding of the career paths and importance of these star scientists, the authors have constructed a database of 5400 such individuals around the world who were reported by their peers to be the most highly cited scientists in their fields. This database draws on information from the Institute for Scientific Information (ISI), which among other things, contains citations of scientists' published work in professional journals. Zucker and Darby report numerous findings from this database in their chapter, several of which we highlight here.

First, while the involvement of a star scientist with a firm has not been a sufficient condition to make that firm commercially successful, it seems to dramatically increase the likelihood of that success. For example, of 38 publicly traded pharmaceutical companies in business as of 1975, 15 had established working relationships with star scientists by 1990, and of these, 80 per cent had survived by 1999. In contrast, only 17 per cent of the other 23 firms, which had no such relationships, were still in business in 1999.

Second, the authors use their database to investigate whether and to what extent star scientists have been important to the entry of firms in different regions throughout the United States and in countries around the world in six specific technology-related sectors (nanotechnology is excluded from the analysis here, but will be the subject of future study, after the authors complete a database specific to this field). The authors' findings are clear: regions or countries with more star scientists in these particular industry sectors exhibit significantly more firm entry. This conclusion holds both for locations within the United States and for 24 other countries outside the United States.

The authors also report a significant amount of immigration of star scientists through the last year of their data, 2004, into the United States, the United Kingdom and Germany. Furthermore, so-called 'round-trip' immigration –a star scientist moves to a country for at least two years then later leaves – accounts for anywhere from one-third to nearly 80 per cent of all star scientists who were ever resident in six key developing countries.

The lesson for policy makers from the authors' database is thus clear: an important key to promoting entrepreneurial growth in technology-related fields is to find ways of attracting and retaining scientific superstars. This requires, in turn, an 'open' labor market, one in which people are mobile within and across countries.

In sum, the papers in this volume suggest a positive relationship between various indicators of 'openness' and entrepreneurship. Openness to competition, domestic and international, seems to facilitate growth and innovation. In a world of open labor markets, in particular, entrepreneurship is most likely to be stimulated by policies that can attract individuals most likely to be successful entrepreneurs – individuals with skills, especially those with strong scientific backgrounds.

A clear lesson from the research reported here, therefore, is that entrepreneurial success requires the right people – both the entrepreneurs and skilled individuals who want to work for them. The more freedom these individuals have to interact with each other, and with their suppliers and customers, the more successful their entrepreneurial endeavors are likely to be. Greater entrepreneurial success, in turn, should lead to faster growth, a central goal of all economies.

REFERENCE

Baumol, William J. (2002), *The Free Market Innovation Machine*. Princeton, NJ: Princeton University Press.

1. Entrepreneurship, trade competition and the explosion of world trade

William J. Baumol

> Without the entrepreneur, knowledge [contributed by the inventor or scientist] might possibly have lain dormant in the memory of one or two persons, or in the pages of literature (J.-B. Say, 1807, 1836, p. 81).

As we are all well aware, recent efforts – however incompetent – to enhance freedom of trade have been a source of marked controversy. One of the main fears they raise is that elimination or even weakening of restrictions will cut into employment opportunities and depress earnings in the economically advanced countries. And it should be clear that if these fears are well grounded, the entrepreneur is high on the list of those imperiled.

Although I take an intermediate position on these matters, believing neither that enhanced trading is *sure* to shower benefits upon the wealthier countries nor that it is likely to inhibit prosperity and growth, that is not my main subject here. All I wish to draw from the preceding observations is that, although its specifics are under dispute, there is obviously a relationship between the volume and degree of freedom of trade and the reward of the entrepreneurs and the incentive for their activities. But, even more, I want to emphasize the other side of the matter: that the volume of trade and the ease with which it is carried out is a function of the degree of exercise of entrepreneurship. Here the story should be obvious, once it is recounted, but it is patently of critical importance both for policy and for understanding of the workings of the world economy.

Basically, my contention here is not only that entrepreneurship affects trade conditions and the quantities exchanged, but that the accomplishments of the entrepreneurs have contributed an expansion of international exchange far greater than can plausibly be expected from the results of any multinational conference dedicated to the reduction of trade barriers. On the other hand, to the extent that trade and dissemination of technology enhance the competition faced by the the wealthier nations and threaten to reduce their gains from trade, the role of entrepreneurship becomes a more urgent matter, serving as an effective way to protect the interests of those nations while also offering benefits to their trading partners.

THE PHENOMENAL EXPANSION OF TRADE IN THE PAST TWO CENTURIES

We are all well aware that the past two centuries have brought to the world's prosperous economies a phenomenal growth in per-capita incomes and a remarkable growth in world GDP in general. But the growth in the volume of international trade puts even those achievements in the shade. Let me quote from a paragraph that I have written elsewhere:

> [T]he share of exports in world GDP has risen more than thirteen-fold in the last two hundred years (Maddison, 1995, p. 38). Considering how rapidly GDP itself has increased over this period, we can conclude that the absolute value of exports has exploded. Angus Maddison estimates (in constant 1990 dollars) that world GDP [has undergone] a 40-fold increase [between 1820 and 1992] – while the value of exports was $7 billion in 1820 and $3,786 in 1992 (a 541-fold increase) (Baumol, Blinder and Wolff, 2003, p. 87).

It hardly needs to be said that this extraordinary (54,000 per cent) increase can be ascribed, above everything else, to the revolutions in transportation and communications technology. From the steamship to the airplane, from the undersea cable to the internet, innovation has caused an explosion in the speed and volume of exchange of output among countries, and an implosion in its costs. To avoid further belaboring of the obvious, let me turn to an insufficiently publicized example that shows that such improvements are still very much under way: this is the case of what is called the 'box' – that is, the giant shipping container, which was effectively introduced in the late 1950s and standardized in dimensions and other features in the mid-1960s.

GROWTH IN TRADE AND THE ENTREPRENEUR'S CONTRIBUTION

Note that the 'box' needed no inventor. Rather, it was arguably the entrepreneur whose alertness pointed out its usefulness in freight transportation. The box was promoted by entrepreneur Morris Forgash, 'who finally got regular intercontinental container service under way' after 1960, and by entrepreneur Malcom McLean, who outraced potential competitors in adopting these containers for the transatlantic trade, soon after (Levinson, 2006, p. 101 ff).

The shipping container brought prosperity to a number of formerly backwater ports and undermined the demand for the services of others. It drastically cut transport expenses, particularly of loading and unloading. 'In 1961, before the container was in international use, ocean freight costs alone accounted for 12 percent of the value of U.S. exports'. [But today], 'it is better to assume that moving goods is essentially costless than to assume that moving goods is an important component of the production process'. '[T]he container not only lowered freight bills, it saved time . . . [and] made it practical for companies . . . to develop just-in-time manufacturing' (Levinson, 2006, p. 8 and chapter 14, with portions quoted by the author from elsewhere and order of the material modified).

It is clear that the entrepreneur played an indispensable role in this process of innovation and stimulation of growth. Even where the entrepreneurs themselves did little that can be labeled 'invention', they played a vital role in ensuring that the great inventions that underlay the explosion of trade did not languish – were not 'many a flower born to blush unseen' – as J.-B. Say recognized two centuries ago. But the 'rules of the game' have changed, and the occupations of the entrepreneurs who have been most successful and most widely publicized have entailed some element of innovation.

Here, it should be emphasized that the term 'innovation' has come to mean much more than just invention itself. It is now taken in the economic literature to connote the entire process, including invention, improvement and development, bringing to market and ensuring utilization. And, accordingly, the innovative entrepreneur's tasks include not only alertness in spotting a promising invention, but in finding new markets for it and disseminating it to those markets. The key point is that one of the main forces that has caused the volume of trade to outpace by far the growth of world gross domestic product (GWP) is not the process of invention itself, but the dissemination of improved technology, particularly transport and communication technology. And that is surely one of the arenas in which the entrepreneur plays the leading role – alertness to opportunities for profitable technology transfer.

That, in turn, reduces the magnitude of the dissimilarities in the productive capacities of different countries, meaning that trade evolves from the exchange of very different products to direct competition in the production of similar products, for example, automobiles. There is much more to the story, but whatever the importance of what remains to be told, the arena I have just described should not be overlooked because it is of prime importance for both entrepreneurship and growth.

THE ENTREPRENEUR'S ROLE IN THE PROCESS

To describe the scenario, we must take note of four aspects: 1) the finding of new markets as a form of innovation; 2) the contribution to the general welfare of quick and pervasive technology transfer; 3) the consequences of increased profusion of transfer for the structure of trade; and 4) the consequences of easier and more frequent transfer for welfare in the country of origin, its labor force and its entrepreneurs.

Appropriately, the literature does emphatically recognize as innovative and entrepreneurial any alertness to the opportunity offered by finding a new market for a product already extant. Discovery of a new market is innovative in itself because it entails a new use for the product, just as finding that a product such as aspirin not only relieves headache, but also helps to reduce the risk of cardiac problems.

ILLUSTRATION: THE WEALTH MIRACLE OF THE NETHERLANDS

A particularly striking example of the place of the entrepreneurs, how their activity was encouraged and what they contributed to trade, is provided by the history of the Dutch Republic, beginning in the fourteenth century but reaching its apex in the sixteenth century revolt of the Netherlands against the overlordship of imperial Spain and the 80-year war that followed. Two quotations sum up the extraordinary accomplishment:

> [N]o one understood how such a magnificent fortune, record prosperity and unexpected power could fall to such a small and, in a sense, brand-new country (Fernand Braudel).

From 1400 to 1700, Dutch per capita income growth was the fastest in Europe [and the world], and from 1600 to the 1820's its level was the highest (Angus Maddison) (as quoted in van Nieuwkerk, 2005, pp. 35, 41).

Thus this country, so insignificant in size, led the world economy for four centuries. Moreover, when the Dutch economy lost its leadership toward the end of the eighteenth century, it hardly declined into poverty but has since remained, rather, toward the head of the queue of prosperous nations. Important here is the fact that the prosperity of the Netherlands was built largely on its role in international trade, as a carrier, a financier and an innovator. And the story entails a sequence of paradoxes: each entails the role of the inventors and the entrepreneurs. And the inventions were abundant. Obviously, they included methods of canal construction and construction of dykes. They also designed ships better adapted to the needs of trade and waters such as the Baltic, but went on to create trading posts in places as far and exotic as New Amsterdam (New York). They also designed new architectural forms that were imitated in parts of England and in New England (by the Pilgrims who came to North America after a ten-year stay in the Netherlands). But, perhaps above all, there were the financial inventions, notably the invention of the Central Bank in the Amsterdam Exchange Bank early in the seventeenth century (1635) that was then followed by the Bank of Sweden and the Bank of England in mid-century. Alexander Hamilton's Bank of New York was not established for about one and a half centuries after that, and the US Federal Reserve System well over a century later.

At least three apparently catastrophic historical phenomena can be deemed to have contributed substantially to the overall Dutch accomplishment. The first was the pervasive threat of flooding, which culminated in the massive breakthrough of the seas on 1 November 1170, when the 200 square mile Zuider Zee was formed, terrifyingly, in a single day. One significant result was the undermining of grain cultivation and the reduction in the agricultural labor force, which was driven to migrate to the towns. At a time when the urban population of Europe was perhaps 10 per cent, that of the Netherlands was closer to 50 per cent. In the country as a whole, such emergencies led to cooperative activity in the construction of flood control barriers and associated projects, thereby making the population customarily accept steps designed to internalize the threatening externalities of processes such as peat harvesting that could open the way to incursion of the sea. The move to the towns also led to expanded handicraft and primitive manufacturing activities, bringing with them the need and incentives for entrepreneurial activity. It also introduced freedom of thought and conscience, with the towns in the middle ages serving as oases of freedom, including freedom from serfdom. This freedom too, as we will see, arguably played an important role in Dutch prosperity.

Another set of events that contributed entrepreneurial talent was the Spanish capture of Brussels and Antwerp. Rather than a calamity, this turned out to be an economic blessing. The Dutch thereafter succeeded in cutting Antwerp off from the Baltic for two centuries, thereby protecting the trading position of Amsterdam and encouraging enterprising foreign trade. More than that, it brought an exodus of enterprising Calvinist refugees fleeing from Spanish oppression, who joined others, such as the Jews who had fled from Spain, in bolstering Amsterdam's entrepreneurial activity.

This is, of course a story repeated many times in history, from Louis

XIV's expulsion of the Huguenots from France, to Hitler's expulsion of the Jews and the exodus of members of the middle class from Castro's Cuba.

Yet another pertinent phenomenon was continued Dutch trade with Spain during its war of independence. As we know, at least until the Napoleonic Wars, trading with the enemy was considered treasonous and blockade of shipping to enemy territory was common practice. But during the war of independence from Spain, the Dutch sold grain, as well as muskets, to the enemy, and even built ships for Spain to replace those that had been destroyed by Dutch naval power (van Nieuwkerk 2005, pp.64–5). This provided wealth to the entrepreneurs of the Netherlands, and arguably helped in achieving the country's ultimate victory, as Spanish payments for the imports contributed to the eight bankruptcies of Philip II and made it impossible for him to pay what he owed to his armies, leading to revolt by the troops.

The net result was expansion of world trade under the leadership of Dutch entrepreneurs, a process that was soon followed by rivals, notably the British.

THE ROLE OF TECHNOLOGY TRANSFER

Transfer of technology often leads to improvement of the product, as when the US imported railroad locomotive technology from Britain. Within one year, the Americans had produced a locomotive with power three times as great as the British champion locomotive and, soon after, the US contributed greatly superior rail design. Thus, recognition of the opportunities for such transfer, and execution of the task, is indisputably one of the innovative actions regularly carried out by innovating enterprises.

Technology transfer is also important for every country because, to keep up with shifts in the world production frontier, every country must take advantage of the gains offered by technology transfer. Even the world's two most profuse patenters – the United States and Japan – each produce less than 30 per cent of the world's patents annually, meaning that each must import the right to use foreign technology that probably entails some 70 per cent of the world's new patents. Such technology transfer, particularly if it entails exchange of one another's intellectual property, ensures that every producing country's products are not bedeviled by a high proportion of obsolete components. If Hewlett-Packard's research and development yields a more powerful memory, while Sony's R&D department comes up with a more reliable internet connection, then technology transfer ensures that the buyers of the product of either firm are not handicapped with either an obsolete memory or an inferior path to the internet. So, in principle, technology transfer – like other innovative acts – potentially serves the general welfare and can serve it substantially.

The improvements in transportation and communication technology have also profoundly changed the composition of the items exchanged in international trade. It used to be true that the preponderant share of items exchanged was dictated by nature and other sources of happenstance. Bananas and coffee were exported by tropical countries and imported by France, the United Kingdom, the United States and other more northerly nations, while iron and steel went in the opposite direction.

BUT WHO GAINS AND WHO MAY LOSE, IF ANYONE?[1]

But as the time and money needed for exchange among nations declined sharply, such fortuitously assigned forms of specialization declined in importance, and it became possible for countries to become profitable producers of items they formerly received primarily via import. The watches and cell phones produced in China and the computer programming and telephone answering services supplied by India are only particularly striking and publicized examples. And the change makes a big difference, particularly for the countries whose intellectual property is undergoing dissemination.

When the forces of nature dictate Central American specialization in the export of bananas and coffee, the effects on Americans engaged in production are minimal, because little of either commodity is produced in mainland US. But when a programmer in India carries out a task similar to what is offered in Silicon Valley, the California job, or at least its wage level, is threatened. The set of traded goods have in effect been transformed from complements into substitutes.

It follows that there are both benefits and costs to US workers: on the one side, American workers are offered products whose price is significantly reduced by the lower-paid foreign producers of the commodities. But, at the same time, American wages, if not American jobs, are put under pressure. And even if, as some observers contend, these effects are *de minimis*, there is another side to this and another potential source of damage to the welfare of the United States. The following hypothetical example describes a before and after scenario – pre-outsourcing and post-outsourcing between two imaginary countries. Let us them the US and India (see Table 1.1).

Initially, the US produces all the world's software and cell phones because Indian productivity in these items is so low that even at its low $6 per hour wage, its prices of those items – $6 and $3 – are higher than those of the US ($4 and $2), so India can only export its inexpensive cottons.

Table 1.1 Hypothetical illustration: outsourcing and share of trade gains

Product	Country	BEFORE OUTSOURCING		AFTER OUTSOURCING	
		Output/ hour 1	Price 1 = Wage/Output	Output/ hour 2	Price 2 = Wage/Output
Cottons	US	**2**	**12**	**2**	**12**
	India	**6**	1	**6**	**1.33***
Software	US	**6**	**4**	**6**	**4**
	India	1	6	**2***	**4***
Cell Phones	US	**12**	**2**	**12**	**2**
	India	**2**	3	**2**	**4***
Wage	US		**24**		**24**
Wage	India		6		**8***

Notes:
Bold = Unchanged Data
Not bold = Changed data, before
Bold with asterisk = changed data, after

But then India increases its productivity in software sufficiently to meet the US $4 price, despite the accompanying rise in Indian wages. Competition for skilled labor then grows and drives up skilled wages throughout India. Now both countries produce software which at least is no more expensive than before for Americans to buy. But with the rise in Indian wages from $6 to $8, Americans find it more expensive to purchase Indian cottons, whose price has gone up from $1 to $1.33, and this is an inevitable cost to the US, making the US poorer in real terms.

It is to be noticed that harm comes to the US consumer not via the commodity, software that India begins to export to the US for the first time. For the price of software remains unchanged or may even be driven lower by the entry of India into that market. Rather, US consumers are harmed by the rise in price of the conventional import, the cottons, that results from the wage rate in India. A little contemplation of the story will confirm that this is the way the logic of the matter must always proceed and it is not a curious consequence of the numbers selected for illustrative purposes. And the conclusion is that even if there is no loss of US jobs or downward pressure on US wages as a result of India's entry into the software trade, the US may be harmed by this outsourcing process. With consumers in the US facing no increase in cost in software, but a higher cost of cottons – that is, facing a lower cost of a new import and a higher cost of a continuing import – the welfare effects can go either way.

The moral of all this is that an increase in the productivity of one or more commodities by a trading partner does not guarantee that the home country will benefit. It still will *usually* remain true that trade will yield benefits to both trading countries, and that the country with the enhanced productivity will increase its gain from trade. But the law of comparative advantage, itself, says nothing about how the total gains from trade will be shared between the countries at issue. Moreover, comparative advantage certainly does not assert that all participating countries will always be better off when there is a rise in the total benefit generated by trade.

A MORE ELEMENTARY EXAMPLE: GAINS FROM TRADE WIPED OUT BY INCREASED PRODUCTIVITY

We can even provide a simpler example showing a more extreme possibility: that a rise in a trading partner's productivity can actually reduce and even eliminate the total gains from trade, as shown in Table 1.2. We see here that India's gain in VCR productivity from 100 to 150 changes India's comparative advantage. As Ricardo showed, and is generally recognized, there are gains from trade only if one of the two trading partners has a *relative* productivity advantage in one of the commodities traded. Here, before the Indian productivity advance, the US productivity ratio in VCRs relative to hats was 200/100 = 2, while that of India was only 100/75 = 4/3, meaning that the US had a clear relative advantage in VCR production. But after India's advance the ratio for the US is unchanged while that of India rises 150/75 = 2, that is, its *comparative* performance has caught up to the US and neither country any longer has a *relative* advantage in the production of either commodity, and the gains offered by trade in this two-good world will have vanished altogether. The obvious paradox is that India will have lost its comparative advantage via a gain in its productivity.

The other side of the matter is that increased trade often returns the favor, so to speak, by increasing opportunity and enhancing real earnings in the home country of the entrepreneur who transfers intellectual property to others. But sometimes it can transpire that this reciprocating consequence

Table 1.2 Productivity (labor output/day) by country and commodity

	United States	India Before	India After
Hats	100	75	75
VCRs	200	100	150

is no favor, and this is something that does require consideration in policy design.[2]

ENTREPRENEURSHIP AND PROTECTION OF THE INTERESTS OF THE TECHNOLOGY OUTSOURCING COUNTRY

I will end by simply asserting that, where such consequences are indeed unfavorable, it is once more the entrepreneur who offers the way out. Thus, competition with cheap foreign labor is nothing new for the United States. But the US has managed to retain its economic leadership position nevertheless, by means of the efforts of its innovators – including its entrepreneurs – who, by offering the world and their own consumers an unending stream of improved products and process, have managed to keep us ahead of the game. And this way of dealing with the problem, happily, is one in which the US has done well by doing good. For it is through the stream of innovation that living standards throughout much of the world have been able to rise so spectacularly in the past few centuries.

The bottom line of all this is that the entrepreneur is deeply involved in the process of trade expansion. The relationship goes both ways. The entrepreneur has played and continues to play a critical role in the enormous explosion of world trade. Without the contribution of the entrepreneur, the subject under discussion might well be a very minor affair. More important from the standpoint of current affairs and currently heated political issues, it is the entrepreneurs and their contribution to innovation that hold the promise of ensuring that the productivity gains of India and China do not become transformed into pains for the US.

NOTES

1. Much of the remainder of this chapter is based on joint work with Ralph Gomory. See, in particular, Gomory and Baumol (2000).
2. The preceding discussion is based on a more recent variant of the analysis in Gomory and Baumol (2000).

REFERENCES

Baumol, William J., Alan S. Blinder, and Edward N. Wolff (2003) *Downsizing in America: Reality, Causes, and Consequences.* New York, NY: Russell Sage Foundation.

Gomory, Ralph E. and W.J. Baumol (2000) *Global Trade and Conflicting National Interests*. Cambridge, Mass.: MIT Press.
Levinson, Marc (2006) *The Box: How the Shipping Container Made the World Smaller and the World Economy Bigger*. Princeton, NJ: Princeton University Press.
Maddison, Angus (1995) *Monitoring the World Economy, 1820–1992*. Paris: Organisation for Economic Co-operation and Development, Development Center.
Say, Jean-Baptiste (1807, 1836) *A Treatise on Political Economy*. Philadelphia, PA: Claxton, Remsen and Haffelfinger.
Van Nieuwkerk, Marius (2005) *Dutch Golden Glory,* Haarlem: Becht.

2. Globalization of venture capital: a Vernon-Dunning synthesis with deal-by-deal data on information technology

Catherine L. Mann

INTRODUCTION

This chapter uses data on individual venture capital (VC) deals to information technology firms to take a detailed look at the globalization of venture capital. The framework for analysis draws on two classic models of product innovation and globalization – Vernon's product cycle of innovation and globalization and Dunning's OLI framework for global ownership and production. The information technology sector is the target of analysis both because the pace of innovation is quite rapid, and because the globalization of production and demand is well advanced. Therefore, evidence on the global production–innovation–ownership nexus may be observed over the relatively short time span of the available data.

There is significant evidence of a product–innovation cycle in the nature of what venture capital finances in its own home market in the United States. Considering deal-by-deal data on software, US VCs invest in young US firms that are engaged in innovative and cutting-edge software applications that are demanded by firms overall in the US economy. For 'older' more commoditized software, there is some evidence of globalized production with US VCs financing foreign firms, although in general these are not start-up firms.

When venture capital goes abroad, there is strong evidence of a foreign innovation–ownership pattern. US venture capital invests in young foreign firms where demand patterns point to fastest market growth, and concentrate on investing in firms in host economies when there appears to be specific niche skills. There is little to no evidence that US venture firms are attracted to start-up activities in perceived low-wage economies such as India and China.

ECONOMIC AND BUSINESS MODELS OF INNOVATION, GLOBAL PRODUCTION AND OWNERSHIP

Why do firms innovate and what underlies their strategy to produce and invest abroad? Economic and business models for such global decisions by the firm draw on two related literatures: Raymond Vernon's classic 1966 product-cycle model (1966) and John H. Dunning's 1976 'eclectic' paradigm of foreign direct investment.[1] Globalization of venture capital synthesizes these two models.

In Vernon's original article on the product cycle, advanced, richer countries with more sophisticated tastes elicit innovative products. As the home market for the product expands, the production process becomes standardized and may exhibit economies of scale. Once production and product are standardized, the driving force under profit maximization is cost minimization. Thus, the product cycle interacts with the global economy as standardized production moves to cheaper locations abroad. The product cycle is complete when foreign firms export back to the originating country the standardized and now cheaper product. Vernon's model did not focus on ownership relations between firms in the home and foreign economies.

In Dunning's eclectic paradigm, a firm considers three factors when making the decision to produce abroad. It considers the advantages of the foreign location (including for example product and transportation costs, local demand and the business environment). It considers its own advantages (including for example technology or management expertise) that will allow it to prosper even when located distant from the home market and subject to competition in the host market. Finally, it weighs advantages and disadvantages of ownership versus forms of contracting out (for example, licensing). Dunning did not originally discuss patterns of innovation between headquarters and foreign firms.

Since Vernon's and Dunning's initial presentations, many related issues have been explored in economic models, empirical analysis, business case studies and management strategies. Some of these ideas include a richer analysis of the supply side of production. For example, how do production characteristics, including fragmentation of the production process, commoditization of parts and network economies (including scale and scope) affect the timing and degree of completeness of the globalized production cycle (Feenstra and Rose, 2000; Clements and Ohashi, 2005)? On the demand side, how do consumer characteristics such as attitudes toward brands, quality and heterogeneity of tastes affect the basic Vernon and Dunning business decision (Windrum, 2005)?

Country characteristics or endowments factor into these newer generation product cycle models: skills, costs, resources and governance (including intellectual property) either speed up or slow down the pace of the product-cycle evolution of globalized production and directly impact the importance of whether to own or contract-out (Bhaduri and Ray, 2004).

Firm characteristics also are important to the Vernon–Dunning choices. How relevant are management issues, labor contracts and Coase-type issues, for example, attitudes toward keeping production within or allowing it outside the boundaries of the firm – which intersects with intellectual property and governance issues, for example (Antras, 2005; Schilli and Dai, 2006).

Many of these characteristics are considered in static models, but of course they are time-varying concerns as well. Which market (home or abroad) is growing faster? Technological change as parameterized in the pace of obsolescence, adoption and fragmentation, also will affect the product-cycle model and eclectic FDI paradigm conclusions (Benarroch and Gaisford, 2002; Deltas and Zacharias, 2006; Balakrishnan and Cheng, 2007; Cutler and Ozawa, 2007).

Globalization of venture capital links Vernon and Dunning by incorporating both innovation and foreign production. Venture capital 'takes a bet' on an innovative product. When venture capital raised at home goes abroad, it concludes that the return to net location advantages (host advantages balanced against distance) plus the unique attributes of the foreign firm (the innovative idea) can only be maximized by taking an ownership stake in the foreign firm.

Some theories of venture capital suggest that close proximity between investor and recipient firm is important for tacit knowledge transfer and explicit business assistance from the VC to the young firm. Tacit knowledge may include experience with successful entrepreneurship. Explicit business assistance may include management, marketing, financial and legal advice. So venture capital going global could mean a weakening of the need for proximity. Or is it that the nature of the relationships between the VC and the young firm are changing such that a greater percentage of VC goes to later stage deals where both tacit and explicit transfers are less important? On the other hand, VC going global may reflect the opening-up of markets heretofore closed. Foreign demands, growing and different from those at home, are two additional reasons for venture capital to go abroad.

This chapter does not reach a definitive conclusion about the relative importance of the various factors engaging global venture capital. But the deal-by-deal database offers some intriguing impressions.

THE DATABASE

The data used for this analysis originates with the Thomson VenturExpert™ database on individual deals between venture capital firms (VCs) and recipient companies (so-called portfolio firms – PFs). The key aspect of the VenturExpert™ data is its international coverage. Thomson compiles information from public sources in the United States, Europe, Asia and Latin America. As neither PFs nor VCs are required by law to divulge transactions, the database may not span the universe of deals. But since both VCs and PFs use such announcements of extension and receipt of funds as a signal to the financial and technology markets of current or impending success, there are incentives to divulge at least some aspects of a deal.[2] The raw downloads from the VenturExpert™ database require a substantial amount of careful handwork to eliminate coding errors, duplication and other inconsistencies.[3]

Our resulting database contains details on venture capital deals for information and communications technology products and services extended by US VCs to foreign PFs. We also have more aggregated data for VC deals to US PFs. The database includes data from 1980 to 2005; the international coverage improves substantially in the mid-1990s. The coverage and classification system is as follows.

All High-Level Groups

We downloaded and compiled data on total value and number of deals between US VCs and US PFs and between US VCs and all foreign PFs in the following 'high-level groups':

- Information technology
- Biotechnology
- Consumer-related
- Industrial/energy
- Medical/health
- Other products.

These relatively more aggregated data are used to evaluate the importance of information technology relative to other technologies or other sectors for US VC firms and the importance of aggregate international exposure for the information technology group.

ICT Products and Services

The so-called (see Table 2.A1) Sub-Group 2 of High-Level Group Information Technology includes information and communications technology products and services, for which we compiled aggregate data on total value and number of deals between US VCs and US PFs, and detailed data by country, company and stage of deal between US VCs and foreign PFs. Data in the following categories are included:

- Communications and media
- Computer hardware
- Computer software
- Internet-specific
- Semiconductor/electronics.

Within each of these categories, there are so-called ‘Sub-Group 3’ categories and further disaggregations, as shown in Table 2.A1. For example, Sub-Group 3 ‘computer services’ includes the more detailed category ‘data-processing, analysis, and input services’.

Information on International Relationships

Because we are principally interested in the international characteristics of VC deals with foreign PFs, we have substantially more detail on foreign PFs than on US PFs. At the level of the individual deal, our database offers information for the international relationships as follows:

- Country and name of US venture capital firm
- Country, name, start date, and detailed activity of foreign portfolio firm
- Details on the deal, including number of VCs involved, dollars extended by ‘stage’ and ‘round’ of finance (startup, seed, early, later expansion, buyout/acquisition).

Table 2.1 gives examples of the detail for three deals within the Sub-Group 2 of ‘Computer Software’.

BIG PICTURE

Why Focus on Information Technology (IT)

When examining venture capital (VC) flows to portfolio firms (PF), why focus on the Information Technology sector? First, the pace of innovation has been quite rapid, so the prospect for observing an innovation-based product-cycle model is greater for this sector (Mann, 2006, chapter 2).

Table 2.1 Example of database detail

Year	Nation	Company Name	Number of firms involved in deal with each company	Total inv. in company by US funds	Fund name	Stage Level Round 1 (also shown for subsequent rounds	Company industry sub-group 2	Company industry sub-group 3	Company business description	Company founding year	Company public status
2005	South Korea	Com2uS Corporation	2	8000	Storm Ventures Fund II, LLC	Expansion	Computer software	Recreational/ game software	Develops mobile games and entertainment	1998	
2001	India	Net Brahma Technologies Pvt Ltd	1	2000	J.P. Morgan Partners – Unspecified Fund	Startup	Computer software	Communications/ networking software	Provides software services	2000	
1997	United Kingdom	4-Sight PLC	1	5300	Geocapital Eurofund, L.P.	Early stage	Computer software	Database & file management	Develops software for graphic file transfer	1989	Private

Second, the behavior over time of total VC investment is characterized by a boom–bust cycle. This investment pattern was accentuated by the high share of IT investment in the overall investment by VCs over almost the last two decades (Figure 2.1). Therefore, for the remainder of the data analysis, we will focus on venture capital investments in the information technology sector.

How Important are Foreign Relationships?

How important are the US VC to US PF relationships relative to the US VC to foreign PF relationships? That is, if our objective is to analyze and assess the implications of the globalized product–innovation–ownership nexus, are we working with a large share of the investment activity, or a relatively small share? Relationships can be measured in terms of dollars or number of deals, but the patterns look quite similar, and are large enough to warrant additional investigation (Figure 2.2).

In dollar terms, the importance of foreign PFs peaked at the height of VC investment activity in 2000. About $13 billion of US venture funds were invested in foreign portfolio firms in 2000; the average flow between 2001 and 2005 was closer to $3 billion. However, in terms of the percentage of VC investment going abroad, there has been a rising share since the mid-1990s and what appears to be a permanent 'step-up' in the share of foreign investments from less than 5 per cent to around 15 per cent. Similarly, the number of foreign PF deals peaked in 2000 at about 1300 individual deals and then fell back to about 300 in subsequent years to 2005. The overall rise and apparent step-up in share of foreign deals mimics the pattern for dollars. The question deepens as to whether there has been an evolution in the type of products or services financed, and whether there has been any change in the country of destination for the VC investments.

EVIDENCE ON THE GLOBAL PRODUCTION–INNOVATION–OWNERSHIP NEXUS

A first approach to investigate a globalized product–innovation–ownership nexus for venture capital is to see how the types of investments financed and target countries change over the sample period. The traditional product cycle emphasizes that innovations begin in the industrial countries and then move abroad when product standardization and cost pressures make lower-cost production platforms attractive. For classical venture capital, in some sense, all their investments should be at the innovative startup stage, but many of the deals that come from the VenturExpert™ database are not

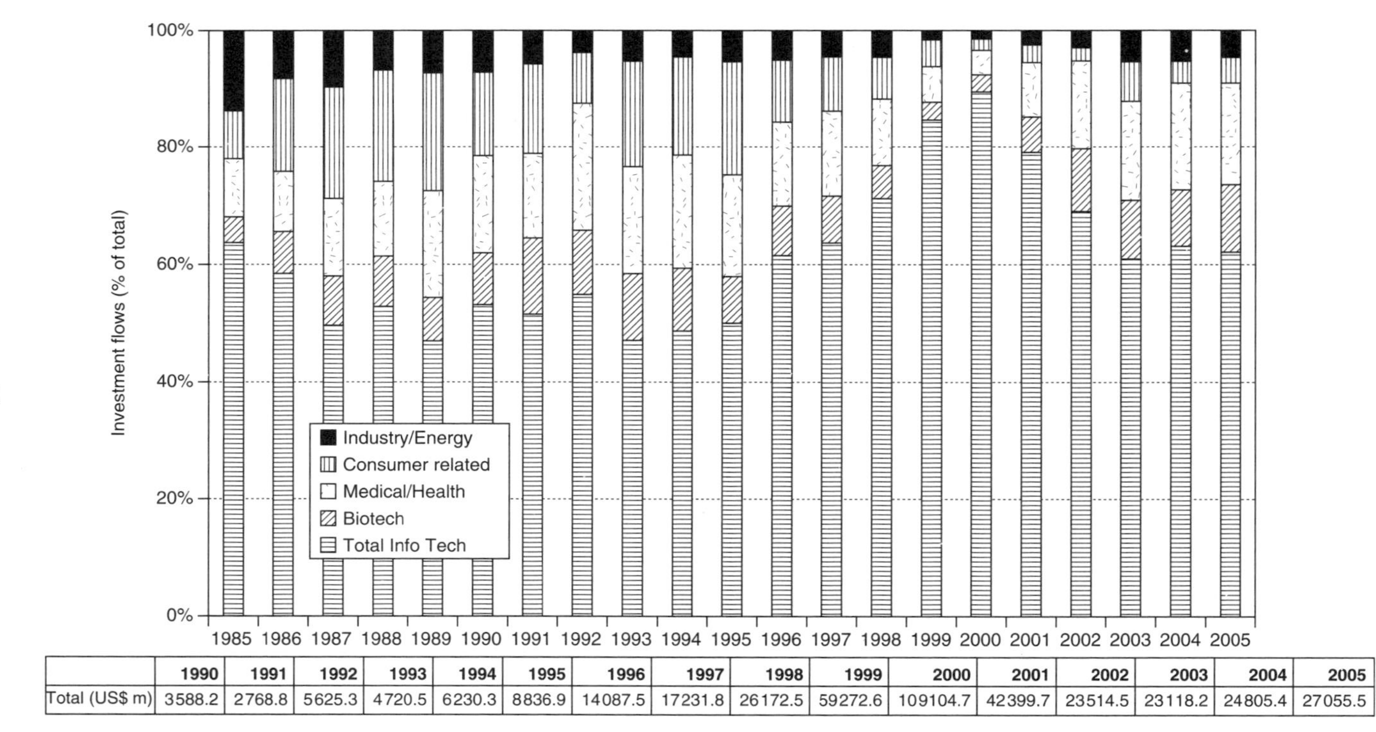

	1990	1991	1992	1993	1994	1995	1996	1997	1998	1999	2000	2001	2002	2003	2004	2005
Total (US$ m)	3588.2	2768.8	5625.3	4720.5	6230.3	8836.9	14087.5	17231.8	26172.5	59272.6	109104.7	42399.7	23514.5	23118.2	24805.4	27055.5

Figure 2.1 VC activity by high-level group: total and composition of flows

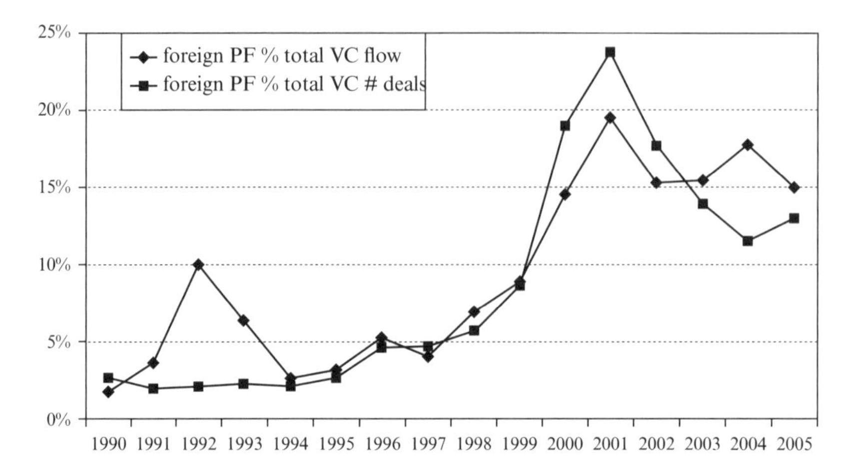

Figure 2.2 VC investments abroad (in the IT sector): share of dollars and deals

seed capital for new firms, but finance expansions, and even buyouts. The behavior of these kinds of investments may be driven less by classic VC motives and more by the product cycle, or even by Dunning's framework for assessing patterns of foreign direct investment.

Simple product cycle: cost-based investments

One model of the product cycle is to invest in lower-cost countries as the product becomes more standardized, and the profit motive demands lower-cost production. Do we see evidence of venture capital firms investing an increasing share in lower-wage economies?

Table 2.2a shows the top 15 countries receiving VC finance for IT portfolio firms from 1999 to 2005. First, only 3 of the top 15 recipients are significantly lower cost (China, India, Brazil). The top two recipients are the UK and Canada. Moreover, looking at the time trend of the share of each country in the funds received in each year, there is no evidence at this level of disaggregation that lower-cost countries receive an increasing share of the VC funds.

A disaggregation of IT funding into sub-group computer hardware (Table 2.2b) and software (Table 2.2c) finds that portfolio firms in the industrial countries still rank first as the destination for VC financing (Ireland and Belgium for computer hardware and the UK, Canada and France for computer software). On the other hand, at this level of disaggregation into types of IT being done at the PFs, there is some evidence

Table 2.2 a, b, c Top 15 countries to receive VC funding in IT: total, hardware, software

	Top 15 countries by Total Funds Received: Aggregate-IT – International flow of US VC-1999–2005														
Country	1999	% for year	2000	% for year	2001	% for year	2002	% for year	2003	% for year	2004	% for year	2005	% for year	Total
United Kingdom	705.99	*22*	2702.58	*25*	873.83	*16*	381.62	*19*	256.63	*11*	306.71	*12*	245.8	*24*	5473.2
Canada	688.33	*21*	1211.46	*11*	673.8	*12*	258.73	*13*	248.47	*11*	293.49	*12*	123.63	*12*	3497.9
China	99.02	*3*	248.04	*2*	971.95	*17*	155.57	*8*	655.94	*28*	445.11	*18*	131.92	*13*	2707.6
France	243.02	*8*	778.53	*7*	580.59	*10*	131.58	*7*	59.43	*3*	331.46	*13*	100.89	*10*	2225.5
South Korea	328.83	*10*	423.02	*4*	314.44	*6*	402.33	*20*	22.95	*1*	356.02	*14*	29	*3*	1876.6
Germany	151.89	*5*	949.31	*9*	215.55	*4*	83.57	*4*	242.45	*10*	28.38	*1*	30.27	*3*	1701.4
India	64.24	*2*	508.48	*5*	397.13	*7*	219.12	*11*	7.4	*0*	162.35	*7*	35.47	*3*	1394.2
Luxembourg	112.69	*4*	1045.25	*10*	0.93	*0*	0	*0*	0.55	*0*	9.4	*0*	192.82	*19*	1361.6
Israel	68.45	*2*	498.19	*5*	266.39	*5*	120.98	*6*	80.43	*3*	167.65	*7*	84.33	*8*	1286.4
Netherlands	229.46	*7*	489.27	*5*	134.06	*2*	15.09	*1*	41.26	*2*	261.62	*11*	0	*0*	1170.8
Brazil	203.34	*6*	511.51	*5*	429.34	*8*	8.22	*0*	13.83	*1*	0	*0*	0	*0*	1166.2
Hong Kong	163.85	*5*	508.48	*5*	47.22	*1*	68.26	*3*	72.46	*3*	39.16	*2*	0	*0*	899.4
Japan	61.22	*2*	243.69	*2*	154.12	*3*	5.72	*0*	389.66	*17*	5.41	*0*	9.32	*1*	869.1
Ireland	31.99	*1*	294.76	*3*	123.23	*2*	81.88	*4*	233.74	*10*	51.06	*2*	31.25	*3*	847.9
Belgium	53.00	*2*	230.71	*2*	422.67	*8*	49.26	*2*	18.32	*1*	9.56	*0*	0		783.5
Total	3205.32		10643.28		5605.25		1981.93		2343.52		2467.38		1014.7		27261.4
% of total int-l flows accounted for by top 15 countries	*77.55*		*81.2*		*81.6*		*83.0*		*89.6*		*92.7*		*76.1*		*82.32*

Table 2.2 a, b, c (continued)

Top 15 Countries by Total Funds Received: IT TECHNOLOGY – Computer Hardware									
Country	1999	2000	2001	2002	2003	2004	2005	Occur.	Total
Ireland	No Inv.	37.15	2.00	0	200.10	No Inv.	0	5	239.25
Belgium	10.73	130.69	2.48	30.00	11.25	No Inv.	No Inv.	5	185.15
China	0	0	No Inv.	No Inv.	55.22	83.25	4	5	142.47
Japan	No Inv.	6.29	6.24	2.53	108.28	No Inv.	No Inv.	4	123.34
United Kingdom	13.41	24.75	18.91	9.86	2.94	3.25	41.89	7	115.01
France	No Inv.	34.45	13.68	7.69	12.84	20.36	10.09	6	99.11
Hong Kong	10.60	25.34	10.50	43.26	No Inv.	No Inv.	No Inv.	4	89.70
India	No Inv.	63.02	9.56	10.26	2.97	1.62	No Inv.	5	87.43
Taiwan	62.00	9.68	0	4.39	No Inv.	No Inv.	No Inv.	4	76.07
Canada	No Inv.	11.77	12.62	1.87	23.40	13.91	8.28	6	71.85
Israel	1.48	34.86	2	No Inv.	2.50	18.97	1.50	6	61.31
Luxembourg	No Inv.	48.51	No Inv.	No Inv.	No Inv.	No Inv.	No Inv.	1	48.51
Germany	0	2.47	13.35	0.28	1.21	0	3.00	7	20.31
South Korea	2.36	12.26	1.13	0.79	No Inv.	No Inv.	No Inv.	4	16.54
Switzerland	1.03	9.30	0.90	1.93	0.91	No Inv.	No Inv.	5	14.07
Total of Top 15	101.61	450.54	93.37	112.86	421.62	141.36	68.76		
15 as % of Total	*92.50*	*97.70*	*85.00*	*94.00*	*94.70*	*97.20*	*100.00*		

Top 15 Countries by Total Funds Received: IT TECHNOLOGY – Computer Software

Country	1999	2000	2001	2002	2003	2004	2005	Total
United Kingdom	117.81	411.90	164.41	161.65	102.97	66.71	101.68	1127.13
Canada	129.31	379.93	104.51	59.30	84.46	35.14	5.12	797.77
France	42.73	106.56	197.00	44.95	7.52	28.19	23.49	450.44
India	5.57	171.70	13.91	151.01	2.75	10.00	12	366.94
Japan	10.52	79.94	8.01	No Inv.	211.66	No Inv.	No Inv.	310.13
Israel	20.88	120.13	60.51	17.08	12.40	23.30	17.25	271.55
Netherlands	0.99	223.03	11.72	10.66	9.06	0.49	No Inv.	255.95
Ireland	17.43	51.88	55.08	36.56	6.34	27.69	22.66	217.64
Sweden	9.33	48.64	16.68	30.29	9.28	14.28	No Inv.	128.50
Germany	14.70	28.09	18.56	36.80	15.88	2.65	1.83	118.51
China	2.21	22.06	27.62	20.46	11.78	28.43	3.5	116.06
Belgium	30.40	29.39	17.53	12.69	1.02	2.63	No Inv.	93.66
Singapore	20.00	47.38	13.98	No Inv.	No Inv.	2.00	No Inv.	83.36
Italy	2.36	70.62	7.85	0	No Inv.	No Inv.	No Inv.	80.83
Denmark	24.27	7.56	27.21	6.92	0.59	0	9	75.55
Total of Top 15	448.51	1798.81	744.58	588.37	475.71	241.51	196.53	4494.02
15 as % of Total	*88.90*	*95.10*	*89.00*	*89.40*	*99.30*	*86.60*	*86.00*	*92.10*

Note: No Investment ('No Inv.') means there were no deals. In contrast a '0' entry means that there were deals, but the $ values were not revealed. So when charts of 'number of deals' are examined, this year will show up as having a deal done, but when 'dollars extended' charts are calculated, there will be no dollar value.

of the product-cycle and FDI models. Of the VC funding extended to the industry, PFs in China have received funds predominantly for hardware – China's lower production costs for IT hardware are well-documented. Those in India receive funds predominantly for software – the lower cost of programmers in India is also well-remarked. Nevertheless, the trends in the percentage received of the total for each year do not reveal an increasing trend toward VC investment in portfolio firms in these locales.

Complex Product Cycle and Location Advantages: Demand Patterns

Newer generations of the product-cycle model and the FDI frameworks acknowledge the differences in the growth of markets and the stage of technological diffusion as well as cost differences when assessing the rationale to go abroad. Is there evidence that VCs target their financing according to similar rationales, such as differences in the nature of demand growth or the stage of technological diffusion in the US relative to foreign markets? One difference between the US and foreign markets is the pattern of demand for the three main components of the IT product basket: hardware, software and services, as well as telecommunications networks. Table 2.3 shows that although the US market continues to be the largest in all four categories, the patterns of growth over the last decade in the four IT product categories and across various countries have been quite different in recent years. These differences in patterns of demand growth could be important factors in the VC decision-making process.

Table 2.3 shows that prior to 2001, demand growth for software and IT services in the United States was greater than the global average, but slowed to below the global average after 2001. Demand in the US for hardware and communications slowed considerably and then fell absolutely. In contrast, in most industrial countries other than Japan, spending in all categories remained strong. In developing countries, the contrast is that their spending on communications and IT hardware is much stronger than their spending on IT software or services.

Based on the newer generation of the product-cycle and FDI models, where demand drives innovation, production and profit, we should see differences in the types of firms the VCs finance in the US compared with in foreign markets: in the US, the VCs should finance software; in the industrial world all range of products might be financed, and in the developing world, communications and especially IT hardware.

Figure 2.3 compares, for each category of IT PF, the pattern of funding to US versus foreign PFs over time. Relatively more US venture capital goes to foreign PFs in hardware, communications and semiconductors; relatively less goes to internet and to software – especially as the time frame

Table 2.3 Global patterns of spending in the ICT sector

Communications Spending				
World Ranking	Country	2003 Expenditure US$m	CAGR 1993–2001%	CAGR 2001–2003%
1	US	459086	4.9	2.1
2	Japan	187353	14.5	0.6
3	Germany	58826	2.9	6.2
4	United Kingdom	55386	9.1	4.3
5	France	43753	4.9	6.9
6	China	40384	26.0	4.7
7	Italy	30017	7.5	5.8
8	South Korea	23762	8.7	4.3
9	Canada	21897	6.6	3.4
10	Spain	19564	5.0	7.9
11	Brazil	18398	19.0	0.8
13	Netherlands	15973	7.4	6.5
14	India	15379	19.6	4.7
16	Mexico	13294	2.2	1.0
18	Taiwan	12520	9.3	2.5
20	Russia	10829	6.5	7.6
22	South Africa	8751	5.8	8.4
35	Malaysia	4904	9.3	4.9
41	Ireland	3705	12.0	2.1
42	Thailand	3674	5.4	4.8
	World Total (70 countries)	1232451	8.5	3.1

IT Hardware				
World Ranking	Country	2003 Expenditure US$m	CAGR 1993–2001%	CAGR 2001–2003%
1	US	119043	6.7	−2
2	Japan	53214	2.4	−9
3	Germany	31967	7.5	7
4	China	24171	29.2	21
5	UK	23125	9.2	1
6	France	17903	5.6	7
7	Italy	12205	7.6	7
8	Canada	10947	7.5	10
9	Brazil	10128	10.2	26
10	South Korea	10090	13.5	10
11	Australia	6502	5.0	12
13	Netherlands	5649	9.5	6

Table 2.3 (continued)

IT Hardware				
World Ranking	Country	2003 Expenditure US$m	CAGR 1993–2001%	CAGR 2001–2003%
14	India	5013	8.8	35
17	Mexico	4370	20.1	15
18	Taiwan	3748	12.5	14
20	Russia	3108	−2.2	21
27	South Africa	2767	5.2	27
31	Malaysia	1463	11.9	9
34	Ireland	1279	16.6	7
37	Thailand	1002	6.0	14
	World Total (70 countries)	402701	13.4	4

IT Services				
World Ranking	Country	2003 Expenditure US$m	CAGR 1993–2001%	CAGR 2001–2003%
1	US	248862	11.7	1.7
2	Japan	68465	7.9	2.5
3	France	38649	14.8	16.9
4	UK	38326	5.3	10.5
5	Germany	37556	9.7	16.5
6	Italy	16949	7.9	16.1
7	Canada	13201	7.7	9.4
8	Netherlands	8031	10.4	15.9
10	Brazil	7432	39.2	24.5
11	Australia	7167	11.0	17.6
15	South Korea	3867	13.2	27.1
17	China	3290	9.6	53.9
20	India	2521	10.9	34.9
21	South Africa	2429	8.9	34.1
23	Mexico	1986	19.0	8.0
24	Russia	1576	7.9	26.9
28	Taiwan	1199	0.8	13.6
34	Ireland	788	10.8	15.6
41	Malaysia	520	10.6	24.2
47	Thailand	317	−4.0	20.6
	World Total (70 countries)	554258	10.2	7.2

Table 2.3 (continued)

		IT Software		
World Ranking	Country	2003 Expenditure US$m	CAGR 1993–2001%	CAGR 2001–2003%
1	US	105035	14.4	3
2	Germany	18459	7.7	19
3	UK	15569	15.3	12
4	Japan	14617	14.4	4
5	France	13033	12.6	19
6	Italy	6627	7.1	18
7	Netherlands	5242	14.2	17
8	Canada	5190	14.6	11
9	Australia	3591	11.7	22
10	China	3065	18.9	36
14	Brazil	2496	19.4	21
18	South Korea	1348	48.5	21
19	South Africa	1325	30.7	35
22	Taiwan	842	6.2	16
23	India	835	14.8	35
26	Mexico	629	6.6	7
28	Russia	585	19.4	22
31	Ireland	531	19.3	17
35	Malaysia	407	14.4	16
38	Thailand	379	15.9	34
	World Total (70 countries)	225217	13.4	10

Note: CAGR stands for Compound Annual Growth Rate.

Source: Mann (2006)

moves from the early 1990s to 2005. On balance, relative funding destinations are as expected based on demand patterns.

Complex Product Cycle and Internalization Choice: Technology Diffusion

Another way to interpret the product-cycle literature in the VC context is to consider whether the VCs continue to fund the ‘newest’ innovations in the ‘rich’ markets, which in the product-cycle framework have the more advanced preferences that support frontier product innovation. In this model of technology diffusion, the rich markets remain the leaders in terms of product innovation, but VCs may support foreign investments as a path to technology diffusion from the advanced to the less-advanced markets,

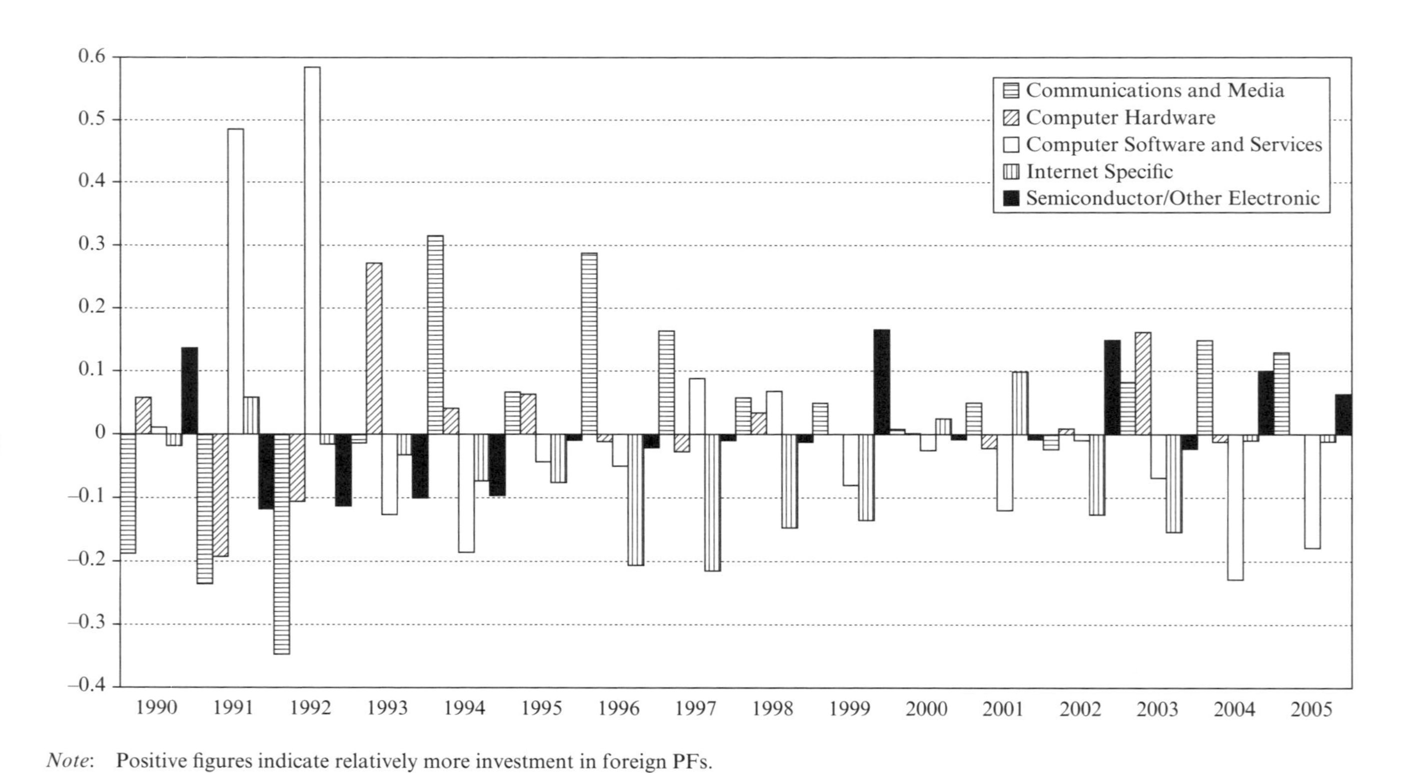

Note: Positive figures indicate relatively more investment in foreign PFs.

Figure 2.3 Investment in foreign PFs relative to US PFs by IT category over time

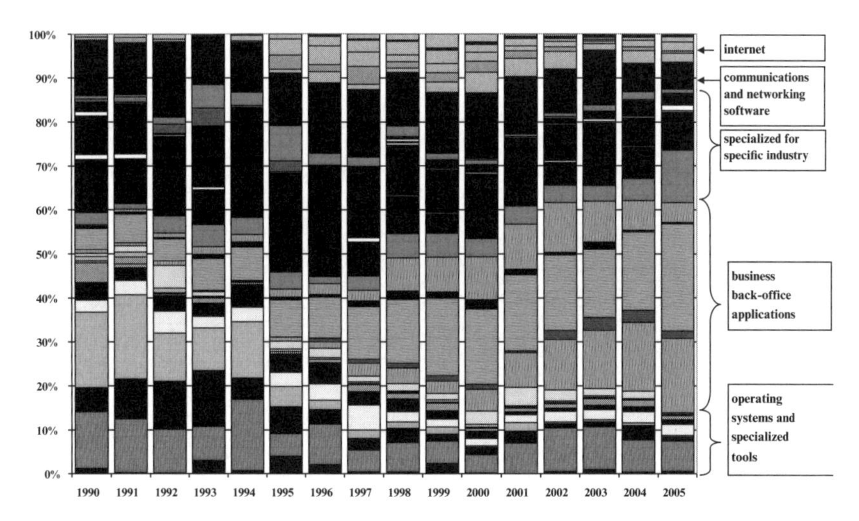

Figure 2.4 US VC investments in US portfolio firms: detailed software investments

particularly if the technology diffusion is associated with tailoring of the product to meet local demand. To analyze this question we disaggregate the VC database further and consider only VC deals in the computer software category.

Consider first VC investments in US portfolio firms (Figure 2.4). There is a clear evolution in VC investments from 'operating systems and specialized tools' to 'business back-office applications', with continued attention to 'specialized software for specific industries'. The surge in internet investments also is apparent. Over time, as the software that controls the inside of the computer has reached the critical mass of users, VCs have moved toward supporting innovative and complex software applications designed to support more effective use of the computer (for example, back-office applications, industry-specific applications and evolving business needs such as security software). This evolution in investment is consistent with macroeconomic analysis, which emphasizes that the productivity-enhancing value of the computer depends increasingly on how it is integrated into the business function (Mann, 2006, Chapter 3). So, within the US, VCs appear to behave as the product-innovation cycle predicts.

Within specialized industry applications, software for the financial sector is most important, as is software for medical applications and health. Previous research indicates that productivity increases associated with the investment in software for the financial sector has been dramatic, whereas the returns on investment in software for health/medical applications appears less so

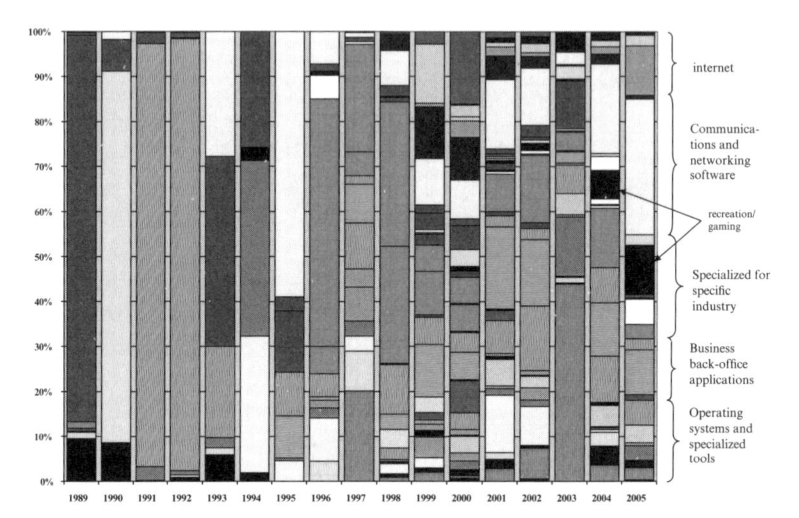

Figure 2.5 US VC investment in foreign portfolio firms: detailed software investments

(Mann, 2006, Chapter 3). Therefore, the prevalence of VC investment does not guarantee either individual profit or economy-wide economic gains.

For VC investment in foreign portfolio firms (Figure 2.5), the offshore element of the product-innovation cycle is less apparent. Prior to 1997, the data are dominated by small-sample issues, with relatively few large late-stage buyouts and acquisitions dominating the sample. After 1997, there is modest evidence of a move to investment in foreign PFs that are in the activities of declining share in the US, which would be expected based on the product-innovation cycle. That is, the share of investments in operating systems and tools and back-office operations was relatively high in the late 1990s and early 2000s, which is consistent with a commoditization and 'offshoring' of this software development process that is no longer cutting edge in the advanced markets.

The relative lack of importance of business applications in the foreign PFs compared to the VC investments in US portfolio firms, suggests that there is a localization component or proprietary knowledge or other factors (such as business demand for these products) that keeps the VC funding of these types of PFs close to the US home market, and, moreover, that there is relatively little local demand in the foreign economies for this kind of application software. Macroeconomic analysis notes that most other economies do not use information technology for enhanced economic performance as effectively as does the US. The lack of VC investment in business applications in foreign PFs is consistent with this macroeconomic observation.

A second observation comparing the domestic and foreign investment shares shows a relatively large exposure to two segments of retail software: entertainment and gaming software, and scientific software. Why would these be important targets for VCs to invest in foreign PFs? Digging deeper into the specific deals for 2004 and 2005 for game software, as an example (Table 2.4), suggests that US VCs search abroad for specific niches of skills, or, perhaps in the case of mobile games and games for China, specific complementarities between skills and demand patterns.

Finally, the comparison of VC investments in US PFs with foreign PFs reveals a relatively greater boom–bust cycle (in the shares) of investments in internet-related software in the foreign PFs (compare shares in Figures 2.4 and 2.5). Although the overall dollar value of the 'bet' taken by VC firms was bigger in the US (and extended over more years before and after 2000), the relative share of the internet bets within computer software investment was bigger in foreign portfolio firms. In the heady days of the dot-com boom, the VCs may have thought that foreign economies could leapfrog directly to internet-based electronic commerce, so they invested accordingly.[4]

Overall, there are some patterns of software investment that support the technology-diffusion cycle which are similar to the product cycle, with the commoditization of software development of some 'older' software moving abroad where, presumably, the cost of further development or enhancement to meet the needs of the local (foreign) market draws on available resources. At the same time, global and local forces appear to be more important in the data, with VCs pursuing niche skills and markets abroad.

Investment Concentration by Country

One question that has arisen in the context of VC investment in foreign PFs is whether US VCs are concentrating their investments in certain countries, particularly in early stage investments in perceived low-wage countries such as India or China. This type of leader–follower regime can result when one VC is thought to have superior information about a type of investment in a country. Is there evidence of this kind of country herding?

Previous discussion indicated that there was little evidence of such country herding when considering VC investment over all stages in the top 15 countries (recall Tables 2a,b,c). Our database disaggregates stages of investment into earlier and later. A herding mentality might be viewed at an early-stage investment followed by a preponderance of later-stage investments in the same country as VCs support expansion in their earlier investments.

Figure 2.6a and 2.6b show the shares of VC investment in selected countries by stage, for the 1994–1998 average compared with the 2003–2005 averages. For almost all these major recipients of VC funding, the later

Table 2.4 Detail on foreign PFs in recreation/gaming software

	Company Name	Total Inv. by US funds	Fund Name	State Level	Company Business Description
2004					
China	Enorbus Technologies	3 000.00	Carlyle Asia Venture Partners II, L.P.	Expansion	Provides wireless entertainment services in China.
Norway	Funcom	599.50	Undisclosed Non Venture Investor	Expansion	Develops computer and console games.
France	In-Fusio	17 072.50	Partech International – Unspecified Fund	Buyout/ Acquisition	Develops video games for mobile phones.
2005					
South Korea	Com2uS Corporation	8 000.00	Storm Ventures Fund II, LLC	Expansion	Develops mobile games and entertainment.
Finland	Fathammer, Ltd.	599.00	Undisclosed Venture Investor	Expansion	Develops advanced mobile gaming software.
Ireland	Havok, Ltd. (AKA: Telekinesys Research, Ltd.)	110.00	Undisclosed Venture Investor	Expansion	Develops and markets computer game software.
Netherlands	JVH Gaming B.V. (AKA: JVH Holding BV)	214.00	Undisclosed Venture Investor	Expansion	Produces and distributes software for the gaming and amusement market.
Ireland	Selatra Limited	1 234.50	Undisclosed Investor	Expansion	Distributes mobile entertainment content specializing in JAVA games.
Finland	Sulake Corporation Oy	18 439.00	Benchmark Capital V	Expansion	Develops multiplayer online games.

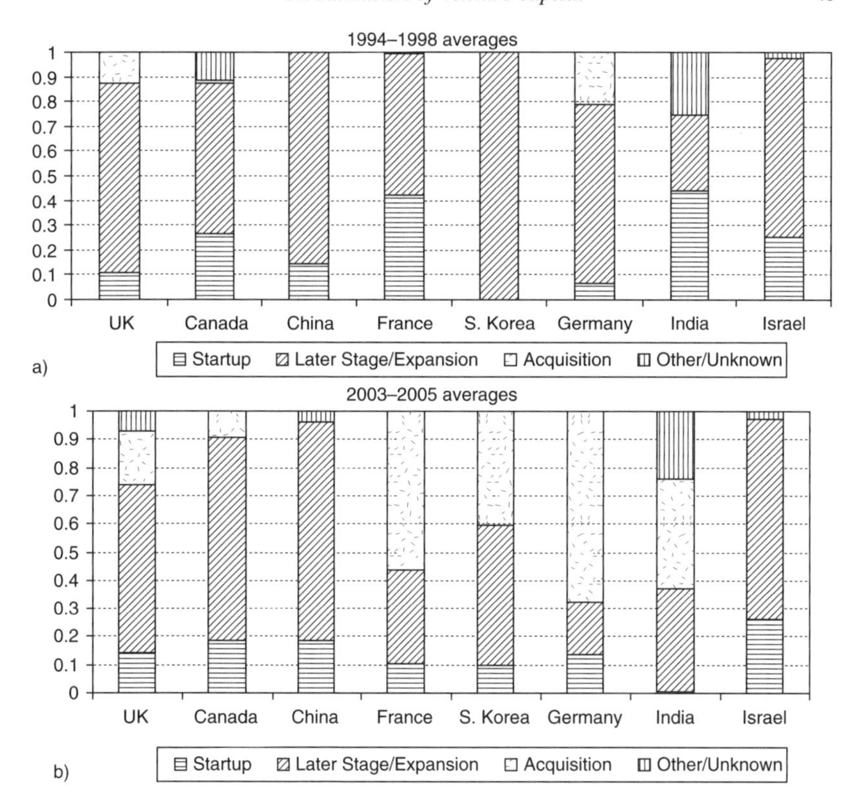

Figure 2.6 a, b Shares of VC investment by stage by country, period averages compared

years show relatively greater funding for acquisition, rather than investments in startups or later-stage development. This suggests that there is some taking stock and wrapping up previous bets, rather than making new bets on new innovations. For US VC investments in India, in particular, this type of behavior is suggested by the data.

If US VCs are not financing startups in China and India, where are they going and what kind of investments are they making? Table 2.5 lists the startups by country, size of investment and industry sub-group. Almost all the investments are in advanced economies, with Sweden, Israel and the United Kingdom most represented, although China has three PFs. The range of Sub-group 3 categories is quite broad, with three security-related PFs, five in the communications arenas, three internet-related firms, four in semiconductors and three in customer services. Therefore, it does not appear that US venture capital firms are inordinately concentrated in financing startups in particular countries or in particular industry segments.

Table 2.5 Start up/seed investments in foreign portfolio firms, 2005

Company Nation	Company Name	Estimated Round Total (in US$m)	Company Industry Sub-Group 3
Canada	Mobidia, Inc.	406	Other Communication/Networking Software
Cayman Islands	Karodpati, Inc.	1 015	Consumer Services
China	Oriental Wisdom Technology Development Co. Ltd.	8 000	Wireless Communications Services
China	Viaon, Inc.	250	Semiconductors
China	Yeelion, Inc.	800	Consumer Services
Denmark	Alight Technologies A/S	562	Laser Components (incl. beamsplitters, excimers)
Denmark	AudioAsics A/S	–	Customized Semiconductors
Finland	UniqMinds	389	Other Communications/Networking Software
Finland	Upstream Engineering Oy	389	Lenses with Optoelectronics Applications
France	GoHalfPrice.com, Ltd. (AKA: Brandalley)	3 869	Consumer Products
Germany	RF-iT Solutions GmbH	118	Database & File Management
Ireland	Channel 6	2 228	Radio & TV Broadcasting Stations
Ireland	Xancom, Ltd. (DBA: Lightstorm Networks)	3 213	Customized Semiconductors
Israel	Aternity	7 500	Other Integrated Systems and Solutions
Israel	Bio-Sense Technologies	450	Security/Alarm/Sensors
Israel	Kidaro, Ltd.	4 000	Security/Firewalls, Encryption Software
Israel	PBC Lasers, Ltd.	1 000	Optoelectronics Semiconductors (incl laser diodes)
Israel	Qumranet	4 753	Other Computer Services
Israel	Xeround Systems	6 500	Data Communications Components

Japan	Business Search Technologies (BST)	1 700	Internet Search Software and Engines
Norway	ReVolt Technologies AS	8 518	Batteries
Portugal	Move Interactive, S.A.	438	Other Internet Systems Software
Russia	Electron-Com PLT, Ltd.	8 000	Internet Access Services and Service Providers
Sweden	Mitrionics AB	1 588	Expert Systems
Sweden	Musicbrigade.com	126	Recreation/Entertainment/Music/Movies
Sweden	Nanoradio AB	2 422	Other Semiconductors
Sweden	Proxilliant Systems Corporation	579	Network Test, Monitor and Support Equipment
Sweden	Syntune AB	1 428	Laser Components (incl. beamsplitters, excimers)
Sweden	ZealCore	129	Security/Firewalls, Encryption Software
Switzerland	Eye P Media	210	Multimedia Software
Switzerland	SpinX Technologies	12 500	Scientific Software
United Kingdom	Njini, Inc.	2 500	Database & File Management
United Kingdom	OmPrompt, Inc.	9 076	Messaging Services
United Kingdom	SiConnect, Ltd.	1 426	Customized Semiconductors
United Kingdom	Undisclosed Company	998	Communications Product/Services
United Kingdom	Vortis Technologies, Ltd.	500	Wireless Communications Services

CONCLUSION

This chapter uses data on individual venture deals to investigate patterns of venture capital investment by country, product and stage of investment. The framework for analysis is the global product–innovation–ownership nexus, where both cost push and demand pull contribute to globalized production by a firm. The data on deals suggest that stronger relative demand and cheaper costs of production abroad for computer hardware and communications equipment move VC investments abroad. In the US, demand for software is relatively stronger, and VCs emphasize software investment in US portfolio firms.

Within the software categories, demand patterns in US and foreign markets are important drivers of VC investment choice. VCs invest relatively more in US portfolio firms engaged in business back-office applications and industry-specific software. They invest relatively more in foreign portfolio firms in computer hardware and communications-related software. Other research reveals that US business firms' use of software applications far exceeds that in foreign economies, so VCs are making financial bets based on patterns of demand internal to the country marketplace.

In addition, evidence supports a globalized innovation product cycle. Within software, VCs fund newer innovations at US portfolio firms (business-related software), whereas older innovations (operating systems and specialized tools) receive VC funding abroad. But global and local forces also are apparent: software that requires a global platform (computer games) is funded more at foreign portfolio firms, whereas software demanding a local platform (medical/health) is funded more at US portfolio firms.

There is little evidence that US venture firms are attracted to start-up activities in perceived low-wage economies such as India and China. The vast majority of start-up activity is in advanced industrial economies where individual portfolio firms have unique ideas and skills.

The Vernon–Dunning frameworks of innovation, global production and ownership are well reflected in the individual deal data on venture capital investments in US and foreign portfolio firms in the information technology sector.

NOTES

1. Dunning introduced his idea at the 1976 Nobel Symposium in Stockholm. Dunning (2001) discusses the heritage of the paradigm.
2. Another data source, Dow Jones VentureSource, includes data on US, European and

Israeli portfolio firms and would provide a useful check on the VenturExpert™ data; we have not pursued this here as the international coverage is our main objective of analysis.

3. Daniel Gould did yeoman's work on the data when he was a research assistant at the Peterson Institute for International Economics in 2005. Daniel is now with Morgan Stanley.
4. On the challenges facing countries to so 'leapfrog' to internet-based e-commerce, see Mann *et al.*, (2000).

REFERENCES

Antras, Pol (2005) 'Incomplete Contracts and the Product Cycle', *American Economic Review*, v. 95, iss. 4, pp. 1054–1073.

Balakrishnan, Jaydeep and Cheng, Chun Hung (2007) 'Multi-Period Planning and Uncertainty Issues in Cellular Manufacturing: A Review and Future Directions', *European Journal of Operational Research*, v. 177, iss. 1, pp. 281–309.

Benarroch, Michael and Gaisford, James (2002) 'Learning-Driven Product Cycles, New Product Adoption and North-South Inequality', *Journal of Economic Development*, v. 27, iss. 1, pp. 1–23.

Bhaduri, Saradindu and Ray, Amit S. (2004) 'Exporting through Technological Capability: Econometric Evidence from India's Pharmaceutical and Electrical/Electronics Firms', *Oxford Development Studies*, v. 32, iss. 1, pp. 87–100.

Clements, Matthew T. and Ohashi, Hiroshi (2005) 'Indirect Network Effects and the Product Cycle: Video Games in the U.S., 1994–2002', *Journal of Industrial Economics*, v. 53, iss. 4, pp. 515–42.

Cutler, Harvey and Ozawa, Terutomo (2007) 'The Dynamics of the "Mature" Product Cycle and Market Recycling, Flying-Geese Style: An Empirical Examination and Policy Implications', *Contemporary Economic Policy*, v. 25, iss. 1, pp. 67–78.

Deltas, George and Zacharias, Eleftherios (2006) 'Entry Order and Pricing over the Product Cycle: The Transition from the 486 to the Pentium Processor', *International Journal of Industrial Organization*, v. 24, iss. 5, pp. 1041–69.

Dunning, John H. (2001) 'The Eclectic (OLI) Paradigm of International Production: Past, Present, and Future', *International Journal of the Economics of Business*, v. 8, iss. 2, pp. 173–90.

Feenstra, Robert C. and Rose, Andrew K. (2000) 'Putting Things in Order: Trade Dynamics and Product Cycles', *Review of Economics and Statistics*, v. 82, iss. 3, pp. 369–82.

Mann, Catherine L. (2006) *Acclerating the Globalization of America: The Role for Information Technology*, Washington, DC: Peterson Institute.

Mann, Catherine L., Eckert, Sue E. and Knight, Sarah Cleeland (2000) *Global Electronic Commerce: A Policy Primer*, Washington, DC: Peterson Institute.

Schilli, Bruno and Dai, Fan (2006) 'Collaborative Life Cycle Management Between Suppliers and OEM', *Computers in Industry*, v. 57, iss. 8/9, pp. 725–31.

Vernon, R. (1966) 'International Investment and International Trade in the Product Cycle', *Quarterly Journal of Economics*, v. 80, iss. 2, pp. 190–207.

Windrum, Paul (2005) 'Heterogeneous Preferences and New Innovation Cycles in Mature Industries: The Amateur Camera Industry 1955–1974', *Industrial and Corporate Change*, v. 14, iss. 6, pp. 1043–74.

APPENDIX 2.1

Table 2.A1 Detailed classification of categories included in the Information Technology high-level group

COMMUNICATIONS
- **Commercial Communications**
  - Radio & TV Broadcasting Stations
  - CATV & Pay TV Systems
  - Cable Service Providers
  - Radio & TV Broadcasting & Other Related Equipment
  - Services to Commercial Communications
  - Media and Entertainment
  - Entertainment ·
  - Publishing
  - Other Commercial Communications
- **Telephone Related**
  - Telecommunications
  - Long Distance Telephone Services
  - Local Exchange Carriers (LEC)
  - Telephone Interconnect & Other Equipment
  - Telephone Answering and/or Management Systems, PBXs
  - Other Telephone Related
- **Wireless Communications**
  - Mobile Communications, Pagers & Cellular Radio
  - Wireless Communications Services
  - Messaging Services
  - Wireless Communications Components
  - Other Wireless Communications
- **Facsimile Transmission**
- **Data Communications**
  - Local Area Networks (incl. voice/data PBX systems)
  - Wide Area Networks
  - Data Communications Components
  - Communications Processors/Network Management
  - Protocol Converters & Emulators
  - Modems and Multiplexers
  - Other Data Communication Components
  - Switches/Hubs/Routers/Gateways/ATM
  - Network Test, Monitor and Support Equipment
  - Other Data Communications

Satellite Communications
  - Satellite Microwave Communications

Table 2.A1 (continued)

Satellite Services/Carriers/Operators
Satellite Ground (and other) Equipment
Microwave Service Facilities
Microwave & Satellite Components
Other Satellite & Microwave
Other Communications Related
Defense Communications
Other Communications Services NEC
Other Communications Products (not yet classified)
COMPUTER HARDWARE
Mainframes & Scientific Computers
Mainframes
Supercomputers and Scientific Computers
Other Mainframes and Scientific Computers
Mini & Personal/Desktop Computers
Fail Safe Computers
Minicomputers
Personal Computers (micro/personal)
Other Mini and Personal Computers
Portable Computers (notebooks/laptops)
Handheld Computing (PDA)
Optical Computing
Servers and Workstations
Servers
Workstations
Thin Client Hardware
Other Servers and Workstations
Digital Imaging and Computer Graphics
CAD/CAM, CAE,EDA Systems
Graphic Systems
Scanning Hardware
OCR (Optical Character Recognition)
OBR (Optical Bar Recognition)
MICR (Magnetic Ink Character Recognition)
Other Scanning Related
Graphics Printers/Plotters
Graphics/Enhanced Video Cards
Other Graphics Peripherals
Other Multimedia NEC
Digital Imaging Hardware and Equipment
Digital Imaging Services
Other Computer Graphics

Table 2.A1 (continued)

Turnkey Integrated Systems and Solutions
Business and Office
Consumer
Retailing
Transportation
Finance/Insurance/Real Estate
Agriculture
Recreation/Entertainment
Manufacturing/Industrial/Construction
Medical/Health
Computer Related
Communications Products/Services
Education
Reference
Scientific
Other Integrated Systems and Solutions
Computer Peripherals
Terminals
Intelligent Terminals
Portable Terminals
Graphics Terminals
Other Terminals
Printers
Laser Printers
Color Printers
Inkjet Printers
DotMatrix Printers
Data I/O Devices
Mouse Input Devices
TouchPad Input Devices
Penbased Computing
Other Data I/O Devices
Disk Related Memory Devices
Floppy Disks & Drives
Winchester Hard Disks and Drives
Disk Drive Components
Other Disk Related
Tape Related Devices
Magnetic Tapes
Tape Heads & Drives
Continuous Tape Backup Systems
Other Tape Related Devices
Other Memory Devices (excl. semiconductors)

Table 2.A1 (continued)

Memory Cards
Sound Cards
Communications Cards
Other Peripheral Cards
Other Peripherals (not yet classified)
COMPUTER SERVICES
Time Sharing Firms
Computer Leasing & Rentals
Computer Training Services
Backup and Disaster Recovery
Data Processing, Analysis & Input Services
Computer Repair Services
Computerized Billing & Accounting Services
Computer Security Services
Data Communications Systems Management
Other Computer Services
Computer Software
Systems Software
Database & File Management
Operating Systems & Utilities
Program Development Tools/CASE/Languages
Graphics and Digital Imaging Software
Other Systems Software
Communications/Networking Software
Security/Firewalls, Encryption Software
Email Software
Groupware
Multimedia Software
Other Communications/Networking Software
Applications Software
Business and Office Software
Home Use Software
Educational Software
Manufacturing/Industrial Software
Medical/Health Software
Banks/Financial Institutions Software
Retailing Software
Integrated Software
ERP/Inventory Software
Recreational/Game Software
Scientific Software
Agricultural Software
Transportation Software

Table 2.A1 (continued)

Other Industry Specific Software
Other Applications Software
Artificial Intelligence Related Software
Expert Systems
Natural Language
Computer-Aided Instruction
Artificial Intelligence Programming Aids
Other Artificial Intelligence Related
Computer Programming
Software Services
Programming Services/Systems Engineering
Software Consulting Services
Software Distribution/Clearinghouse
Other Software Services
Other Software Related
INTERNET SPECIFIC
Internet Communications and Infrastructure NEC
Internet Access Services and Service Providers
Internet Multimedia Services
Internet Backbone Infrastructure
E-Commerce Technology
Internet Security and Transaction Services
E-commerce Services
Other E-commerce
Computers Hardware
Web Servers
Internet Software
E-commerce enabling software
Internet Systems Software
Site Development and Administration Software
Internet Search Software and Engines
WebServer Software
Web Languages (Java/ActiveX/HTML/XML)
Web Authoring/Development Software
Other Internet Systems Software
Internet Programming
Internet/Web Design and Programming Services
Internet Graphics Services
Other Internet Software Services
Internet E-commerce
Internet and Online Related
E-Commerce–Selling Products Online or Internet
Business and Office Products

Table 2.A1 (continued)

Consumer Products
Retailing Products
Publishing Products
Transportation Products
Finance/Insurance/Real Estate Products
Agricultural Products
Manufacturing/Industrial/Construction
Medical/Health
Computer Related
Communications Products
Education Products
Reference Products
Scientific Products
Legal Products
Other E-commerce Selling Products
E-commerce – Selling Services Online/Internet
Business and Office Services
Consumer Services
Retailing Services
Publishing Services
Transportation Services
Finance/Insurance/Real Estate Services
Agricultural Services
Recreation/Entertainment/Music/Movies
Manufacturing/Industrial/Construction
Medical/Health Services
Computer Related Services
Communications Products/Services
Education Services
Reference
Scientific
Legal
Recreation/Entertainment Services
Other E-commerce Selling Services
Internet Content
Business and Office Information/Content
Consumer Information/Content
Retailing Information/Content
Publishing Information/Content
Transportation Information/Content
Finance/Real Estate/Insurance Info/Content
Agriculture Information/Content
Recreation/Entertainment/Music/Movies

Table 2.A1 (continued)

Manufacturing/Industrial/Construction Information/Content
Medical/Health Information/Content
Computer Related Information/Content
Communications Information/Content
Education Information/Content
Reference Information/Content
Scientific Information/Content
Legal Information/Content
Other Aggregation/Portal/Exchange Sites
Internet Services
Internet Marketing Services
Data Warehousing Services
Other Internet and Online Services NEC
COMPUTER OTHER
Voice Synthesis
Voice Recognition
Other Computer Related (not yet classified)
SEMICONDUCTORS ELECTRONICS
Semiconductors/Other Electronics
Electronic Components
Semiconductors
Customized Semiconductors
Standard Semiconductors
Flash Memory
Optoelectronics Semiconductors (incl. laser diodes)
Other Semiconductors
Microprocessors
Controllers and Sensors
Circuit Boards
Display Panels
Batteries
Power Supplies
Uninterruptible Power Supply (UPS)
Electronics Equipment
Semiconductor Fabrication Equipment & Wafer Products
Component Testing Equipment
Other Electronics Related Equipment
Laser Related
Laser Components (incl. beamsplitters, excimers)
Other Laser Related
Fiber Optics
Fiber Optic Cables
Fiber Optic Couplers and Connectors

Table 2.A1 (continued)

Fiber Optic Communication Systems
Other Fiber Optics
Scientific Instrumentation
Analytical & Scientific Instrumentation
Chromatographs & Related Laboratory Equipment
Other Measuring Devices
Other Analytical & Scientific Instrumentation
Electronics, Other
Other Electronics Related (including keyboards)
Military Electronics (excluding communications)
Copiers
Calculators
Security/Alarm/Sensors
Other Electronics Related (incl. alarm systems)
Optoelectronics
Photo Diodes
Optoelectronics Fabrication Equipment
Lenses with Optoelectronics Applications
Advanced Photographic Processes (incl. lithographs)
Other Optoelectronics Related
Other Electronic Semiconductor

Note: Other high-level groups are: Biotechnology, Consumer-related, Industrial/Energy, Medical/Health, Other products.

3. Offshoring: why venture capital-backed businesses stay at home*

Amar Bhidé

INTRODUCTION

Colonial powers once went to war to secure overseas markets, but today, export opportunities, or the lack thereof, do not have a significant place in the popular consciousness. Rather, offshoring – which leads to the import of goods and services – dominates the discourse on trade. And some pundits and politicians seem particularly agitated by venture capital-backed businesses, whose innovative activity is supposed to offset the offshoring of low-wage jobs, joining the exodus and relocating their own development activity to low-wage locations overseas. In this chapter, I will not analyze whether offshoring by VC-backed businesses helps or hurts their home countries. Rather, I discuss the extent of offshoring by the venture capital-backed businesses that I studied and what encouraged or discouraged them from going offshore.[1] The findings are part of a broader research effort involving interviews with 106 CEOs of venture-backed companies which covered two other facets of the globalization of their companies, namely their efforts to serve international markets and the role of immigrants (as founders and employees). The broader effort is expected to culminate in a book, and in this chapter I will make some references to findings covered in more detail in that work.

In my interviews I found that offshoring was indeed of great consequence to some companies, whose entire development staff was located abroad. All they had in the US were their headquarters, sales and marketing staff. Others, like CiDRA's founder and CEO, had become satisfied customers of outsourcing companies (instead of having their own off-shore development staff)

* Much of the material contained in this Chapter has been previously published in, Bhidé, A. (2008), *The venturesome economy: how innovation sustains prosperity in a more connected world*, Princeton, NJ: Princeton University Press. Princeton University Press give permission for this chapter to be published.

> CiDRA was one of the first companies to use the off-shore model for product development. I had worked with Tata [the largest of the Indian outsourcing companies] before and this development went extremely well. Infosys wanted to use us as a case study, and they ended up featuring us in their annual report. The talent they sent us was incredible. They had five to six people working with us in the US and 30 in India. The arrangement gave us lower costs and faster delivery. Infosys is an amazing company. They have a software factory approach. They give you a date and then meet it – for us, the cost of software pales with the cost of being late. When you have top tier investors who want you swinging for the fences, you need to get to market as quickly as you can.

But the companies that relied on offshore development to a significant degree were outnumbered by those that didn't. The experiences of the many companies that were considering but had not yet tried, had tried and failed, or had decided not to try to offshore development were reflected in these comments:

> We will outsource someday, but not now. Right now, we need to focus and we don't need a lot of people. All I have now are a couple of Stanford PhDs, Masters from MIT and a few industry-experienced people.

> We gave it a try. It did not matter how good they were in India, we could not make it profitably work for us.

> We have analyzed outsourcing every year, and every year we've concluded it doesn't make sense. Our company is very high-end and specialized. We have historically put everyone, not just in the US, but in the same building.

> We're *just* getting to the scale where it might make sense. We have enough of a backlog of initiatives and enough modularity to the product so that we could take pieces of a development and push it to an outsource provider.

Overall, offshoring development was apparently no more significant or widespread than initiatives to serve international customers; in fact, by some measures, offshoring was less significant. Twenty-nine companies undertook sales and marketing out of an overseas office. In nine such cases, sales and marketing was the only activity undertaken out of their overseas offices. In contrast, there were 24 companies that used their offices for performing some form of offshoring activity (and in 10 cases, exclusively for an offshoring activity). Of these 24, 19 only used their offshore facility for the development of new products, rather than to manufacture parts or to provide technical support to customers and so on. And of the 19, only 11 were involved in developing a core product or a critical component thereof, as opposed to ancillary sub-components or software testing.

Similarly, 28 companies had relationships with other businesses abroad that sold or distributed their products overseas. In contrast, 40 had offshoring relationships, but only 29 used these relationships for any kind of product development activity, and of the 29, only 8 were used to develop core products or components of core products.

In this discussion, I will start with the reasons for offshoring, and then I will examine the problems and drawbacks. I will also discuss how the general pros and cons affect 'what, where and how' choices, the special case of FDA-regulated businesses, and the contrasts with large and incorporated Fortune 500 companies.

NO-CHOICE OFFSHORING

Most of the companies which said they had to offshore – or at least would have found it highly problematic not to offshore – fell into one of three categories. One group comprised companies whose innovations had to be embodied in physical goods, typically upstream components, and produced in high volumes. In many cases, particularly for the designers of semiconductors, using sub-contractors who had the necessary capabilities and cost structures was virtually inevitable. 'In our business, which is making novel miniaturized components,' said one CEO, 'we could not function without a supply chain outside the US. Fabrication, packaging, and testing of semi-conductors all have to be in Asia.' Another consideration, according to a CEO, was time and capital:

> You could build a fully automated, 24/7, 365-days-a-year, high-quality manufacturing facility. This is what the Japanese did in the 1990s, and because labor costs wouldn't have mattered, the facility could have been located anywhere. But this would have cost at least $100 million and taken several years to develop the competency. That would be very challenging to a VC-backed start-up. Instead, we decided to use the manufacturing base in China. China provides a manual or semi-automatic manufacturing alternative that isn't quite as good as the Japanese methodology for quality. But it has been proven over the last 10 years to be adequate, the variable and startup cost is lower, and the people availability is great. So we were able to enter the market with reasonable volumes and supply batteries to tier-one customers on a price-competitive basis.

A second category, comprising four firms, 'had to have' offshore relationships because they served as value-added resellers of offshore resources: Vivre was a reseller of European luxury goods; Odyssey was a global logistics management outsourcing company; E-Silicon helped small- to medium-sized developers of customized chips (including one in my sample) use the fabrication, packing and testing services offered by providers in

Asia; and Virtusa – which had programmers in ten locations abroad – was, according to its CEO, 'an IT services company, pure and simple'.

Notice, however, that for both these categories, the 'unavoidable' offshoring did not involve the development of new products or technologies, although in many cases, it did utilize specialized skills and assets of the offshore provider.

This was not the case for the third category of the 'no real choice' companies – six businesses that had started overseas. Unsurprisingly, their development teams were located overseas as well.[2] Although in principle, the developers could have been relocated to the US when the headquarters and sales marketing staff had 'migrated' to the US, this would have been disruptive and expensive for a small company. Moreover, the CEO of a company that had started in the UK told us that when he tried to move some of the engineers to the US, they refused. So practically speaking, these companies didn't have much of a choice.[3]

We could also reasonably include in (or place at the periphery of) the third 'no real choice' category, companies that acquired their offshoring facilities through the acquisition of another company. Overall, about a quarter of the companies in my sample had acquired another company.[4] In twelve such cases, the acquisition brought with it an overseas facility, and in five cases, the overseas facility was used for some form of offshoring. Here too, in principle, the inherited offshore facilities could have been shut down and the staff (or projects) repatriated to the US. And indeed, in one case, the CEO had tried to do precisely that with a facility based in Israel. But according to the CEO, the supply of engineers at home had become very tight and visas to relocate the Israeli staff to the US were unobtainable. So he reluctantly kept the facility open. But in the other cases, the CEOs saw no reason to shut down the acquired facility. In one instance, of a company in the telecommunications industry, the CEO expected to expand the acquired facility, based in Belfast (in Northern Ireland), because

> we need to augment our development quickly. British Telecom has a large operation in Belfast, and the area has a highly skilled and stable workforce. There is not the turnover that we've seen in California. And, they are in the same time zone as our European customers.

OFFSHORING, BY CHOICE

Box 3.1 contains the comments of the CEOs whose companies weren't impelled by the lack of a domestic manufacturing base or the happenstance of their origins or acquisitions. The comments point to three kinds of

BOX 3.1 REASONS FOR CHOOSING OFFSHORING

There is a wealth of highly educated resources abroad available at a fraction of the cost here. That was a key motivator for us; and, honestly, if anyone says it's anything other than cost, they're lying.

We started out just with Quality Assurance. I say 'just' but it was, in fact, very important because it allowed 24-hour development. Our programmers here would send off the code they had written during the day to China, and when they arrived the next morning, they would have a long list of bugs they needed to fix.

Our majority shareholder has investments in a number of outsourcing companies. They have whispered in my ear – they are marvelous, they never shout – for a long time, to continue to look at it for our back office operation and our customer support function. We found some things that might otherwise have been put on the backburner, and we are doing a science experiment on it now.

Two years ago, we hired someone who was born in Pakistan who had extensive experience outsourcing major projects to India. At about the same time, we had a project that some of our customers wanted us to do, but we didn't want to spend too much money or resources because it wasn't critical to our business in the long term. Also, all my competitors were outsourcing – every entrepreneur I knew was doing some form of outsourcing – and my VCs told me that around 80 percent of their companies were.

Our concern was, if our competitors outsource, would they have a competitive advantage? Moreover, in today's business environment, you have to take it seriously. If you expect to be a world-class organization today, and you are not doing some things offshore, you are probably not a world-class organization.

We tried outsourcing, and it failed. So then for about two years we didn't bother. Then I started feeling pressure. It was clear that we had to dramatically increase our development capacity, and we just could not hire people at that rate here. Our motivation wasn't cost – I want to be clear about that – it was capacity. We just needed more output. Customers were demanding more functionality, the rate of innovation was increasing, and we just could not service that demand.

We were 18 months into the company when it became hard to hire in the DC area. We said, 'let's go to other places where there is an abundance of competencies in software for call processing'. We went to Dallas, where my co-founder had managed a site for Nortel, and Montreal, where I had managed a large R&D team. The folks in Montreal were more interested, and we felt we could hire people there that wanted to work for us.

Last year the unemployment rate here was less than five percent, and we had an average of 15 open positions in our operations department. I hooked up with a portfolio sister company, and they were able to fill those positions in India.

We started using an outsourcing company in India close to a year and half ago. There are three principal value adds that we get. The first is a skilled labor force. We're having a tough time finding the kind of software developers we need here. It's amazing to me. We have job requisitions open with high pay, and we're having a tough time filling them. Secondly, it's a flexible workforce. We can flex up, we can flex down. It's not like turning a light switch on and off, but it's less pain than doing it here. Third, and I ranked it in priority, is cost. And it's not an 80 percent reduction, it's 50 percent.

We started doing off-shore development in India from day one. We raised money at the end of 2002, which was a difficult year to raise financing, and we wanted to figure out cost-effective ways to make that money last. One of the VCs was recommending that startups establish offshore development. They had invested in an outsourcing company and were great believers in the capital efficiencies even a startup can get from offshore. My co-founder had 10 years of experience in offshore development and knew how to organize teams here and offshore so that you could get 18-hour productivity days from the engineering team.

reasons: the pursuit of competitive advantages; the experience and outlook of the founding team; and the strong encouragement of their investors.

The comments in Box 3.1 also indicate that CEOs had a variety of views about the role of costs. Two said that the only reason to offshore was to reduce costs, while one insisted that costs had not played any role. A more common response was that costs did matter but played a subsidiary role to other considerations – particularly tightness in the local labor market and the speedier development that could be realized using round-the-clock development.

Cynics might suggest that even if cost savings were paramount, very few CEOs would admit this. But whether or not the CEOs revealed the true reasons for offshoring, one thing seems fairly clear. As mentioned in the introductory section, few companies were developing their core products offshore. And the number that had actually chosen to do so was extremely small. Development facilities that originated abroad with the company itself (or had later been inherited through an acquisition) accounted for all but four of the offshore facilities used to develop core products or components of core products. Most of the offshoring that companies started after they were up and running was for activities such as data entry, customer support and testing (also known as Quality Assurance). In the sections that follow, I will examine why.

EXTERNAL AND INTERNAL COMMUNICATION

The value of an ongoing dialogue with customers ('co-development partners') discouraged many CEOs from locating their R&D personnel offshore. As one CEO said:

> I have an Indian friend who lives in Portland but has an outsourcing company in India that sells programming services to large US companies. He tried to sell me on the idea they could develop our core development as well. We talked about it, and I ultimately decided not to do it. We are developing a product for an emerging category where interaction with customers drives innovation. All of our customers are now based in the US, and it's very important that the people who are developing our software are in regular communication with our customers, and not just by talking with them on the telephone. They need to be visiting the customer's physical locations, see how the software is being used, talk with the end users, take that knowledge back to the company, and use it to design new features and capabilities. I just didn't see how that could be effectively done overseas.

Keeping the R&D staff at home facilitated communication with sales and marketing staff, who might have even closer contact with customers. One CEO said the value of putting the engineering staff with sales, marketing and product managers in a single location close to customers precluded offshoring:

> If you're outsourcing a function where all the processes are very well defined, then it could be interesting. But, where you need responsiveness and constant innovation, it is better to deal with local people. It's not just the time difference and language barrier of dealing with a country like India. You also struggle with communication in the same country, even in the same location, because engineers speak a different language from salespeople and product-marketing people. Even with everybody being American, if you have a development center somewhere in the middle of the US and the rest of the team is in California, you really run into problems. It's not a question of cost. You want people right next to you, not in India or Alabama. If it's purely repetitive work and there is no need for constant communication and feedback, I'm sure outsourcing could work. But here, we're constantly dealing with customers, who constantly give us changes.

One of the very few companies that apparently didn't have a problem with a remote development facility was Cybrel, which from the start, had located its R&D in Israel. But as its CEO explained, this may have been related to its staffing policies and the nature of its product:

> Coordinating the R&D staff – which is still all based in Israel – with sales, business development marketing, and professional services – which are based both in Israel and the US – has never been an issue. We don't have a head of Israel

> and head of America. We have functional departments, and except for R&D, the departments have people in both countries. It's never been a major problem bridging the gap, probably because we have moved a lot of people from Israel to the US. They bring along all the knowledge and contacts – they know the people there – and then you have just a two-minute call or IM [Instant Message] and you get things done. It also helps that many of the Americans we have hired are fluent Hebrew speakers; we have just three flat-out Americans. And, the nature of our projects didn't require you to be on-site with customers much. You needed a kick off, a couple of follow up meetings, and three or four face-to-face meetings in a six-month period.

The other company which had started and continued with Israel-based R&D, had faced more significant coordination problems, its CEO (a 'flat-out American' by all appearances) said

> The R&D organization had a product focus, not a customer focus. They developed what they thought was needed and wouldn't accept feedback the US team got from customers. There was a large emotional and political gap and a lot of conflict between the two teams.
>
> When I arrived, Israel was not even on the same e-mail system as the US. Then after we merged the e-mail systems, I once sent an e-mail to all employees announcing a successful sale we had made. I got an e-mail back from the manager in Israel saying: 'Don't tell my people anything – they will just ask for raises.'

PARTITIONING PROBLEMS

Communication of the development staff with customers and the other members of the organization does not, however, require all the developers to be in the same location. Why not have development teams where some members are located in the US, close to customers, and the sales and marketing personnel with the others in low-cost, offshore locations? One of our interviewees said that his company couldn't because they were developing hardware – physical objects that could only be worked on in one place. Software development, he volunteered, might be different. And indeed, the development of open-source software such as Linux and Firefox suggests that software can be developed by a widely dispersed team – a model that had, in fact, been used by two companies (see Box 3.2).

The CEOs of other companies were aware of the open-source model, but they believed that their particular software (including an application based on Linux!) could not readily be developed by dispersed teams. In part, the problem derived from the complexity of what they were developing – Swiss Army knives as it were, rather than meat cleavers. The blade, the bottle opener, screwdriver and wire opener of the knife had to

BOX 3.2 VIRTUALLY OFFSHORE

One company, using dispersed programmers offshore, was developing an interactive web access tool – a 'social browser' whose features included tools for blogging and sharing photographs and bookmarks. Its founder had previously headed marketing and business affairs for the Mozilla Foundation and coordinated marketing activities for Firefox, its open-source browser. The 'social browser' incorporated some of Mozilla's technology as well as its open-source approach – including widely dispersed programmers. Virtually all 'telecommuted' from their homes over the internet – 18 from locations within the US and 7 abroad.

The other company was developing software for law enforcement. Its founder and CEO, who was a proponent of 'extreme programming' and remote development, explained:

> In extreme programming, new features do not go through the old school marketing requirements and external specifications and internal specifications routine. We create 'use cases' that come directly from end users. We then code a unit to 'solve' that case. We then implement that module as part of the whole project. Developers are closely involved with users in that process to make sure that what they code is what the case represents, or to figure out if the user interface is easy to use.
>
> In the past, the user and the programmer would have to sit next to each other. But now with IM, with 'live person' types of technologies, that's no longer necessary. We take an extreme view of extreme programming and of remote development. I don't care if I have a developer in the Midwest or in New York or in Florida. They just basically get onto our virtual development site and are constantly in contact through IM or other communication mechanisms. We use Skype regularly for conferencing. There, electronic mechanisms bring you close to the customer without the need to be there.
>
> It happens that all six of our programmers are in Vancouver, Canada. We have a small office outside Simon Fraser University, where our base technology was originally developed. Four out of the six people typically work out of their homes. The office is primarily used when our VP of engineering and products and our CTO [Chief Technical Officer], who live in California, travel up there. They go over when we need large changes in the architecture and technology and to discuss next versions. We have toyed with using people overseas in Japan and Indonesia, but that hasn't happened yet.

fit together; they could not be developed independently. In principle, a master designer could specify rules and interfaces so that the designer of the bottle opener did not have to interact with the designer of the wire stripper. In practice, this was hard; so many companies apparently saw great benefits to team members working side by side. As one CEO said,

> We need tremendous interaction between the teams working on the different components of our product; what we do is not something that can be reduced to a tight requirement and thrown over the ocean for a development team to work off.[5]

But open-source applications also have a large number of components that have to be compatible. Yet Linux and Firefox have been developed – and continue to evolve – through the efforts of individuals whose interactions are usually limited to periodic exchanges over the internet. Why shouldn't this also be a good model for the innovations of VC-backed businesses? Indeed, according to one CEO, the inability of early-stage companies to use offshore development was a function of the inexperience of their technical leadership.

> If you have a seasoned engineering chief who has defined your procedures, selected good development tools, instituted a well-documented Quality Assurance Process, and you have excellent market requirement documents and product requirement documents, there is no reason why even if you are a small company, you can't hand over pieces of your development to an outsourcing organization. But an awful lot of start-ups lack that discipline.

This was, however, very much a minority view. Most CEOs apparently felt that the dynamics of the process through which they developed new combinations made it difficult to partition development into tasks or sub-projects that could be undertaken by remote individuals or teams. Sending detailed market or product requirement documents to an offshore organization was, for an early-stage enterprise, neither feasible nor desirable. Their case against the partitioning is described below.

VC-backed businesses develop 'new combinations' through an iterative process, adding or removing features as they sequentially discover what 'bundles' their customers value. Sometimes, they also have to stabilize and extend their base technology. Moreover, competitive races and financial pressures demand rapid progress. In contrast, developers of open-source software like Linux and Firefox work off a stable kernel or code base, and many of the features they add are not 'new', in that these features have already been implemented in an earlier operating system or browser. And because Linux and Firefox are not commercial products, the problem of determining the optimal bundle comprising the most attractive trade-off of cost and specific features doesn't arise. Nor does speed particularly matter – the developers can set their own pace, usually while holding down paid jobs.

The fluidity and pace of development in turn, as the CEOs told us, make it difficult to make plans for who would do what, and when:

> We often don't know what we want until the day before we do it. There are many spontaneous 'A-Ha!s' in our technical development. We are building and piecing together things that have never been put together before. There are a lot of moving parts and there isn't a clear roadmap to follow.
>
> We've found that no matter how much you try to define something upfront, it's going to be somewhat wrong. Moreover, in the very early stages, when you are building a team, you don't have a product manager, let alone a product management process. A formal development process is fine if you are a mature company with long development cycles. It's much tougher when you have only one product that you need to get out quickly. Our iteration cycle has to be very, very fast. If we get a request from a customer, we have to respond very quickly.

The need to make frequent, coordinated changes apparently requires, according to one CEO (who as it happened, had instituted a sophisticated product management process), co-location of the entire development team:

> We have communications challenges, just with one product manager and 15 developers. There are times when you have to grab everyone, put them in the room, and sit at a white board. I have personally pulled developers for three or four sessions in the last four weeks, where we made major breakthroughs in terms of what we were trying to do. You couldn't do this on e-mail. You couldn't do this even one-on-one . . . If a customer has an issue or we have an idea for a new feature, because we have all our developers in one place, we can turn around our software in a big hurry. I know it's conceptually possible in offshoring mode, but in practice, I think you lose the speed and that spark of innovation you have with a lot of really top-quality developers in one room.

BANDWIDTH CONSTRAINTS

The experience of the companies that had developed their products abroad suggests that the coordination problems of offshore development go beyond those of simply exchanging information – they include basic organizational and cultural conflicts. And while these problems may not be intractable, they consume managerial bandwidth. The experience of companies that had offshore development centers suggests that to start making it work consumes precious top management time and effort. As one CEO said:

> During the bubble years, we had money and wanted to expand our development team. My co-founder's brother had an outsourcing company in India and he dedicated about 50 people for us. It took three years to get it to work – it was a

> constant battle. We had several problems. One big one was the reporting structure. We had one guy responsible for the overall management in India and the US. We also had directors who were responsible for different functions. The developers were confused about who they were supposed to report to. To make things worse, there were conflicts between the functional directors, and the organizational structure was constantly evolving. Managing people itself is different in different places. You can't apply the way you manage people here to India. India is very process focused. The US is more fluid. We needed systems in place to make sure that the definition of the work is very clear. Now everybody is very happy.

The previously mentioned CEO who had problems coordinating the company's developers, who were based solely in Israel, with the staff in other functions, who were based mainly in the US, said:

> We had to change the manager of the development unit. The new guy is an Israeli who has worked in the US. We changed the development process; the team had been very bootstrapped in their approach. They had taught themselves how to develop the system by reading a book. We installed a video conferencing system and hired a US-Israeli consultant for cultural training. We made lots of trips back and forth. We got a few customers in Israel so the development team would have direct contact with some real users and not just a marketing team in the US. A lot of the tension has gone, and the relationships are more positive. But it took a lot of effort.

The question of whether to offshore therefore depended on whether the benefits would exceed the disruptions and costs (including 'management bandwidth'). For many manufacturing companies, having facilities and suppliers in Asia created serious coordination challenges; however, low manufacturing costs – and access to resources that weren't available in the US – compensated for the difficulties, as the CEO of a company developing advanced batteries told us:

> Co-location of your engineers, marketing people, and sales people is much more efficient – no question about it. Relatively simple concepts can be difficult to get across on the phone. You can try various tools: web-casting, PowerPoint presentations, the like, but it takes longer and the language difference makes it likely that you will make some errors that will have to be corrected later. I tell people that 25 years ago, I was in a technology startup company in Boston, and we were struggling with trying to coordinate our marketing and manufacturing, when the president moved the manufacturing facility to Vermont. Every time we had a meeting, we had to drive two and a half hours each way. I used to curse that guy. Now I've started this business where the manufacturing is a 24-hour flight away in China. But what is the alternative? If we could co-locate everyone efficiently from a cost perspective, and if the facilities we needed were here, we would.
>
> But our strategy was to focus on high-volume applications. We could have been a niche player making specialty products in low volumes for specialized military, aerospace or medical applications. We could then have done all our

> manufacturing in North America. But we made the decision early on that we would be a tier-one supplier globally. That meant that we had to have high-volume, high-quality, and low-cost manufacturing, otherwise even with our technology differentiation, we would not long survive.
>
> Now North American companies abandoned the advanced battery market 10 or 15 years ago, and all the advanced technology work has been done in Asia, principally in Japan, secondarily in Korea and then third, in China. Ninety-percent of the equipment manufacturers that serve this market are in Asia, 90 percent of the materials that are utilized in the industry are procured from Asian sources, and a very large part of the intellectual knowledge base resides in Asia. So, if we were going to play on a global basis, we'd have to have a presence in Asia.

Next, we will see why many companies did *not* believe that offshoring their development activities would offer benefits that offset the disruptions and costs.

A FEW GOOD DEVELOPERS

According to some advocates, offshoring can help businesses accelerate innovation, because the same amount of capital can pay for larger development teams. Skeptics, however, question whether team size actually increases the speed of development. Nine people may dig a ditch in a third of the time as it takes three people; however, as Frederick Brooks wrote in his celebrated book, *The Mythical Man-Month: Essays on Software Engineering*: 'When a task cannot be partitioned because of sequential constraints, the application of more effort has no effect on the schedule. The bearing of a child takes nine months, no matter how many women are assigned.' In fact, 'Brooks' Law' suggests that increasing the size of software teams may delay development, one significant reason being that large teams entail high communication overheads.[6] Many believers in the 'small is beautiful' mentality go one step further to argue that it is better to pay a premium for a few star programmers than to employ many average programmers.

Star programmers may not, however, be abundant in low-wage locations – among other things, the willingness to work for a low wage invites questions about an employee's 'star-worthiness'. Moreover, all things being equal, small teams can make the economics of offshoring unattractive: the total savings on the wage bill of a small team may not offset the irreducible out-of-pocket and management bandwidth costs in setting up and managing an offshore facility.

The skeptical view was by far the dominant one among the CEOs we interviewed. As Box 3.3 indicates, CEOs believed that the optimal size of their teams was too small to justify offshore development.

BOX 3.3 HOW SIZE MATTERED

Great code can be worth millions and millions and millions of dollars very quickly, so fewer, higher-end people that are more expensive sometimes is a better way to do things.

We are an ASP [Applications Service Provider]. Our process is highly integrated and dependent on doing everything quickly – we are making changes to the software all the time. It's not like enterprise software with big but infrequent releases. We need tight-knit, small teams.

The concept of software factories with the people as cost is wrong. I'm willing to pay four times the money for somebody who is really good because they are going to generate 100 times the value. Running around to get programmers for $20 thousand a year makes no sense when what's between their ears is incredibly important.

The right engineers who are really top-notch will vastly outperform large numbers of novice engineers.

What we needed when we were starting was very deep but not very broad. We didn't need a lot of people to do standard stuff. We needed a few people to do very specialized stuff.

The bottom line:

We have 16 developers. Even if we offshore the whole thing, the economics don't work out.

If you have development teams of 1,000 or 1,500 people, and you have specific applications that can be compartmentalized, then offshoring is fine. We have a development team of fewer than 30. I cannot be convinced that the economics outweigh the value of having all of them in the same building.

We did some calculations and found we would need at least 15 overseas developers to support the additional management overhead, and we're not there.

Starting a development center in the US made it more economical to add additional capacity there as well. Just as it is cheaper to add sales staff at home than in a new sales office abroad (because no additional set-up or fixed costs have to be incurred), it is also cheaper to add another developer to an existing development team. Moreover, the fixed costs of coordinating the work of developers abroad and at home tend to be much larger than the fixed costs of managing a sales office. Therefore, where businesses might think of opening a one- or two-person sales outpost abroad, they have to decide whether to add many developers or none. At home, developers can be added in one at a time. And, as the following quotes indicate, the quirks and nuances of complex projects and technologies and the norms and interactions of social groups also favor adding staff in existing locations:

> Our software has these enormously complex econometric models. When we hire scientists here, it takes them months to understand what's going on inside the models. How do you hand that knowledge to a team in Shanghai? It's not a language issue – it's the fact that they're at the end of a telephone line and not sitting next to you for months.

> The easiest time to [offshore] is when the company is being formed or is changing a different technology path. Neither is true for us. Our technology was created here and in the US. We have programmers who have been here from the start, are very loyal to the company, and are a close-knit group. Their knowledge base is pretty deep, but a lot of it is almost tribal knowledge that they carry around in their heads – I wouldn't say that all our design documents and structural documents and coding reports are always detailed or up-to-date. At this time, it would be hard to do any offshore development. If we got to an inflection point, where we were starting something totally new, we'd think about it.

> We [a provider of health care services] were approached by an outsourcing company from India. They were part of a group that runs a chain of hospitals. They came over to us and said, 'We know hospital stuff. We'd like to be in the US, and you might want to do something in India. We'd be a great partner for you.' They have very aggressive people and so we tried it.
>
> It was a dismal failure. At some point, people have got to understand what you are doing and develop a bunch of company-specific knowledge – and our stuff is very specific. Even though this group knew something about health care, their productivity was unbelievably low. They were two and a half times cheaper than people here, but they did one fourth the work.

A SUITABLE SUPPLY

As mentioned, the battery and semiconductor developers used facilities and suppliers located in Asia not just because of low costs, but also because the capabilities were not readily available in the US. Similarly, a document processing company had set up a software development center in Antwerp, Belgium, because a department in the university was a leading center for research in computational linguistics and graduated many well-trained students in the field. Conversely, many CEOs said they had been discouraged from undertaking development in low-cost locations abroad because of the scarcity of the skills they needed.

In a few cases, the CEOs said that developers were unavailable because of differences in 'downstream' markets. For instance, the developer of an advertising network for online games wanted programmers who were avid 'gamers', who would have knowledge of the context for the code they wrote. But low-cost locations like India had few 'gamers' because not many young people could afford the high-speed internet connections needed for online games. The CEO of another company said that it had to develop the core part of its application in the US because it needed actuarial expertise in health insurance:

> You might find actuaries in the property and casualty field – for instance, Lloyds of London has many. But you don't have many medical insurers outside the US – it's all government-run, so you just don't have people with the skill sets to underwrite and predict medical costs.

CEOs cited problems with the 'style' of overseas developers. One said that the software developed by his company's center in Switzerland 'was less clever, more process-oriented. Its look and feel wasn't particularly innovative – it just seemed like old things being reused.' Another said that his previous business had used an outsourcing company in India and found that 'the style of coding was different and it was difficult for us to look at the comments in the code and understand'. A third said his company had stopped using programmers in Russia because of 'language issues and a different focus on quality – the code wasn't as buttoned up as we expect it to be here'.

A more common issue with offshoring from India was the scarcity of productive mainstream programmers there. One CEO (of British-Pakistani heritage) whose company had a small engineering team in India because 'one of our key guys wanted to move back to India', said he wouldn't have done it otherwise because 'software engineers cost a third as much, but are only half as productive. It's not worth the hassle.' Moreover, as the quote of a CEO in Box 3.4 illustrates, the challenge of attracting and retaining capable programmers in the face of competition for their services from large multinational companies compounded the problem of low productivity.

Why should the experiences of my interviewees be so contrary to the popular notion of India containing a limitless supply of hard-working, highly talented software engineers? Could this, for instance, be the result of a fluke or bias in my sample? Or is the popular notion mistaken?

Certainly there is no shortage of individuals in India who are willing to offer their services as software programmers. The outsourcing company, Infosys, famously receives more than a million applicants for entry-level jobs each year. But the number of capable programmers is much smaller: if the supply really was abundant, companies like Infosys, which in 2006 hired fewer than three out of every 100 applicants, would not have to raise wages by 10 to 20 per cent a year, and face similar levels of employee turnover. Moreover, research that Professor Kumar of the Indian Institute of Management,

BOX 3.4 A DIFFICULT HOMECOMING

We launched this company after the bubble, and because my co-founder and I are from India, we tried to figure out how to leverage our dollars there. We couldn't, for a number of reasons. One was domain expertise. We are a systems management company, and we wanted very sophisticated, OS- [Operating System] level developers; those people are tough to find, although there was a plethora of people with backgrounds at the applications level. We also wanted people with 10 to 15 years of hard-core development experience, but most of the people had less than four years of experience. In India, people always seem to aspire to get into management. If they haven't become managers after four years, I think their parents would start wondering, 'Is this person an idiot or what?' But once people get into management, they lose technical skills. In the US, there are people who thrive on working on complex development architectures – it's what they want to do as a career.

We also found that professionals wanted to work for large US brands. I think it was important for them to tell their parents or their spouse: 'I'm working for GE or Microsoft or HP or IBM.' If they worked for a startup with no name recognition, I think it would be viewed as 'OK you weren't good enough for IBM so you had to settle for the second or third choice.' Also, good people want to see some long-term commitment by the US company – they don't want to work for a fly-by-night operation. They want to see a team of 20-plus in place for them to feel comfortable. That's easy for Microsoft, HP, Sun and IBM, but hard for us. And we're not going to have the big glass tower building and our name on the outside of the building in lights.

So we had a tough time really attracting the best of the best in India. And if we could find someone good, they'd leave – the turnover was tremendous.

We retrenched, but not fully, at first. We still had a core group of people here in the US, so we tried co-development; we naively thought we could do round-the-clock work on the same projects between the US and India. But time and distance made interactivity between the US and India very problematic. Then, we gave them a project that they could manage on their own. That didn't work either: as a startup, you don't spend much time dotting every 'I' and crossing every 'T' when you're doing technical specifications. You use gut instinct, you build something, you test it in the market, come back and iterate. But you can't say to a team in India: 'Here's kind of what I want … can you go take a crack at it?' You end up with huge disconnect in terms of what they thought they were supposed to do versus what your expectations were, because they don't have a really good appreciation of your core business. Ultimately, we just gave up.

Bangalore, and I have done suggests that VC-backed businesses have an especially hard time competing for the good or even acceptable talent against the large multinational companies or companies like Infosys, whose principal clientele comprises large companies in the US and Europe.

PUSHBACK AND PREDISPOSITIONS

Two CEOs said they had encountered resistance from their US development staff to offshoring. 'To some degree, they were concerned about their own jobs', said one CEO. 'They also seemed to be genuinely concerned about the quality of the work being done in India'. The other recalled:

> Early in 2003, we decided to move a component of R&D to a low-cost region to be competitive over the long term. Nevertheless, employees in the US, especially the Indian community, got very upset. They thought we were going to shut down the US operation and didn't believe us when we said we wouldn't. We stopped and waited until 2004. The business grew substantially in the meantime, and when one of us restarted the process, young star employees came forward and asked to head up the Indian organization. Now, we have a sizeable staff in both countries.

Similarly, the CEO of a company whose development was based in Israel, said the Israeli programmers weren't 'culturally and technically' comfortable moving software development out of Israel and vetoed starting a development center in India. Ultimately, by way of a 'compromise', the company decided to move Quality Assurance to India because the function could be 'easily expanded and contracted'.

One CEO said: 'Our customers have made it very clear to us that they don't want us to outsource. There have been real issues created by outsourcing; Americans are frustrated by that.'

These few cases apart however, the strongest 'attitudinal' resistance to offshoring came from the CEOs themselves. 'I already have enough risk in building a business. Why add to it at such an early stage, when so many other things could also go wrong?'

Some were disinclined to offshore because they had tried it in their previous ventures without much success:

> In my previous startup, I worked with an offshore team in India. The time differences involved and the quality of engineering and the discontinuity of language made it very, very difficult to do.

> In my prior company, we tried outsourcing product development, but it failed. The product just didn't work very well. I think it failed because we couldn't communicate the requirements.

> Our head of engineering was an Indian national who had wanted to move back. He was thrilled when I told him that he could be our Indian development officer. The set up seemed perfect. The guy knew the code inside out, he wanted to be there, and he hired a dozen people. But guess what, within six months it made no difference if we knew him or not. It all comes down to how well you can prepare the work. If your specifications are absolute by the time they leave your desk in North America, maybe it will work when it's being developed in India, but I don't know anybody who is that perfect, so it ends up requiring midnight conversations with the team in India. And the number of change order requests makes the price of whatever you are trying to develop about the same as having done it here.

Others had been involved with successful initiatives – but in large companies. These experiences had convinced them offshoring development was not suitable for a startup:

> Multi-site management is hard and expensive. I used to work at Nortel [a large telecommunications company]. We had 100 people in Bangalore, with three senior-level people in North America managing them, traveling back and forth, training them and making sure they were on track.

> I used to work for a multinational. The company was so big that we could put our own bricks and mortar in India, hire our own people, and not just bring people from North America. We had 300 people there and guess what, when you do it that way, it does work out very nicely. The results were the exact opposite in one venture-backed company I worked with.

A third – and the largest – category had no first-hand experience, but had been discouraged from offshoring by others' experiences and opinions:

> I know a lot of people who have chosen to outsource, who have not gotten the price benefits they thought they would get because they end up spending a lot more time. The price per hour of work is a lot less. But if it takes three times as many hours to get the job done, you haven't saved any money.

> What I'm finding from other colleagues is that it takes a tremendous amount of effort to get it up and running properly and to really get any time to market advantage and to really get any reasonable cost saving. Yes, there are cost savings, but they're not to the magnitude that people have been talking about. The only reason to move overseas is if you really need lots and lots of people to do something who can be quickly trained up on what you need them to do, and then they're going to be very productive and deliver to you in time to market advantage for lower cost. I mean significantly lower cost, because other than that, it's not worth it.

> A company of our size really does not have the corporate infrastructure to effectively manage a significant remote technical development initiative, in my opinion and in the opinion of the technical experts of my board. Once or twice

> per year, a subcommittee of my board comes together to look at our technical direction. One of our board members is the former CTO [Chief Technology Officer] of Texas Instruments, the other one is CTO of United Healthcare. These are executives with vast experience in development around the globe. One of the questions we asked them last week is: 'We have an application that we want to enhance and probably rewrite; is it time now to think about possibly doing this offshore?' They said, 'Absolutely not. You're just too small to manage it remotely.'

WHAT TO OFFSHORE

The problems VC-backed businesses encounter (or anticipate) with the offshore development of new products are apparently less troubling with what one CEO called 'operational things like data entry and call centers'. Tasks are more easily routinized and partitioned. The activity doesn't change very much; therefore, there is plenty of time to amortize the set-up costs. The skills required typically aren't deep or specialized – data entry, for instance, doesn't require much more than the ability to read and type. And the basic technology and managerial know-how necessary for remote data entry and telephonic sales and support were refined well before the current offshoring boom got under way. For instance, banks had long figured out how to operate remote call centers and data processing operations in places like Arizona and Utah rather than at their branches and headquarters. It was therefore not a huge leap – at least technically and managerially – to replicate these activities in places like India, once the necessary communications infrastructure was established. In contrast, the remote development of software is of fairly recent vintage. Through about the 1990s, most outsourcing companies sent programmers to work on their customers' premises and indeed, as of this writing, companies like Infosys still get nearly half of their revenues from the so-called on-site projects.

But VC-backed businesses that are usually still developing their products and building a customer base do not generate a high volume of transactions or phone traffic. Therefore, even if the obstacles to offshoring are modest and the economics attractive, many VC-backed businesses don't have the need for offshore call centers and data entry. In our discussions with CEOs, although the problems were rarely mentioned, as Table 3.1 indicates, only four CEOs said their companies had outsourced transaction processing and other such routinized, ongoing services to vendors abroad. (Six companies had established their own centers, but these all provided high-end services to local customers, such as design support, and were located in the UK, continental Europe and Japan.)

Similarly, with offshore manufacturing, except in some process industries,

Table 3.1 Distribution of offshore outsourcing by function, number of companies and location

Function Performed	Number of Companies	Location of Facilities
Product or infrastructure development	29*	Bangladesh, Canada, China (2), Denmark, Germany (2), India (19), Indonesia, Ireland, South Korea, Poland, Russia, Singapore (2), Ukraine (2)
Core products	5	Germany, India (3), Ukraine (2)
Infrastructure	1	India
Components	9	Canada, China (2), Germany, India (6), Russia, Singapore
Ancillary products	9	Bangladesh, China, Denmark, India (6), Ireland, Russia
Testing	14	China (2), Germany, India (9), Indonesia, South Korea, Poland, Russia, Singapore, Ukraine
Ongoing inputs	14*	Asia, Canada (2), China (5), Denmark, Europe, Germany (2), Japan, South Korea (2), Mexico, Taiwan (4), India
Contract manufacturing	10	Asia, Canada, China (4), Denmark, Europe, Germany, Japan, South Korea (2), Mexico, Taiwan (4)
Other	6	China, Germany, India, Japan, Korea, Taiwan, Western Europe
Ongoing services	4*	Canada, China, India (2), worldwide
Software maintenance	1	India
Technical support	0	
Transaction processing	1	Canada, India
Other	3	Canada, China, India, worldwide
Complements	6*	China, Europe, France (3), Germany, Japan, Sweden, UK, Western Europe, worldwide
Services	3	France, Sweden, Western Europe, worldwide
Hardware	2	China, France (2), Germany, Japan, UK
Other	2	China, France, Japan, UK

Note: *Some companies had more than one functional relationship in each category.

the decoupling and partitioning of the stages of production is commonplace. And in several businesses, using offshore suppliers is considered unavoidable. For instance, fabless semiconductor companies have to deal with remote silicon foundries. Moreover, the path to contract manufacturers in the Far East is even better trodden than the path to Indian outsourcing companies. Therefore, in my sample, all but two companies that could use offshore manufacturing had done so. But, given the preponderance of companies that developed software and other services, the total number of companies that had their own manufacturing facilities offshore or used third-party suppliers was relatively small. As seen in Tables 3.1 and 3.2 (respectively), 14 used third-party suppliers and only 2 had their own manufacturing facilities abroad.

Offshore testing (QA) was slightly more prevalent than offshore

Table 3.2 Distribution of in-house offshore facilities, by function, number of companies and location

Function	Number of Companies	Location
Product or infrastructure development	19*	Australia, Belgium, Canada (2), China (3), Denmark, India (5), Israel (3), Switzerland, UK (5), Ukraine
Core products	11	Australia, Canada (2), China, Denmark, India (2), Israel (2), UK (3)
Infrastructure	1	Ukraine
Ancillary products or components	6	Belgium, China (3), India (3), Israel (2), Switzerland, UK (3)
Testing	1	Belgium, India
Ongoing inputs	14	Asia, Canada (2), China (5), Denmark, Europe, Germany (2), Japan, South Korea (2), Mexico, Taiwan (4)
Purchasing	1	Western Europe (various)
Contract manufacturing	2	Asia, Canada, China (4), Denmark, Europe, Germany, Japan, South Korea (2), Mexico, Taiwan (4)
Ongoing services	8*	UK (2)
Software maintenance	3	UK (2)
Technical support	4	UK
Other	6	China, Germany, India, Japan, Korea, Taiwan, Western Europe

Note: *Some companies had more than one functional relationship in each category.

manufacturing and considerably more common than the offshoring of services like data entry and call centers: as shown in Tables 3.1 and 3.2 (respectively), 14 companies used outsourcing companies and one had its own facility for testing abroad. Although offshore testing was not a 'must' like offshore manufacturing, more companies needed to test, and like data entry, testing was not as problematic as complete product development. There was less ambiguity about the task, so offshore staff didn't have to 'guess' what they were expected to do. The problems of labor availability and turnover were less acute – unlike programmers, testing staff didn't have to be 'outstanding', and replacing someone who left in the middle of a project was less disruptive. And, as one CEO pointed out, testers in the US and offshore could more easily collaborate on the same project:

> Our QA runs around the clock with a combination of US and Indian resources. People here in the US do testing during the day and then hand it off to people in India who do further testing overnight. Next morning, when we come in here, we see the results of those tests. It is hard to imagine John in the US writing code for 10 hours and handing it over to Ashok in India to write additional code. Ashok would have to spend a lot of time trying to figure out what John wrote and vice versa.[7]

Similarly, several companies that kept their 'main' development activity at home had tried to develop components of their core or ancillary products offshore. These efforts were usually relatively recent (and had sometimes followed prior QA or data entry offshoring) and invariably cautious. As the following comments indicate, even though some CEOs said that their primary reason for offshoring was to reduce costs, their choice of projects suggested that they were more concerned about minimizing the problems and risks of offshoring rather than maximizing the cost savings.

> We build and test components of the product in India that are relatively easily partitionable or jobs that no one really wants to do in the US. For instance, they are developing a couple of adapters that allow our products to integrate with other products. We created a general template, and they just need to populate the template with the specifics of the product that we are integrating into. They also do the 'build engineering' – the not-exactly-sexy, 'does it work' stuff.

> We are pushing a project out that really isn't core to our application. It's adding some things to a dashboard and reporting and some other stuff that is more commoditized than the IP [intellectual property] that we rely on. I just don't see us ever outsourcing that.

> We started with data entry and that turned out to be a home run. We now do 70 percent of data entry overseas and 30 percent in the US. Offshoring software development, however, has been slow. You have to tell the people offshore

exactly what you want. Programmers in the US can figure things out for themselves because they are involved in developing the prototype; they go to customer meetings, and they understand the underlying business process. Offshore programmers are one step removed. So when time is critical, when you have a rapid development cycle, you don't go offshore. You put your maintenance projects or stable stuff overseas. Our approach is to get it started in the US, and when it's scaled up, we send it offshore.

We've learned it's just too hard to hand off anything complex – all the big decisions are being made in California, and it's very hard to create a spec and hand it to someone in China and get good results.

We send off stuff we don't like to do – for instance, getting rid of the duplicate data items. Non-core stuff that's on the periphery but needs to get done and can be clearly identified.

We have a product that has evolved over five years. The team that built it here knows its inner workings, and it's not productive to train anyone on it, let alone a team in India. One of our rules is, if it needs legacy proprietary knowledge, it's based here; new – but not too new – over there.

In one telling instance, a company had brought back a development project to the US after it unexpectedly turned out to be of strategic importance.

A few customers asked us to implement a new standard. Our developers didn't think the standard was going anywhere, so we decided to do the implementation in India. But the standard became a big deal, and important customers started asking for it. Fortunately, our chief architect had been attending all of the meetings of the body that was setting the standards, and he had the expertise from a design and conceptual point of view, but from an actual hands-on development point of view, all the expertise was in India. Nevertheless, we didn't bring anyone over from India. We just built the expertise from scratch here.

Some CEOs said that what they could offshore was limited by the skills available abroad:

Very early on, we created a company in India. We hired engineers who supplemented our own technical staff, for the more mundane technical activities, such as the lower-level identification of certain pieces of information that needed to be gleaned. We found an abundance of people who could perform tasks that did not require the deep technical expertise and they were much less expensive. That has been very useful for the preliminary work that we do. But even after five years we have not found a source outside the US that has the deep expertise to do the refined work that is required for a final product.

Arguably, criteria used to select offshoring projects that reflect concerns about the quality and turnover of overseas personnel may have, in fact, exacerbated these problems. As one CEO said:

> There is a high turnover rate in India. That's because so much of the work done there is considered lower level. If you want to attract and retain people you have to give them something they can sink their teeth into – something they will be proud to own.

At another point during the interview, however, the same individual said that his company's developers in India were working on 'projects that do not require a deep knowledge of the core technology, are generally add-ons – like more ways for customers to slice and dice data – and don't require senior architects and aren't threatening to the team in the US'.

An unusual perspective on what to offshore was provided by a CEO who said:

> Companies produce proprietary software by assembling components. The highly proprietary, highly competitive pieces are developed at home. When teams of people from engineering, product management, and marketing develop something with a lot of messing and tweaking of prototypes – that's difficult to offshore. The rest, if it can be properly documented, you can send offshore. But on-shore and offshore aren't the only two options: there is also now open source. We are evolving to a three-tiered process of developing software: utilizing open source where we can and offshoring the things that have less competitive advantages, and then developing the pieces that are high competitive advantage at home.

Although no other CEO raised this as a third option, many did mention in different contexts that they were using open-source components in their products. And to the degree that open-source components are developed by individuals dispersed all over the world, we can regard their use as a disguised form of the offshoring of non-core development.

MAKE OR BUY – AND WHERE?

Companies that chose to offshore had to decide whether or not to outsource. In some cases, this was mainly a classic 'make or buy decision' that had little to do with offshoring issues. For instance, many semiconductor companies outsourced their manufacturing because their requirements were too small to support an in-house facility; whether to use a domestic or overseas foundry was a separate issue. Conversely, the CEO of a software company we interviewed was reluctant to outsource because of the problem of specifying the work. His observations happened to concern Indian outsourcing companies but his general problem would also apply to a US-based outsourcing company as well:

> A lot of outsourcing shops in India are set up for big companies. They want all the data before they bid on contracts. Now when a Citibank says, 'I want to

> move my trading system from Cobol to C++ on a Sun server,' it's easy for the outsourcing company to reply, 'that will cost $3 million, we'll have it in seven months.' But that's the wrong model for a startup. You don't know much – you can come up with a specific plan that isn't real world, but then if your product requirement changes, engineers in India will say, 'Oh my god, you can't do this. It's going to cost you another $500 K.' Or, you can do time and materials, but then you can't control over your costs.

Similarly, another CEO described his reservations about using an Israeli outsourcing team:

> The challenge for a small company is that you get 10 engineers in Israel who build something great for you in six months. But then suppose a year later, we have to modify. Now what? Am I going to generate a long-term contract for these guys? Probably not. I need people on staff even if this means we're paying substantially higher prices.

The same concerns would presumably arise if the outsourcing company was located in California rather than Israel.

The standard 'make or buy' considerations – of low internal demand compared to the minimum efficient scale – help explain why the offshoring of manufacturing was also outsourced to another firm, rather than done in-house (compare Tables 3.1 and 3.2). Similarly, the greater severity of writing and monitoring contracts for 'complete' product development helps explain its low incidence, compared to the outsourcing of testing and the development of modules. But these weren't the only factors. For instance, as mentioned, many offshore in-house development centers can be traced to the national origins of the businesses or their acquisitions of other businesses. And, as we will see next, there were subtle interactions between outsourcing and offshoring problems. Although analyzing these interactions does not add much to our understanding of why certain activities are more likely to be outsourced than others, it will help clarify why many VC-backed businesses didn't have any small-scale or mundane offshoring, even of activities such as testing.

Outsourcing apparently mitigates some of the problems of offshoring and amplifies some others. For instance, CEOs said they had chosen to outsource because a small and not particularly critical operation could not justify the considerable time, money, and effort required to start and manage an in-house offshore operation:

> Even though it's more expensive per person, we just didn't have the infrastructure to rent buildings, hire people, pay taxes, and do whatever the hell else we'd have to do to have a facility in India. And we couldn't build the infrastructure because we didn't have the economy of scale – we started with five people.

> I didn't think we're large enough to have our own center, though, I've seen this done with companies of our size. We didn't have anyone on staff that has experience in managing a remote facility, so it's just not something that we pursued.

> I'm not an expert on international business and law, but I know it was a lot easier and a lot faster for a US company than starting a subsidiary in India.

On the other side, some CEOs said outsourcing increased the problems of getting and retaining good staff abroad:

> Outsourcing companies can't attract the top talent in engineering. If you are a product company and your stock options are worth something, then you can attract talent. A lot of these outsourcing companies hire a lot of junior-level people who are not as productive. I once ran development for a large company. We used an outsourcing company in Romania. They were using right-out-of-school grads. I shut it down and moved everything to our own center in Israel.

Moreover, outsourcing might reduce the time and expenses necessary to start an offshore operation (because some of the organizational and physical infrastructure was already in place), but it did not eliminate the set-up costs. As one CEO, who was eventually pleased with his outsourcing arrangements, said:

> The process was quite grueling and very expensive. I hired a consultant who had set up relationships there before. We set up strict criteria for evaluations. We set up pilot projects. Getting it to work has been more difficult than we would have expected.

Similarly, the costs and problem of coordinating activities across time zones, languages and national cultures did not go away, and may well have increased because communications also had to cross organizational boundaries. Several CEOs said, for instance, that it was important to have a liaison from the outsourcing company in the US to 'translate' their exchanges with the remote staff.

> There is a Srinivas in India and a Srinivas here in the US. They've worked together over many years. Our core technical team tells the Srinivas here what they want built in India – generally stuff like management consoles and reports that the core team doesn't want to do. The Srinivas here then deals with the Srinivas there who manages the six developers who do the coding.

Typically, the outsourcing companies share in, if not fully pay for, the start-up costs and the ongoing management costs (for example, the salaries of the Srinivases), but from the point of view of a VC-backed business, this arrangement has a downside. Outsourcing companies prefer clients with large, long-term projects where they can more easily recover their set-up and management costs. But even the projects of VC-backed businesses, especially the non-core or peripheral candidates for offshoring, don't require a large development staff. And VC-backed businesses also have short time horizons. 'My goal is to accelerate development', one CEO said. 'When outsourcing companies talk to me about two-year development time frames, I start to sweat. I can't think that far ahead. I'm thinking about six-month development – that's the longest possible lead time that I can think about.'

Unsurprisingly, many CEOs we interviewed had found that the premier outsourcing companies did not devote much attention to small customers or did not allocate their most talented staff to their projects:

> I have worked with [a large Indian outsourcing company] in my last startup. We suffered a little bit from that. They tried to give us the attention we needed, but I don't think we got as much attention as we would've gotten from a smaller company.
>
> We then tried working with three different outsourcing firms. But, because we couldn't commit to the number of heads and the duration of contracts that a larger firm could commit to, we couldn't get the best talent in the talent pool of the outsourcing company. We always got the B or C teams – the A team would work on large projects for some Fortune 500 company.

There were a couple of exceptions. In one case, the CEO said:

> We are a customer of Wipro – probably the smallest customer they have. We've never had more than six or seven people assigned to us when they typically have six hundred. They aggressively sought our business because they said they wanted to break into the advertising industry. My friends who had worked with them said we'd be crazy to try to work with them because they're such a slow, bureaucratic, careful organization. But we thought, if we put in the right processes, we could use them for things like very routine data infrastructure management projects. It's been going on for about a year. They have one employee here and their engineers there are queuing up trying to work on our projects because normally, they only get to work for large banking clients.

In the normal course however, the smaller companies who couldn't easily compete for Fortune 500 clients were more interested in serving VC-backed startups – and vice versa. As one CEO said: 'We're looking for outsourcing companies that have between 500 to a 1,000 developers. That is still relatively large, but a contract to engage between twenty or thirty of their developers is more meaningful to them than it is to somebody that had 6,000 developers.' Another said, 'we gravitated to a small company where we could have reasonable mindshare'.

But the mutuality of interest doesn't solve the basic problem of the mismatch between high set-up and overhead costs on the one hand and small, short projects on the other. One way or the other, market forces tend to drive scarce resources – the good engineers – into their highest valued use, namely the large, long-term projects. The mechanism for this in India appears to be through a combination of immigration to the US and steep wage differentials in the local labor market. The premier outsourcing companies bid up wages to attract the best talent. The smaller outsourcing companies that undertake the less economically attractive projects can't afford to pay for high-quality talent and have to make do with the candidates who have been rejected by the larger companies.

Moreover, the interviews that Professor Kumar and I did in Bangalore suggest that smaller outsourcing companies keep losing their good employees. One owner of a small outsourcing company told us that his firm had become 'a training and recruiting ground for the large companies'. His engineers were 'all looking for their "Infosys" card. And when they get the call, how can I tell them not to go?'

Another problem reported by a CEO (of Indian origin) was keeping the interest of a small company after they had become successful:

> Our partner had originally been started as a product company – by someone I had known for a long time and had run out of funds. We provided a financial lifeline. Our understanding was that if this project worked out, we would acquire them. We carved out something that one customer wanted but wasn't strategic for us. We provided most of the architecture and design.
>
> But apparently our interests weren't aligned. When they found a more attractive opportunity they lost interest in our project. Also there didn't seem to be the notion of consequences for them – they were far away and they didn't have a name to lose in the US. We disengaged as fast as possible, and have decided not to think of doing any more development abroad until we have enough heft, so that vendors in India will pay attention to us.

To get around the lack of interest of large outsourcing companies, one CEO said his company had joined up with three other companies of similar size to set up a dedicated outsourcing operation. The circumstances were unusual: all four companies were 'telecom-centric', but they weren't competitors. All of them had data entry tasks, which made it easy (compared to developing software) to redeploy staff across projects. And the four companies could among them support about a thousand 'seats'.

A more common approach to solving the problem was the hybrid, 'build-operate-transfer' model: a local entrepreneur would take responsibility for setting up the offshore center and hire its staff ('build'), manage the operation for some transitional period and ultimately transfer ownership of the operation (or sometimes just its staff) to the US company. Throughout the period, as the CEO of Stoneriver[8] explained, the offshore staff would be treated 'as if they were employees of the US company':

> They call themselves Stoneriver India. They spend a hundred percent of their time working for us. They have company e-mail addresses. As soon as they're hired, they come here for a five-week stint, they work in our offices, they go back, and then they come back here seven or eight months later. We even paid them a bonus this year, when my VP of engineering went over there last week. That's very unique. We weren't obligated by contract, but we're trying to engender some good will and some loyalty, and boy, that went over really well.

It was not clear to me, however, that the hybrid model could fully square the circle, as it were, in attracting and keeping top talent. The CEO quoted above, for instance, also said that 'we now have just a handful of employees; we will get it to about 20 by the middle of the next quarter when we have our next big product release. Then we will pare back the team by about five.' A flexible workforce has many benefits, but presumably employee retention is not high on that list. In any event, for the companies we interviewed, it was early days for the build-operate-transfer approach; in most cases the experiment had been in operation for about a year and only one company had actually reached the 'transfer' stage.

The pattern of offshore locations seemed to track the kinds of activity undertaken. Offshore manufacturing (which, as mentioned, was predominantly outsourced) was concentrated in the Far East, although NAFTA countries (Canada and Mexico) and Western Europe were also represented, as Table 3.1 indicates.

As also mentioned, the development of complete core products offshore was predominantly undertaken in in-house facilities; in turn, most such in-house facilities had been started offshore along with the companies themselves or had been secured through acquisitions. All were located in advanced economies. This was also the pattern with the other kinds of in-house offshoring operations as well. For instance, all the in-house service operations abroad were in Europe or Japan.

India, it will come as no surprise, was a favored location for outsourced development activities such as testing and outsourced services such as data entry. To a considerable degree, this reflects a snowball effect: India became, early on, a low-cost source of programming labor, initially on site and then increasingly offshore. Over time, the number of Indian vendors and their total capacity for providing outsourcing services grew substantially, as did a number of individuals in the US who had used their services. Therefore, when we asked CEOs why they had chosen an Indian outsourcing company, a typical answer was: 'Our VP of engineering and I had both worked with people in India, and we knew how outsourcers in India work'. Some CEOs also mentioned receiving e-mails and phone calls from Indian outsourcing companies 'practically every day'.

Although to some degree the success of Indian outsourcing fed on itself – awareness and knowledge begat more awareness and knowledge – there was also a self-limiting element. Labor shortages in India, and the emergence of competitors in other countries attracted to the business by the success of Indian outsourcing companies, had encouraged some CEOs to look elsewhere:

> We are looking at the Ukraine and the ex-Soviet Republics – one of our partners has an operation in Ukraine and perhaps we will get some people through them. India strikes us as overplayed – the price advantage is not as great as it once was – and there is an employee loyalty issue. We hear it's a very cash-driven market now. A software developer is paid about $30,000 to $36,000 a year. Guys will go across the street for another thousand a year.

Two CEOs said they had set up outsourcing relationships in China because of personal relationships there. One had gone to Canada because of 'the difficulty of managing outsourcing in India – the savings of going to India weren't worth it, and we wanted something safe and predictable'. Nevertheless, overall, India was the location of choice: 16 of the 28 companies that had outsourced development (to any degree) had done so only in India, 9 had not outsourced in India and 3 had outsourcing relationships in India and some other country. Similarly, of the 14 companies that outsourced testing, nine had done so in India.

LEGAL ISSUES

Concerns about the loss of IP (intellectual property) affected choices of whether, what, and where to offshore. My interviews suggest that the core value of the innovations of many VC-backed businesses cannot be secured by patents. Often the only legal protection is through copyright laws, trade secrets or confidentiality agreements with employees. Several CEOs lacked confidence about such protections outside the US and were hesitant to let the crucial features of their IP 'out of the building', let alone outside the country:

> I don't feel comfortable with our IP traveling all over the world to different cultures and morals and laws. What is actual law in one place and what is actual law in another place is different. And then there is standard practice – doing business in Italy is an entirely different scenario, whether it's against the law or not.

It's a very long, drawn out process abroad for defending your IP and prosecuting those who took it. Things that we just take for granted in the US are vulnerabilities abroad.

We are very careful about not handing enough of the product over to be an IP risk. We have different levels of trust with our outsourcing partners, and we don't trust *anyone* to handle the complete IP.

We do QA and documentation outside the US, but we are not ready to move our engineering. We might save 60 percent on our development costs, but it's not worth the risk – one weird guy could destroy the business.

The core team here in the US has all of the intellectual property. The things that are given to the offshore team are things that, even if they stole it, we would be happy.

The decision of where to offshore was also influenced by CEOs' beliefs about the safety of their intellectual property. For instance, a CEO whose company was about to start outsourcing from India said, 'I believe that the Indian outsourcers have a process and a method for maintaining confidentiality. I don't have any clue about whether folks in other countries have that process or not.' Another said he had ruled out Korea because, in his previous venture, he had found that although the quality of programmers was high, 'they steal everything – there is no way you can protect your code there'.

Concerns about China seemed widespread. In some cases, the cost advantages made it worthwhile to offshore in China – after taking elaborate measures to protect the company's intellectual property (see Box 3.5). In other cases, the companies decided that the benefits weren't worth the risk:

We were approached by a competitor to our current Taiwanese supplier. They had better costs for us, and certainly [we] were intrigued by the costs. But they were based in China, and the intellectual property situation in China is such that we did not want to risk it because if our IP gets out, that's the end of the company.

In China, they steal. I don't know how else to say it. They steal. They'll take a picture of Snoopy and sell it as Shoopy. What I'm told by people from China is that when somebody sees a CD, their immediate thought is, 'How many copies can I make from this, and how many can I sell?' Maybe it's not really rampant, but I didn't have the time to get the data to find that out. We went with India with people that we knew and we trusted.

My CTO [Chief Technical Officer] is from China and is paranoid about outsourcing from there.

BOX 3.5 DIVIDE AND DEFEND

A CEO whose company's manufacturing operations and suppliers were located in the Far East described the steps they had taken to protect their intellectual property:

There are four steps to making our product. The first is making the ingredients. We developed one of the ingredients – a unique powder. We make that ourselves, because it is the most unique differentiator for our technology, in China. We've split the process across two factories that are an hour apart by car so that the employees don't have access to the entire process: A lot of the trade secret theft in China occurs by the employees at the engineering level who start their own business.

Sometimes the management team sets up a satellite operation to produce the same material for the China market without the parent company being aware of it. So the Chinese nationals who we hired to run the plant are Western-educated, with families and a legal resident status in the US. If they get caught stealing, they'd be subject to North American courts. They are also highly compensated with stock and have a significant upside in the success of the company.

In step two of the process, the powder is blended with other ingredients to make a liquid coat that is applied to a metal foil. A subcontractor does this for us in Korea, which is a little bit more secure than doing it in China. The coated materials get shipped back into China, where a subcontractor assembles the 'guts' of the product in a remote location. There is some intellectual property in the mechanical aspects of assembly, and we do run some risk that people could knock off some of the things we've done. The output is then sent to a subcontractor in Taiwan for the final step.

It would have been nice to use a single facility but five facilities in three countries protects our IP.

CEOs were also skeptical about the enforceability of contracts:

There's a written contract governed by both US and Indian law. Now contracts in India may be difficult to enforce, but the person we are dealing with has a US-based company. As it happens though, we couldn't really enforce the contract. In the end, people can get out – there are tons of holes in the contract, and there are tons of things you can do to stall.

We have a long-term contract with a Canadian manufacturer, but it's more of an understanding – it's not really enforceable.

Contracts are not, let's say, adhered to very religiously in China or other parts of Asia for that matter. You sign a contract, and two months later they come back to you and say, 'Well, we didn't realize that we have to . . . so we have to charge

> more.' What you have to do is make the best possible deal and understand that it'll be a continuous negotiation process every month for the rest of your relationship. Sometimes this happens right up front. With one company, we had months of discussion at long distance and over a couple of visits we negotiated a contract. We then spent eight hours going through every line of the agreement. When we were done, we went to dinner, we had lobsters, we had wine. The next day, they came in at noon, sat, and said, 'We don't think that contract's fair.' I ripped up the contract in front of them, threw it in the trash, and said, 'What would you like to do?' They were very happy.

The aggravation apart, the contracting problems did not seem to have much of an impact on concrete decisions, especially in comparison to concerns about intellectual property. This is hardly surprising: flagrant breaches of contract or take-it-or-leave-it demands for renegotiation are a normal fact of entrepreneurial life, even in the US. And as Howard Stevenson and I once found, the strong routinely get away with a lot: the usual response is to accommodate or terminate the relationship when firms or individuals who have more market power or financial clout breach their contracts or promises. Retaliation or suing to recover damages is a last resort:

> Retaliation is a double loss. First you lose your money; now you're losing time.

> Bite me once, it is your fault; bite me twice, my fault. But bite me twice, and I won't have anything to do with you because I have better things to do with my life. I'm not going to litigate just for the pleasure of getting even with you.[9]

Therefore, even if contractual safeguards are somewhat, or even considerably weaker, doing business abroad may not be vastly different in this respect from doing business at home.

Why, then, did the businesses bother with negotiating contracts? One CEO said, 'because it makes you feel good'. Another said his VCs had insisted he negotiate the right to hire the employees of the Indian outsourcing company who worked on his company's projects, even though such a contract would be unenforceable – anywhere in the world.[10] A third said that even though his Chinese suppliers had a 'relaxed attitude' toward contractual obligations, they believed that 'Western companies are contract-oriented, and they would think us not very serious if we didn't negotiate a 30-page contract and just shook hands instead'.

But there were more substantive reasons as well. Some CEOs regarded contracts with suppliers as useful 'mutual-planning devices'. For instance, a fabless semiconductor company had entered into a contract with a foundry to reserve line capacity for $10 million worth of goods a year.

The supplier couldn't really 'hold the customer's side's feet to the fire', on this, but it was useful in establishing production schedules. Contracts similarly helped clarify mutual expectations (for instance, about service levels) and provided a modicum of protection against personnel changes. If, for instance, individuals moved on, their successors would have some knowledge of what their predecessors had agreed to. Negotiations could help build relationships, because 'when you spend day after day going over a contract you get to know each other better'.[11] And given the significant potential for miscommunication and misunderstandings in cross-country commerce, it is reasonable to expect serious negotiations over contracts, regardless of the legal problems of enforcement.

SPECIAL CASES: DRUGS AND DEVICES

Interviews with CEOs engaged in developing pharmaceutical products and medical devices regulated by the FDA suggested that their innovative activities have some distinctive features. Notably, the time and expense required to commercialize new drugs and devices encourages high levels of specialization. On the pharmaceutical side, for instance, companies tend to focus on some part of the process – in my sample, many companies had licensed promising compounds, which they expected to 'develop' (or what in other industries would be called 'test') through a few phases of clinical trials. They were also highly virtual; they expected to retain a Contract Research Organization (CRO) to manage the trials. And FDA regulations made it difficult to 'try-it-fix-it'. Once a testing protocol had been approved by the FDA, midstream changes were usually not permitted, and the drug or device would either 'pass' or 'fail'. Below, we will see how these distinctive features affected offshoring.

One problem faced by the companies developing drugs was that the top-tier CROs (like Paraxel), which had the capacity to manage trials in many different countries, were regarded as insufficiently attentive or too expensive for a small business. The smaller CROs offered more attention or better prices – but they lacked the capacity to manage overseas trials:

> If you are working with a global CRO and you wanted an international trial, it would be a touch more expensive because you would incur translation costs and things. But as long as that CRO has clinical management people abroad, these additional charges would be relatively small. But we work with smaller, unglobal CROs who are well less than half the cost of the Paraxels. We are basically shopping the K-marts, and the difference in cost is incredible.
>
> Paraxel and all the big guys will tell you that they care just as much about small companies as they care about Merck, but in my experience, that's not true.

> I think that the small, domestic CROs care about your business a lot more than do big, huge companies for whom you're a fraction of their business.

But why not use one or several small overseas CROs? This option, however, would require more 'bandwidth' than could be justified by a small, early stage trial. As the CEO of a company developing a drug to treat diabetes said:

> We have three sites in the US for our initial clinical trial, but we also evaluated a site in Lima, Peru, of all places. South America has a very high incidence of diabetes and is an excellent place to do diabetes research. But we concluded that given the small size of our initial studies and given that we are dinky players with limited management ability, we had to stay in the US. With just 45 people, we couldn't afford to lose one or two spending time in Peru.

A third issue was the competence of CROs in low-cost locations – a matter of much greater concern in drug trials than in software testing. One CEO (and an immigrant from India) explained:

> You can do clinical trials in India for a third or a fourth of what it would cost in Europe or the United States. There are a significant number of patients available, and their compliance rate is very high, because they don't get the drug for free.
>
> The problem is you don't want to use a bad CRO even if they were willing to work for you pro bono. CROs can screw up by misdosing – giving the wrong drug, giving the wrong dose, or forgetting. These kinds of screw ups are critical. The regulations describe pretty much to a T what needs to be done, and any deviation from that is not acceptable. And, you have to report everything to the FDA. So, if an accident takes place in India, you have to report that to the FDA.
>
> All this requires a great deal of technical skill. These people have PhDs, and like MDs, they have to go through board certification and keep taking continuing education credits to keep their board certifications active. But you still don't have CROs in India and other developing countries who have this kind of ability yet.

Some companies had started trials in Europe because of the availability of patients and samples, not lower costs.

> We were driven to doing trials [for a treatment of Crohn's disease] in 10 countries in Europe because there is less competition for patients and more availability. There are places in Eastern Europe with a high incidence of Crohn's disease. And we were looking for patients who have not been previously treated by a certain compound that is used broadly and aggressively in the US, but not in Europe.

> We want to enroll as many patients as quickly as we can because the clock is ticking, and in Eastern Europe, they are incented to enroll much more quickly. For example, in Prague, cardiologists only make the equivalent of 500 US

> dollars in a month, but if they participate in our clinical trial they can make a year's salary with just a few patients. So they're very much incented to enroll patients. The price per patient is a little bit less over there, but not significantly so.

> 'We're developing a non-invasive test [for endometriosis]. All we need is a little vial of blood [taken from patients before the patient gets the traditional laparoscopic test]. We found clinical researchers in Europe who had been collecting samples for other trials, and they were able to share those samples with us. When we approached physicians in the US who had been doing studies on endometriosis, more often than not, the physician would say: 'I'm sorry, I can not share my samples because your use is different from what's allowed in my IRB [Institutional Review Board] approval.'

CEOs also anticipated doing more overseas trials in the future for marketing reasons and for getting approval abroad.

> We'll run our phase one and phase two trials domestically. But if we get to phase three, we will think about doing that globally. We're very active, even today, in engaging overseas opinion leaders in what we're doing and getting their thoughts on our next set of trials. And if want approval to sell in Japan, we will have to run Japanese trials.

On the preclinical side, one CEO said his company had used labs in the UK, because 'they had the competencies we needed. They weren't cheaper by more than 10 percent, if that. I'm a firm believer in competence over cost.'

Only one CEO said his company had tried to take advantage of lower labor costs abroad:

> We started off as a virtual company, but then because we advanced our pipeline faster than we had expected, we needed a lab to do a lot more pre-clinical work. We selected Shanghai because of cost savings.
>
> I wouldn't say that we do cutting-edge work in China. The people all happen to have PhDs, but the work could be done by well-trained technicians. We do a lot of high-throughput work. We run an awful lot of in vitro and in vivo studies – for about 10 percent of the cost in the US, and coordination hasn't been a big problem. And it's not like IT. Say you develop a new process in IT. By the time you have that set up in China, it's already outdated. In biotech, you have a longer cycle and there are components of preclinical development that are pretty standard and straightforward. We can define the work very specifically with very clear outputs. Also, we only have 14 people, which we could grow to 30 – it's not like we have a hundred people.

Developers of medical devices routinely undertook (or seriously considered undertaking) human trials abroad before doing so in the US. CEOs said this was because the more flexible regulatory regimes outside the US facilitated the trial and error necessary to develop the devices.

> There is a lot of iterative invention in devices, and we need clinical input. But doing that in the US is very time consuming. We first did animal studies and bench work here, and the first patient we treated was in Melbourne, Australia. We then aggressively recruited sites outside the US, based on their regulatory hurdles or lack thereof. So, after Australia, we ended up in Hong Kong, Brazil, and then throughout Europe. Fortunately for us, whatever you figure out through iteration abroad will also work at home, but it would have been much more convenient for us if we could have done the trials here first. This is our primary market – there are 3 million people in America who could use our device. In fact, there are a lot of reasons why we would have focused on the US, were it not for that regulatory component.

> We're not in humans yet; we do expect that when we go into humans, our first human implants will be outside of the US. That's largely because the regulatory bodies of other countries are less risk-averse. Obviously, no matter what the regulatory body is, you would never put anything in a person that you thought would harm them. But going overseas does allow you to quickly determine safety and efficacy. Then, you and your investors have the confidence to proceed into the more difficult regions. It also allows you to refine your product before you take on the system in the US. It's very difficult and very expensive to make changes once you start the US process, so you really want to make sure the bugs are worked out somewhere else first.

> Do not attribute this to me, but I think the FDA prefers testing to be done outside the United States first. That's not a politically correct statement, but that's my impression. And it's easier to do testing in other parts of the world because the regulatory hurdles are lower. However, we were able to find a clinical pathway that allowed us to do our testing in the United States first. That was a big boon for us.

CEOs of companies that performed human trials abroad did not, however, favor offshoring their other functions:

> Our product is unique, and what we do is very specialized. It is very difficult to find people who can have the necessary skills. And, when the skills you need are scarce, you have to go to where it is. For us it's the United States. There are other medical devices that are more commodity products that can be developed with low-cost labor overseas because those skill sets may exist there.

> We have only two employees outside the US. We service everything else internationally by flying people out of California. We do all our R&D out of one facility. In fact, early stage companies should have R&D, manufacturing, quality control, regulatory, marketing in one contiguous facility.

> If you're making a commodity medical product, say saline or infusion lines, you have to produce it in a low-cost location. But costs aren't the driver for us

now – it's getting it right, quickly. Everything is fast-paced, and if you have to communicate by e-mail or by phone or even by video conference, you lose the ability to make things happen quickly. You can't have hallway meetings spontaneously – unscheduled meetings where somebody has a problem, and suddenly everyone gathers around and comes up with a plan to address it. Also, if you have multiple locations, you need more people. For instance, a team that only does manufacturing and another team focused on R&D. Now, because everything is in a single location, we have R&D and manufacturing people that will sometimes do more manufacturing and sometimes do more R&D.

I've been at early stage companies that didn't co-locate their staff. They always lived to regret it. For instance, I was in a company located in a modular business park with many bays. We were running out of space, and the company next to us wasn't going to move, so we jumped a bay. All of a sudden, part of our organization got disconnected even though it was only 50 yards away. It was as if that team didn't exist; they weren't engaged in what their colleagues were doing. Another startup company I once worked at was in the Bay Area [in San Francisco]. They had developed a product they were ready to go to market with. They decided to build a huge manufacturing plant down in Temecula, in the desert east of San Diego, where the land was cheap. But then the engineers were flying north and south every week, and it was really disruptive. So, whatever cost savings they may have gained were lost in efficiency, and quality, and the ability to innovate.

CONTRASTS WITH LARGE COMPANIES

Fortune 100 companies, especially in the IT and pharmaceutical sectors, derived a significantly higher share of their revenues from overseas customers than did the VC-backed businesses in our sample. We do not have a similar measure to compare offshoring; by all accounts, however, large companies have also been ahead in taking advantage of this as well. For instance, nearly every IT company in the Fortune 100 has a large and visible presence in Bangalore, whereas only a handful of the VC-backed businesses had operations in Bangalore and none of them on the scale of the Fortune 100 companies. And Bangalore is, of course, just one of the offshore locations from which large companies secure goods and services and undertake their R&D.

Large companies apparently enjoy several advantages in offshoring. These include ample financial resources, managerial bandwidth and extensive experience of doing business abroad. Multinationals like General Electric, Citibank and American Express, whose in-house and outsourced activities catalyzed Indian offshoring, had been operating subsidiaries and joint ventures in India for many decades before that.

The activities of large companies are also more suited for offshoring.

A large proportion comprise stable, high-throughput operations (such as sending and collecting on bills) that can be codified and consolidated in one low-cost offshore location. Moreover, even though routine activities may dominate innovative activities, because of the enormous size of Fortune 100 companies, their portfolio of innovative projects is large. And at least some projects from this portfolio are attractive candidates for offshoring because the requirements can be specified up-front, and they do not require ongoing interactions with customers. Examples include the development of utilities (such as printer drivers) for existing products, the porting of software from one hardware platform to another, and upgrades of in-house mainframe systems.

Furthermore, large corporations undertake some basic – or what I have called 'upstream' – research (that VC-backed businesses typically use but do not produce). Such research, too, can be done without interactions with customers – and at a more measured pace than commercial development.

Their size and scope provide large companies advantages in recruiting local staff and building relationships with high-quality outsourcing companies. The former are attracted by the job security and career opportunities available in the international networks of large employers. The latter find the economics of working on the kinds of projects that large companies outsource more attractive: routine activities like billing are more 'contractible' (because, for instance, the requirements can be more easily satisfied), and the fixed costs of marketing and maintenance of the relationship can be amortized over multi-million-dollar, multi-year deals.[12] And, as mentioned, these advantages of large companies allow them to pay wages that make them the employer of first resort for the best local talent, leaving VC-backed companies with somewhat slim pickings.

RECAP AND BROADER IMPLICATIONS

The tight capital constraints that may encourage VC-backed companies to focus on the domestic market create pressures in the opposite direction when it comes to offshoring. Many VCs apparently strongly encourage their businesses to try to take advantage of low development costs overseas. Nevertheless, the use of offshoring by the companies we studied was limited. Very few businesses chose to develop their core products in low-cost locations because of the value of proximity and the difficulties of partitioning. Companies that focused on relationships with domestic customers from whom they could get rapid feedback also wanted their developers close to these customers and to the other members of their staff.

Several other factors also reinforced their reluctance to offshore. These included the scarcity of managerial bandwidth, the relatively small savings that could be realized from offshoring small teams, the limited supply of capable staff available in offshore locations, the competition from large companies for this staff, the difficulty of communicating across time zones and cultures, and the fear of losing their intellectual property.

These difficulties, however, appear to have been less of an impediment in the offshoring of activities such as testing and the development of ancillary products. Here, proximity to customers was not critical, and the tasks could be more easily partitioned and sent off to a remote location. These activities also did not require as much managerial attention or the brightest and the best talent and did not put the company's intellectual property at risk.

Looking beyond the trade-offs facing just the VC-backed businesses, the analysis in this chapter suggests generally that there are many impediments to the offshoring of midstream innovative activity, whether or not it is undertaken by VC-backed businesses. There isn't a single floodgate that, if opened, would unleash a torrential outflow of innovative activity. Moreover, the impediments to offshoring don't appear to be ones that will decline as quickly or even at the same rate. For instance, as people and firms in more low-cost locations abroad learn how to outsource – and knowledge of their capabilities disseminates – the scarcity of labor could decline. It is not at all clear, however, when – if at all – technology will allow full and deep communication, not just the exchange of words and numbers across time zones, cultures and working styles, or provide a good virtual substitute for real meetings around a white board or an actual visit to a customer site.

The offshoring of manufacturing and of routine services, it is also worth noting, wasn't restrained by many of the problems that hold back the offshoring of midstream innovation. First, specifications of what is to be manufactured can be precisely communicated. Then, there is little need for ongoing dialogue – the buyer can simply examine the goods produced and see if they meet the agreed specifications. This is rarely the case with midstream development projects – the outputs are difficult to specify in advance. Therefore, ongoing engagement with remote staff is important. Second, in many manufacturing activities (and in some routine services), the notion of an unbounded supply of unused labor (that can do the job) is closer to reality than is the case with innovative activities, where the supply is limited. Moreover, when a source arises (as might happen when garment exporters set up shop in Bangladesh), it is not difficult for customers to test whether they are up to the mark. Therefore, additional supply can enter the market with relative ease. Third, in manufacturing (although usually not in services), an intermittent supply can be satisfactory. For instance, the requirements of a small semiconductor company can be satisfied by a day's output from a production line in a foundry once every quarter. With software development, however, a continuous supply, preferably from the same programmers, is necessary. Labor requirements cannot be satisfied by securing the services of the entire staff of an outsourcing company for a day or two.

That said, innovators are increasingly undertaking some activities, such as testing offshore, whose significance should not be underplayed. Testing may not be glamorous, but it does account for, according to many experts, about half the time and expense of developing software. There are two ways to interpret the significance of such offshoring. One is that it takes away the jobs of US workers who would otherwise have been employed in such activities (or, at least, reduces their wages). The other interpretation, which the analysis in my book (Bhidé 2008) but not in this chapter favors, is that the total output of innovations increases because more projects can be undertaken with the same capital, and some of the labor that might have been absorbed in routine activity becomes available. As a result, employment in higher-paid and more interesting development work increases. Even more importantly, from the point of view of the overall good, the innovations enhance the productivity of their users.

NOTES

1. The why (and why not) questions are important because this will help the reader (as it did me) assess whether the patterns I report are an artifact of my sample or in fact are representative of the universe of VC-backed businesses. They are also helpful in judging whether the patterns are likely to be transitory or be sustained over the long haul.
2. I include in this count a company started by Israeli founders that was incorporated in the US and had some sales and marketing staff in New York. Everything else was in Israel.
3. It is also worth noting that it probably was not low wages that encouraged these companies to keep their development centers in their countries of origin. The companies had originated in advanced economies, where wages were not much lower than US wages.
4. The seemingly high proportion is explained by the bursting of the internet bubble, after which a number of struggling companies were up for sale. Also, the difficulty of going public (for companies that weren't struggling) meant that more companies remained under VC ownership when they reached the 'normal' stage for undertaking acquisitions.
5. Another CEO said: 'What we do requires a deep understanding of communication protocols. Our software has to communicate with highly complex applications that our customers have installed and there are no open APIs to write codes to.'
6. The number of 'communication channels' increases as the square of the number of people: with twice as many people you have four times the number of possible interactions.
7. A few CEOs did say that they used offshore and US programmers to work on the same project. In all such cases the actual number of offshore programmers was small (four or fewer) and most CEOs thought it was a really bad idea.

8. Disguised name.
9. Bhidé and Stevenson (1990).
10. 'Imagine what would happen in the US', he said, 'if we fire an employee with whom we have a non-compete agreement, and he then goes and works for a competitor. The only way to keep your employees is to have them want to work for you, not because of a contract.'
11. Although I am not aware of any research about this, it is reasonable to assume that similar benefits help explain some of the effort that goes into negotiating contracts within the US as well.
12. The effort required to start and manage software development projects is certainly more substantial, but the magnitude of the projects justifies the considerable time put into the planning and oversight. Moreover, in large, complex projects, the additional effort required for remote development represents a small proportion of the total effort that would normally be put into an equivalent on-site project.

REFERENCES

Bhidé, A. (2008), *The Venturesome Economy: How Innovation Sustains Prosperity in a More Connected World*, Princeton, NY: Princeton University Press.

Brooks, F. (1995), *The Mythical Man-Month: Essays on Software Engineering*, 2nd ed., Indianapolis, IN: Addison-Wesley.

4. Entrepreneurship, culture and openness

Edmund Phelps and Gylfi Zoega

INTRODUCTION

Advances in scientific knowledge – in technology – are made by scientists working in research labs around the world. At any point in time there is multidimensional frontier technology that consists of technological breakthroughs made in each industry and each country. Conceiving of new products and new methods against the background of existing technologies and the accessible stock of past products and methods is generally the contribution of business people, as Hayek (1967/1978) understood – the knowledgeable and imaginative businessmen or financiers or end users. Developing and marketing such visions requires the undertaking of entrepreneurs (often the conceivers), whose range and zeal were prized by Schumpeter (1911). Evaluating and trying the new products and methods is done by the cutting edge managers of Nelson and Phelps (1966) and the venturesome consumers of Bhidé (2000). The Hayekian innovators, drawing on the expertise that comes from their specialized experience and close observation, think of new ideas for possible development and subsequent sale in domestic or overseas markets. Schumpeterian entrepreneurs monitor developments in technologies, products and methods at home and abroad and contemplate how profitable it would be to adapt or improve or cheapen existing goods or methods. It follows that while productivity improvements receive a huge boost from technological progress, the two are only loosely linked. A period of significant technological progress can at the same time witness very low rates of productivity growth; and, vice versa, one can have periods with rapid productivity growth and little technological progress.

Those who conceive, develop and try out a novel product or method are hoping for some combination of pecuniary profit and personal satisfaction in the process. When they find an opportunity that passes that market test they improve welfare – widening the set of goods and methods available and offering satisfaction from the conceiving, developing and trying a new good or method. (When they fail either to make a profit or gain satisfaction, thus burning up resources that could have been spent otherwise without generating the hoped-for benefits, they may reduce welfare – though the attractive jobs they created in the attempt may have reduced involuntary unemployment.) In analogy to scientific discoveries, one can talk of a business discovery whenever the 'discovery procedure' hits upon and implements a plausible innovation and the latter passes the market test.

Like technological discoveries, business discoveries fall into two groups. The entrepreneur may discover ways in which he can import foreign business discoveries and adapt them to local circumstances. He spreads foreign business knowledge to his country and improves local welfare as a result. Such an entrepreneur would need to have a feel for the nuances of local markets, local tastes and the ability of the local workforce to provide the service. Amar Bhidé has pointed out (2000) the importance of the ability of local consumers to enjoy the new technology. But none of this is obvious *a priori*. A systematically successful local entrepreneur has the ability to gauge these factors fairly accurately and to detect those business innovations that are capable of earning a profit. In this he is facing Knightian risk (Knight 1921) because he is doing something for the very first time and no prior experience will enable him to calculate the probability of success.

The second type of entrepreneur is one who makes genuinely original business innovations, not modelled on any existing ones. Such an entrepreneur pushes out the frontier of business knowledge in the world. He may, however, benefit from the vast array of existing business practices, each being an innovation inherited from the past. Standing on the shoulders of giants may help the would-be entrepreneur in miscellaneous ways. Past entrepreneurs may have created a climate of creativity, self-reliance and ambition that affects the behaviour of current would-be entrepreneurs. Casual evidence suggests that successful individuals in different professions have a performance-enhancing effect on others by setting high standards of achievement, demonstrating that success is possible and showing the path towards success. Success often breeds further success. Past entrepreneurial successes may also have affected the institutional environment by breaking up the pattern of entrenched interests and their hold on the power of the state. Laws are often passed, thrown aside or modified following successful innovations, either to promote further innovations or to prevent excesses and market failures that were not previously known.

MEASURES OF DYNAMISM

Our measure of dynamism goes beyond the simple notion of labor productivity or labor productivity growth. While labor productivity may seem

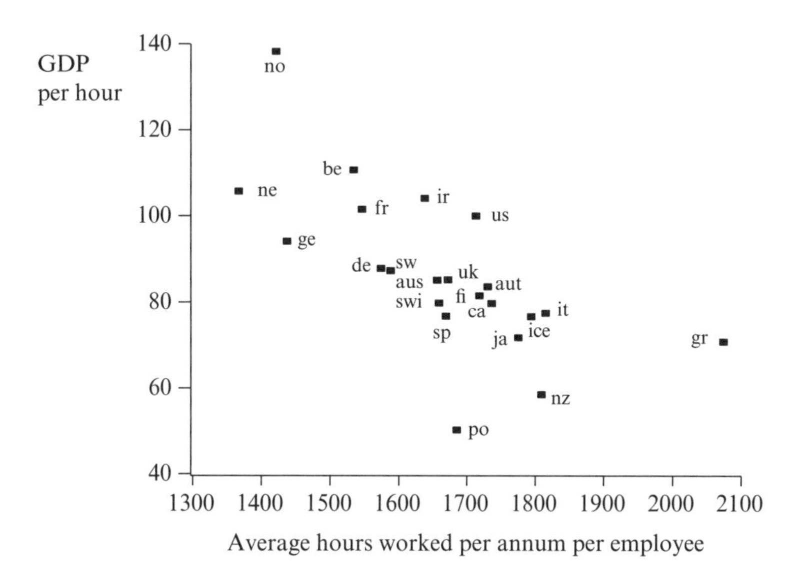

Figure 4.1 Hourly productivity and hours of work

to be an obvious measure of dynamism, it suffers from a couple of rather obvious shortcomings in this regard. First, the hourly productivity figures in Europe are skewed by the absence of many low productivity people, particularly the young ones, who are counted as unemployed. Second, as shown in Figure 4.1, the level of hourly productivity is also an imperfect measure in that hourly productivity is related to the number of hours worked. This may be either because longer hours cause fatigue, which lowers output per hour, or because shorter working hours put pressure on workers to perform well on the job. This helps explain why, to take just one example, output per hour is high in France where there are comparatively few hours worked. It has been suggested that in addition, firms only hire when the workforce has been stretched thin compared to most other countries owing to their exceptional firing costs. In contrast, productivity in the US is high despite the much higher number of hours worked.[1]

Instead of using labor productivity in levels or growth rates, we follow Phelps (2005) by defining a dynamic economy as one based on creativity – innovative ideas, problem solving and the discovery and development of human talents – where the work offered by the business economy must offer mental stimulation and challenges in the form of problems to solve, and in this way lead to the discovery of talents. In the spirit of Dewey and William James, the rewarding life then consists of problem solving, taking action and putting one's ideas to the test – whether that is the market, a sporting match or the laboratory experiment. Hence, our appropriate measure of dynamism becomes job satisfaction. Our thesis is hence that a dynamic economy is primarily bound to yield high levels of job satisfaction.

We use the World Values Survey (Inglehart, 2006) to get a measure of job satisfaction. The question used to measure the level of job satisfaction in the survey is:

> Overall, how satisfied or dissatisfied are you with your job? a) Dissatisfied; b) 2; c) 3; d) 4; e) 5; f) 6; g) 7; h) 8; i) 9; j) Satisfied

We take the proportion of respondents who express satisfaction 8 and above and use this as a measure of absorption in one's work and deep gratification from it rather than merely a cheerful nature. This gives us 14 observations for the OECD countries in year 2000.

Richard Layard (2005) has in his recent book *Happiness: Lessons from a New Science* come close to defining happiness along similar lines. Following his lead we can use reported happiness as an alternative measure of dynamism. Again, using the World Values Survey we find responses to the following question:

> Taking all things together, would you say you are: a) Very happy; b) Quite happy; c) Not very happy; d) Not at all happy.

We take the fraction of respondents who pick 'very happy' as a measure of happiness. The correlation between our measure of job satisfaction and our measure of happiness is 0.63 but the benefit of the happiness measure is that we have observations on a larger sample of 22 OECD countries.

Our measure of job satisfaction is correlated with a number of other measures of economic performance. The labor force participation rate and the unemployment rate can be interpreted as proxies for the degree of prosperity in the sense of the discovery and development of talents. See Appendix 4.1 for more data. Figure 4.2 shows that across the sample of 14 OECD countries, job satisfaction is inversely correlated with unemployment and positively correlated with labor force participation of the young, both men and women, and of women in the 25–64 years category. The correlation between job satisfaction and the overall unemployment rate is −0.63 and the correlation with the rate of participation of young men is 0.60; the correlation for young women is 0.73; and that for women aged 25–64 is 0.57. This supports the thesis proposed by Phelps (2005) that a dynamic economy may have an impact on unemployment and participation through job satisfaction.

We are left with the fundamental question: what are the ingredients or

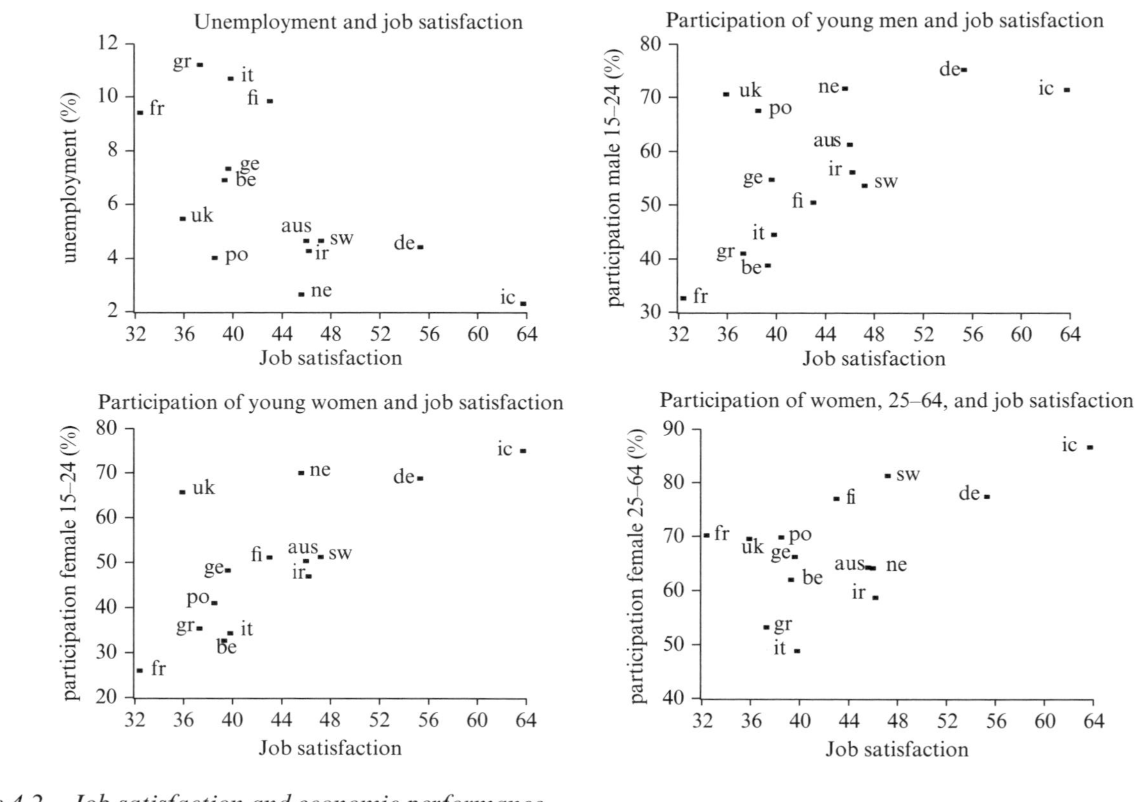

Figure 4.2 Job satisfaction and economic performance

the social recipe for an entrepreneurial economy? Ever since Adam Smith, economists have focused on institutions, the underlying assumption being that all humans are alike and given the right set of institutions they will be guided by an invisible hand to deliver maximum social welfare. Yet many attempts to export institutions to other cultures, such as those in Africa, South America and the Middle East, have been far less than successful. There remains the question of how the spirit of creative entrepreneurship can be started. One possibility is that the answer is found in a nation's culture. While Marx took culture to depend on the economy's structure, the Enlightenment thinkers all took it for granted that culture – meaning values, attitudes, morals and beliefs – mattered for the effectiveness of business life. This Enlightenment view lives in Weber's Protestant ethic (1905) and Schumpeter's theory of economic development (1911).

THE DETERMINANTS OF JOB SATISFACTION AND HAPPINESS

One obvious candidate variable for determining job satisfaction and happiness is gross domestic product (GDP) per capita. In fact, macroeconomics textbooks sometimes focus on output without discussing the relationship with happiness and job satisfaction.

The use of GDP per capita as a sole measure of economic welfare is so commonplace that we would like to discuss its significance briefly before continuing our exploration of the determinants of happiness. A higher level of GDP makes it possible to improve the standard of health care and education as well as a higher level of private consumption. For this reason, it has come as a surprise that the relationship between GDP and reported happiness appears less than robust (see, for example, Layard, 2005). Thus, happiness does not appear to have an upward trend from one generation to the next. It is also apparent when looking at current generations that a high level of income does not always guarantee happiness. There are other factors that are important, such as marriage, good health, a rewarding and challenging job, friends and family. Clearly, a high level of output per capita does not guarantee any of these things. More public holidays and a longer annual vacation could thus strengthen the family at the expense of output. Culture also matters. It is partly manifested in work ethics and hence output but it also affects institutions and output as well as other determinants of job satisfaction and happiness. For this reason it appears to be more reasonable to model the relationship between culture and institutions, on the one hand, and job satisfaction and happiness, on the other hand. Focusing exclusively on GDP – its level and rate of growth – can be

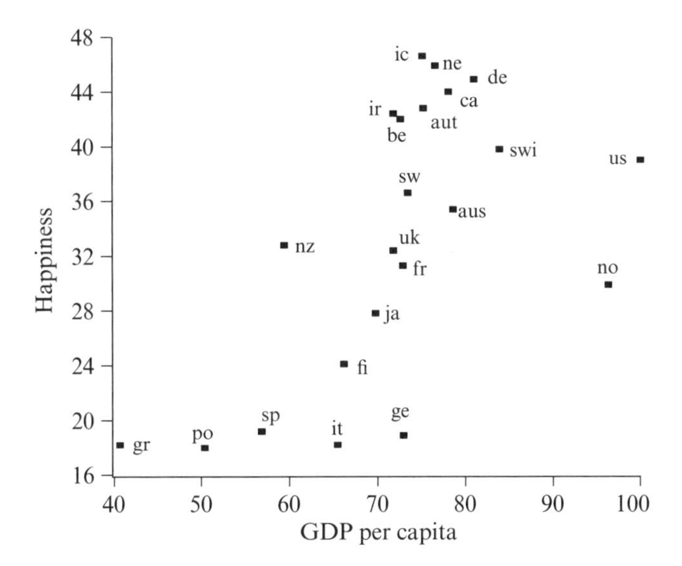

Note: GDP per capita is normalized by the corresponding value for the US.

Figure 4.3 Reported happiness and GDP per capita

misleading because a higher rate of growth can possibly adversely affect workers and households due to the stress of work, long working hours and so on. However, money and consumption have enormous attractions, as described in the writings of Thorstein Veblen and his followers. But, as Veblen (1934) pointed out, it is not clear that money and consumption, hence also output, feeds into family happiness.

Figure 4.3 shows the relationship between GDP per capita and reported happiness for 22 OECD countries[2] for the year 2000. GDP per capita for each country is normalized by the corresponding value for the United States so that the values given on the horizontal axis show GDP per capita in each country relative to that of the US. There is a positive relationship between the two variables. However, this relationship is far from being exact. When GDP exceeds 70 per cent of the US value, the relationship appears to disappear. There is a relationship for the whole sample because reported happiness is lower in Greece, Portugal and Spain and GDP per capita is also lower in these countries than in others. Note that reported happiness is greater in New Zealand and lower in Norway than what these countries' income levels would suggest. Denmark, Iceland and the Netherlands have the highest reported levels, higher than that for the US, which has a higher level of GDP per capita.

In the light of a less than precise relationship between GDP and happiness, our next step is to estimate an equation that has more explanatory variables,

$$H = A\Gamma \tag{4.1}$$

where we let H be a 22*1 vector of happiness measures for our sample of 22 countries in year 2000 and A is a vector of coefficients for matrix Γ, which has 22 observations for a host of variables in the same year. The results are shown in Table 4.1.

In column (1) we show a positive relationship between happiness and the log of GDP per capita. A 1 per cent rise in GDP per capita, from one country to another, increases the share of respondents who claim to be very happy by a large fraction. Note, however, that the explanatory power of this variable is not great, only about 38 per cent. Our next variable is a measure of economic freedom,[3] on a scale from 1 to 100 where 1 implies minimum freedom and 100 maximum. It measures, amongst other factors, the cost of setting up, operating and closing down enterprises, government interference in capital and labor markets, and the effects of public spending and taxes. This variable turns out to have a positive and statistically significant coefficient. Together, GDP per capita and economic freedom explain around 54 per cent of the variation in reported happiness across the sample of 22 countries.

We next add a measure of openness to international trade, measured by the ratio of the sum of imports and exports, on the one hand, and GDP on the other hand. As described by William Baumol (Chapter 1), entrepreneurship both affects the volume of trade as well as being affected by it. This variable has a positive and statistically significant coefficient, so that when openness rises by 10 per cent of GDP, the fraction of respondents claiming to be very happy rises by 1 per cent. Inflation does not have a statistically significant coefficient, but do note that inflation was nowhere a serious problem within the club of 22 OECD countries in year 2000. Our remaining variables are average hours of work (OECD),[4] mandatory annual leaves (OECD),[5] the number of paid public holidays (OECD)[6] and the rate of unemployment. Of these, the average hours worked comes out strongest. When the number of working hours per year goes up by 50, happiness goes up by 1.5 per cent. Note that more work implies greater happiness, supporting our thesis of dynamism generating interesting and challenging jobs. Both the length of annual leave and the number of public holidays come out as insignificant. Finally, unemployment (Source: OECD) has a negative coefficient but is not so significant; a 1 per cent increase in unemployment (let's say from 2 per cent to 3 per cent) will make just under 1 per

Table 4.1 Estimated happiness equation (4.1)

	Dependent variable: happiness									
	Constant	**GDP**	**Freedom**	**Open**	**Inflation**	**Hours**	**Leave**	**Holidays**	**Unemp.**	**R^2**
(1)	−288.29	31.82								0.38
	(4.00)*	(4.43)*								
(2)	−253.41	24.35	0.57							0.47
	(3.30)*	(2.86)*	(2.10)*							
(3)	−247.51	22.73	0.61	0.11						0.64
	(3.41)*	(2.81)*	(2.29)*	(3.38)*						
(4)	−252.00	23.31	0.57	0.10	0.74					0.65
	(3.32)*	(2.76)*	(2.25)*	(2.63)*	(0.74)					
(5)	−366.59	32.76	0.42	0.13	0.28	0.02				0.67
	(3.56)*	(3.45)*	(1.50)	(2.69)*	(0.28)	(1.09)				
(6)	−413.47	35.55	0.50	0.12	0.05	0.02	0.27			0.69
	(3.24)*	(3.22)*	(1.92)	(2.58)*	(0.06)	(1.21)	(1.19)			
(7)	−379.70	32.66	0.41	0.13	0.88	0.02	0.30	−0.47		0.72
	(3.04)*	(2.92)*	(1.88)	(2.46)*	(0.71)	(1.56)	(1.29)	(1.55)		
(8)	−345.53	30.83	0.19	0.12	0.99	0.03	0.27	−0.44	−0.81	0.74
	(2.68)*	(2.72)*	(0.67)	(2.08)*	(0.75)	(1.89)	(1.25)	(1.46)	(1.28)	

Note: White heteroskedasticity-consistent standard error and covariances. Significance at 5% level indicated by a star.

cent fewer people happy.[7] Note that the inclusion of the unemployment variable makes the coefficient of economic freedom drop because the two are correlated in the data: the OECD countries with a low value on the freedom index also have higher than average rates of unemployment. We also experimented with adding a measure of tertiary education (Barro and Lee, 2000) and a measure of the frequency of divorces and separations. None of these variables had a significant coefficient when added to the list of variables in Table 4.1.

In sum, the list of statistically significant variables includes GDP per capita, economic freedom and openness to international trade. In addition there is a positive relationship between the number of hours worked and reported happiness. In Figure 4.4 we show the relationship between happiness, on the one hand, and economic freedom and openness, on the other.

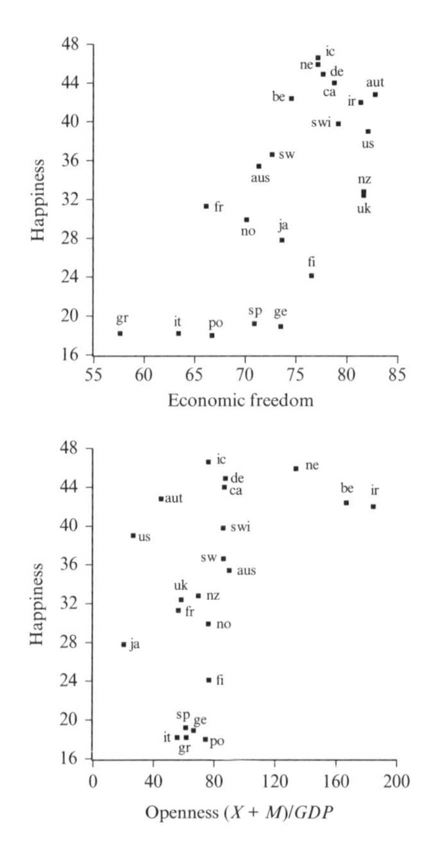

Figure 4.4 Reported happiness, economic freedom and openness

CULTURE AND VALUES

We now move on to discuss which factors determine GDP per capita, economic freedom and openness to international trade. The estimated equation is the following

$$\Gamma^r = BC \tag{4.2}$$

where Γ^r is a 3*22 submatrix of Γ in equation (4.1) with observations on GDP per capita, economic freedom and openness, B is a vector of coefficients and C is a matrix of cultural variables for the 22 countries. We would like to find differences in culture and values that can explain the differences in these three variables across our group of 22 OECD counties. Here we follow in the footsteps of Phelps (2006a), who explained European economic performance – measured by its unemployment rate, its labor force participation rate and the rate of productivity growth – by a set of cultural variables. The findings suggested that the Continent's economic performance was weighed down by several elements of its economic culture.

We use the World Values Survey to measure cultural differences; in particular, we take the responses to the following questions as a measure of work ethics and report the proportion of respondents who choose the answer written in bold letters.

1. Here are some more aspects of a job that people say are important. Please look at them and tell me which ones you personally think are important in a job:
   A job in which you feel you can achieve something: a) **Mentioned**; b) Not mentioned.
   An opportunity to use initiative: a) **Mentioned**; b) Not mentioned.
   A job that is interesting: a) **Mentioned**; b) Not mentioned.
2. People have different ideas about following instructions at work. Some say that one should follow one's superior's instructions even when one does not fully agree with them. Others say that one should follow one's superior's instructions only when one is convinced that they are right. With which of these two opinions do you agree?
   a) **Follow instructions**; b) Must be convinced first; c) Depends.
3. Now I'd like you to tell me your views on competition.
   a) **Competition is good. It stimulates people to work hard and develop new ideas**;
   b) Competition is harmful. It brings out the worst in people.
4. Here are some more aspects of a job that people say are important. Please look at them and tell me which ones you personally think

are important in a job: Generous holidays: a) Not mentioned; b) **Mentioned**.

5. Here are some more aspects of a job that people say are important. Please look at them and tell me which ones you personally think are important in a job: Not too much pressure: a) Not mentioned; b) **Mentioned**.
6. Here are some more aspects of a job that people say are important. Please look at them and tell me which ones you personally think are important in a job: Good job security: a) Not mentioned; b) **Mentioned**.

Answers are measured by the proportion of respondents that answered each question most favourably as indicated in bold letters above. Table 4.2 shows the responses for each of the 22 OECD countries.

What emerges is a difference between the English-speaking countries and the continental European countries. The former group puts greater emphasis on being able to achieve on the job, on showing initiative and that the job is interesting; they also have a more favourable view of competition. The English-speaking respondents are also more inclined to follow instructions. Finally, they put less emphasis on vacations. The Nordic nations have values that fall somewhere between those of these two groups. The Japanese are similar to the Continental Europeans except that they emphasize job security more than anyone else. We put Iceland in a separate line at the bottom of the table because its culture appears to be a mixture of the English speaking and the Continental cultures: work ethics resemble the former while in terms of religion and social capital it is closer to the latter. Surprisingly, it differs from the larger Scandinavian countries in terms of a lower level of trust.

We next turn to different cultural aspects. These are, first, what we can call social capital, and second those having to do with religion. When it comes to social capital we are referring to the level of trust that exists between citizens as well as confidence in the authorities. The role of trust has been described by a number of authors. One of the earlier ones is Banfield (1958).[8] Knack and Keefer (1997) find a relationship between trust and economic growth. They cite Arrow (1972) in support of their findings; he claimed that 'virtually every commercial transaction has within itself an element of trust, certainly any transaction conducted over a period of time'. They then go on to explain that trust is important in the relationship between an employer and his or her employees as well as in the relationship between a government and its citizens. Trust facilitates the writing of contracts, and lawsuits become fewer in number. However, as pointed out by Baumol *et al.* (2007) the causality can sometimes be reversed when economic growth creates increased civility and trust.

Table 4.2 Work ethics. social capital and religion

	Work ethics								Religion		Social capital	
	achieve	**initiative**	**interest-ing**	**obedience**	**competi-tion**	**leave**	**no pressure**	**job sec.**	**God**	**god. pol.**	**trust**	**confid. p.o.**
Australia	71.6	52.3	74.1	48.9	26.4	13.7	23.6	58.5	21.1	–	38.1	3.5
Canada	72.7	49.9	70.4	57.2	23.6	26.4	27.8	64.9	36.9	6.6	38.4	7.1
Ireland	71.2	58.9	72.2	36.8	19.7	45.9	44.2	68.5	36.1	4.0	35.2	13.0
N. Zealand	82.5	72.5	83.7	33.6	24.1	32.3	35.4	72.0	23.3	–	47.5	2.6
U.K.	57.9	39.2	67.9	43.5	11.6	39.3	28.3	65.1	13.9	3.3	28.5	3.3
U.S.	83.7	61.7	81.5	64.5	28.9	36.6	37.8	71.8	58.2	17.6	35.5	10.4
Average	**73.3**	**55.8**	**75.0**	**47.4**	**22.4**	**32.4**	**32.9**	**66.8**	**31.6**	**7.9**	**37.2**	**6.7**
Austria	56.5	48.5	57.3	24.8	22.6	20.3	17.8	75.4	24.6	4.6	31.3	4.8
Belgium	46.7	49.1	56.0	30.7	10.3	33.9	31.9	47.1	14.7	3.3	29.4	3.0
France	50.3	42.8	65.6	33.3	15.8	19.8	11.5	46.3	8.3	3.9	21.4	4.2
Germany	49.1	51.2	68.5	34.6	14.7	23.6	22.7	78.0	9.1	3.6	31.2	2.3
Greece	60.2	56.2	68.9	26.4	15.0	32.4	53.5	65.3	30.1	17.5	20.5	1.4
Italy	75.4	64.4	75.5	26.3	17.8	34.7	60.3	76.1	32.3	4.4	31.8	3.5
Netherlands	40.0	62.0	55.7	27.5	4.8	27.7	33.0	28.6	11.7	0.6	59.4	1.7
Portugal	48.1	35.4	45.0	42.1	17.5	37.3	24.4	64.4	35.7	2.6	9.8	3.0
Spain	47.7	35.0	53.2	35.1	12.7	40.2	39.0	74.7	17.8	1.8	36.3	6.3
Switzerland	56.3	61.4	72.1	33.8	26.3	26.1	30.5	64.4	16.3	–	37.8	2.0
Average	**53.0**	**50.6**	**61.8**	**31.5**	**15.8**	**29.8**	**32.5**	**62.0**	**20.1**	**4.7**	**30.9**	**3.2**
Japan	**69.7**	**49.8**	**63.7**	**28.0**	**10.6**	**70.6**	**69.1**	**80.3**	**6.0**	**2.2**	**39.6**	**1.7**

Table 4.2 (continued)

	Work ethics								Religion		Social capital	
	achieve	initiative	interesting	obedience	competition	leave	no pressure	job sec.	God	god. pol.	trust	confid. p.o.
Denmark	54.9	49.5	64.7	34.5	13.3	16.1	13.9	50.0	6.5	1.3	64.1	3.5
Finland	56.1	48.1	76.0	30.0	10.6	20.8	30.9	68.2	16.2	3.5	56.8	3.2
Norway	74.4	49.7	70.1	59.7	17.5	10.7	23.8	69.3	11.9	–	64.8	2.1
Sweden	72.3	51.9	69.9	37.6	17.7	19.5	35.0	51.0	8.8	1.7	63.7	2.4
Average	**62.8**	**52.1**	**70.6**	**39.1**	**17.1**	**19.3**	**26.8**	**60.6**	**10.9**	**2.2**	**62.4**	**2.8**
Iceland	**80.6**	**63.1**	**76.1**	**42.0**	**33.7**	**17.6**	**32.4**	**58.4**	**15.2**	**2.6**	**39.3**	**5.3**

Note: job sec. = job security; god. pol. = godly politicians; confid. p.o. = confidence in public officials.

We use the answers to the following two questions to measure social capital.

7. Generally speaking, would you say that most people can be trusted or that you need to be very careful in dealing with people? a) Most people can be trusted; b) Can't be too careful.
8. Could you tell me how much confidence you have in the civil service: a) A great deal; b) Quite a lot; c) Not very much; d) None at all.

The table gives the proportion of respondents who have a lot of confidence in the civil service and trust their fellow citizens (answers indicated in bold letters above). Note that the four Nordic countries have a high level of trust. In contrast, there is little difference between the English-speaking nations and the Continental Europeans. Confidence in the civil service is greatest in the English-speaking countries.

Finally, we turn to religion. The table gives the proportion of respondents who answered the following two questions in the affirmative.

9. How important is God in your life? Please use this scale to indicate – 10 means very important and 1 means not at all important: a) Not at all important; b) 2; c) 3; d) 4; e) 5; f) 6; g) 7; h) 8; i) 9; j) Very important.
10. How much do you agree or disagree with the following statement: Politicians who do not believe in God are unfit for public office: a) Agree strongly; b) Agree; c) Neither agree or disagree; d) Disagree; e) Strongly disagree.

The proportion of respondents who express a strong belief in god is greatest in the US and thereafter in the Catholic part of Europe. Only in the US and in Ireland do people put much weight on politicians being religious.

We now use factor analysis to derive principal components for the matrix of values shown in Table 4.3. We proceed by summarizing work ethics by deriving the principal components of the 8*22 sub-matrix containing information on those factors. The first principal component, PC1, explains 40 per cent of the variation in the matrix, the second principal component, PC2, explains 27 per cent of the variation and the third, PC3, explains 14 per cent of the variation. Table 4.3 has the eigenvectors for the three principal components.

The first principal component, PC1, emphasizes achievement, initiative and interesting jobs, and values competition. This captures what we can call 'good work ethics'. The second principal components emphasizes

Table 4.3 Principal components for work ethics

	PC1-good work ethics	PC2-low pressure	PC3-initiative
Achievement	**0.53**	0.03	−0.08
Initiative	**0.38**	0.07	**0.60**
Interesting	**0.49**	−0.05	0.21
Obedience	0.26	**−0.33**	**−0.50**
Competition	**0.43**	−0.24	−0.12
Vacation	−0.01	**0.60**	−0.19
Low pressure	0.16	**0.61**	0.08
Job security	0.24	**0.31**	**−0.53**

Note: Bold indicates a factor loading higher than 0.30.

annual leave, a job free of stress and job security, while willingness to follow instructions receives a negative factor loading. We can call this factor ‘low pressure’. The third principal component, PC3, has a positive factor loading for initiative, while willingness to follow instructions and job security get a negative loading. We can call the variable ‘initiative’.

Our one remaining step is to take our measures of trust and work ethics to explain the pattern of GDP per capita, economic freedom, openness to international trade and hours of work, the four variables that were positively related to reported happiness above.[9] The results are shown in Table 4.4. Trust has a positive impact on GDP as does economic freedom. Confidence in the civil service has a positive relationship to GDP, economic freedom and openness to trade. The first PC – good work ethics – has a positive relationship to GDP but a negative relationship to openness. The second PC – low pressure – has a negative impact on GDP per capita. The third PC – initiative – has a positive effect on openness to trade. Hours of work are a positive function of good work ethics as measured by PC1.

We also explore an alternative model where GDP per capita, economic freedom, openness, hours worked and the cultural variables are put on equal par instead of making the first three a function of underlying cultural variables. We then reduce equations (4.1) and (4.2) so that they become

$$H = C\Gamma^r + DC \qquad (4.3)$$

where H, Γ^r and C have the same interpretations as above. The results (not reported here) indicate that all the cultural variables apart from the third principal component, which we labelled initiative, become insignificant at

Table 4.4 Happiness, trust and work ethics

	Log(GDP)	Log(GDP)*	Freedom	Freedom	Open**	Open**	Hours***	Hours***	Happiness	Happiness
Constant	9.73	9.80	64.05	67.29	42.21	35.51	1786.37	1897.25	16.15	20.91
	(79.37)*	(69.91)*	(16.61)*	(3.88)	(3.89)*	(2.29)*	(11.11)	(13.98)	(3.06)*	(3.60)*
Trust	0.01	0.01	0.09	0.05	0.44	0.38	−3.73	−4.16	0.30	0.16
	(2.80)*	(1.92)	(1.21)	(0.59)	(1.46)	(1.15)	(1.38)	(1.81)	(2.69)*	(1.26)
Conf. civil	0.02	0.03	0.74	0.31	7.34	9.182	2.75	−13.88	1.27	1.49
service	(1.86)*	(2.01)*	(2.68)*	(0.91)	(2.93)*	(4.40)*	(0.25)	(1.11)	(3.10)*	(3.19)*
PC1-good		0.01		1.74		-5.83		52.42		0.11
work ethics		(0.58)		(2.58)**		(1.91)		(3.37)*		(0.11)
PC2-		−0.09		0.09		1.76		54.93		-2.54
low pressure		(2.83)*		(0.13)		(0.64)		(1.71)		(1.47)
PC3-		0.01		−0.08		10.40		−0.55		3.43
initiative		(0.25)		(0.07)		(1.98)*		(0.02)		(2.03)*
population					−0.38	-0.00				
					(6.32)*	(4.87)*				
R-squared	0.34	0.58	0.15	0.39	0.74	0.85	0.21	0.56	0.28	0.51

Note: * Japan is an outlier. ** Belgium is an outlier. *** Italy and Japan are outliers. Significance at 5% level indicated by a star.

the 5 per cent level. These variables hence affect H mainly through Γ^r; that is output per capita, economic freedom and openness.

We finally estimate the reduced form relationship between happiness, social capital and work ethics. The results are reported in the right-most column, and show that happiness has a negative relationship with PC2 and a positive relationship with PC3. Trust and confidence in the civil service has a positive coefficient.

CONCLUDING REMARKS

We have found that it is not just income that generates happiness, but also opportunities in the form of economic freedom and international trade. In addition, good work ethics, initiative and a level of mutual trust between citizens pay off in terms of greater happiness. We have also found cultural patterns within the group of OECD economies. The English-speaking world appears to have better, or at least different, work ethics from Continental Europe, and Scandinavia falls somewhere in between. Moreover, the Scandinavian countries benefit from a higher level of trust. Japan differs mainly from the rest in putting much greater weight on annual leave, public holidays, job security and not facing too much pressure at work.

The Continental European economies of Spain, Portugal, Greece, Italy, Germany and France have low levels of reported happiness, which could be explained by lower levels of economic freedom, less trade with the outside world, fewer hours of work, a culture which does not yield trust comparable to that of Scandinavia, and lower levels of work ethics than the Anglo-Saxon countries. In short, these economies are lacking in dynamism. This is then manifested in higher unemployment rates and lower labor force participation rates. In contrast, reported happiness and job satisfaction are greater in Scandinavia and the English-speaking countries due to more trust, greater economic freedom, more openness and different work ethics. There remains the question whether institutional change on the Continent can occur in spite of its culture and, if so, if culture may change as a consequence.

NOTES

1. The high level of productivity in Norway is an anomaly in that it is partly explained by its income from oil production.
2. The countries are: Austria (aus), Australia (aut), Belgium (be), Canada (ca), Denmark

(de), Finland (fi), France (fr), Germany (ge), Greece (gr), Iceland (ic), Ireland (ir), Italy (it), Japan (ja), Netherlands (ne), Norway (no), New Zealand (nz), Portugal (po), Spain (sp), Sweden (sw), Switzerland (swi), the UK (uk) and the US (us).

3. Source: *Index of Economic Freedom, The Heritage Foundation* (http://www.heritage.org/research/features/index/chapters/htm/index2007_chap3.cfm). The index is a simple average of measures of ten types of freedom: business freedom, which measures the ease of creating, operating and closing a business; trade freedom, which measures tariff and non-tariff protection; monetary freedom, which measures price stability; freedom from government, which measures public expenditures; fiscal freedom, which measures the tax burden; property rights, which measures laws protecting property rights: investment freedom, which measures how freely capital flows between countries; financial freedom, which measures banking security and the private ownership of banks; freedom from corruption; and labor freedom, which measures the freedom workers and business have to interact without any restrictions imposed by the state.
4. Average hours worked per employed person per year.
5. Statutory annual minimum leave.
6. Paid public holidays.
7. See also Eurobarometer Survey, 1975–1991, http:ec.europa.eu/public_opinion/archives/eb_arch_en.htm, accessed 10 October 2008.
8. See also the Russell Sage conference on altruism, Phelps (1975).
9. In the openness regression we correct for the size of the population and find, not surprisingly, that smaller nations trade more with other countries.

REFERENCES

Aghion, Philippe and Peter Howitt (1998), *Endogenous Growth Theory*, Cambridge, MA and London, UK: MIT Press.

Arrow, K. (1972), 'Gifts and exchanges', *Philosophy and Public Affairs*, I, 343–362.

Banfield, Edward (1958), *The Moral Basis of a Backward Society*, New York: Free Press.

Barro, Robert J. and Jong-Wha Lee (2000), *International Data on Educational Attainment: Updates and Implications*, NBER Working Paper No. 7911, Cambridge, MA: NBER.

Baumol, William J., Robert E. Litan and Carl J. Schramm (2007), *Good Capitalism, Bad Capitalism and the Economics of Growth and Prosperity*, New Haven and London: Yale University Press.

Bhidé, Amar (2000), *The Origin and Evolution of New Businesses*, Oxford: Oxford University Press.

Clark, Gregory (2007), *A Farewell to Alms: A Brief Economic History of the World*, Princeton, NJ and Oxford: Princeton University Press.

Dewey, John (1920), 'The School and Society', Chicago, Illinois: University of Chicago Press.

Hamilton, Barton, H. (2000), 'Does Entrepreneurship Pay? An Empirical Analysis of the Returns to Self-Employment', *Journal of Political Economy*, 108 (3), 604–631.

Hayek, Friedrich A. (1967/1978), 'Competition as a Discovery Procedure', in his *New Studies in Philosophy, Politics, Economics and the History of Ideas*, London: Routledge, 179–190.

Inglehart, Roland (2006), *World Values Surveys 1981–2004*, Ann Arbor: University of Michigan (http://www.worldvaluessurvey.org).

Knack, Stephen and Philip Keefer (1997), 'Does Social Capital Have an Economic Payoff? A cross-country investigation', *Quarterly Journal of Economics*, 112, 1251–1288.

Knight, Frank (1921), *Risk Uncertainty and Profit*, New York: Houghton Mifflin Co.

Layard, Richard (2005), *Happiness: Lessons from a New Science*, New York: Penguin.

Moskowitz, Tobias J. and Annette Vissing-Jörgensen (2002), 'The Returns to Entrepreneurial Investment: A Private Equity Premium Puzzle?' *The American Economic Review*, 92 (4), 745–778.

Nelson, Richard R. and Edmund S. Phelps (1966), 'Investment in Humans, Technological Diffusion, and Economic Growth', *American Economic Review*, 56 (2), 69–75.

Phelps, Edmund S. (1975), *Altruism, Morality, and Economic Theory*, New York: Russell Sage Foundation.

Phelps, Edmund S. (2005), 'The Continent's Poor Economic Performance Stems from its Economics Institutions and Economic Culture – and Little, If at All, from the Classical Welfare State'. Paper presented at an OECD seminar on *Addressing the Economic Performance in Continental Europe*, Paris, 28 October 2005.

Phelps, Edmund S. (2006a), 'Economic Culture and Economic Performance: What Light I Shed on the Continent's Problem?'. Paper presented at the Venice Summer Institute 2006, *Perspectives on the Performance of the Continent's Economies*.

Phelps, Edmund S. (2006b), 'Further Steps to a Theory of Innovation and Growth: On the Path Begun by Knight, Hayek and Polanyi', *American Economic Review, Papers and Proceedings*, May.

Schumpeter, Joseph A. (1911), *Theorie der wirtschaflichen Entwicklung*, Leipzig: Duncker and Humblot.

Veblen, Thorstein (1934), *The Theory of the Leisure Class: An Economic Study of Institutions*, Modern Library.

Weber, Max (1905/1958), 'Die protestantische Ethik und der 'Geist' der Kapitalismus', Archivder *Sozialwissenschaften und Sozialpolitik*, 20 and 21. Trans. Talcott Parsons, *The Protestant Ethic and the Spirit of Capitalism*, London: Allen and Unwin; New York: Scribner.

William, James (1916), *Talks to Teachers on Psychology, and to Students on Some of Life's Ideals*, New York: Holt.

APPENDIX 4.1: ECONOMIC PERFORMANCE

Table 4.A1 Unemployment rate

	1960–64	1965–69	1970–1974	1975–79	1980–84	1985–89	1990–94	1995–99	2000–2004
Australia	1.94	1.71	2.20	5.52	7.49	7.33	9.27	7.91	6.20
Canada	5.85	3.98	5.80	7.55	9.88	8.88	10.27	8.80	7.26
Ireland	5.25	5.15	6.24	8.97	12.19	16.27	14.54	9.48	4.34
New Zealand	0.07	0.27	0.23	0.95	3.84	4.86	9.21	6.65	5.00
UK	1.38	1.63	2.30	4.38	9.40	9.29	8.68	7.19	5.06
US	5.72	3.84	5.41	7.02	8.32	6.23	6.59	4.93	5.21
Austria	2.01	1.61	1.01	1.47	2.55	3.96	4.81	5.52	4.59
Belgium	1.48	1.56	1.49	5.25	9.33	9.24	7.69	9.28	7.52
France	1.20	2.04	2.71	4.88	7.92	10.08	10.48	11.53	9.19
Germany	0.49	0.67	0.71	2.15	4.44	5.90	6.28	8.41	8.29
Greece	6.16	4.59	2.92	1.90	5.72	7.54	8.52	10.34	10.48
Italy	3.46	4.13	4.27	5.09	6.99	9.88	9.57	11.75	9.06
Netherlands	0.56	1.08	1.79	3.85	7.99	8.03	6.20	5.31	3.13
Portugal	2.22	4.40	2.86	6.91	8.21	7.20	5.13	6.10	5.22
Spain	1.87	2.14	2.29	4.53	12.41	15.17	14.29	16.00	11.04
Switzerland	0.02	0.01	0.01	0.43	0.57	0.78	2.67	4.13	3.42
Japan	1.34	1.22	1.29	2.04	2.39	2.60	2.35	3.74	5.05
Denmark	1.14	1.08	1.23	4.82	7.38	5.82	8.18	5.61	4.85
Finland	1.41	2.52	2.16	4.98	5.15	4.65	10.91	12.89	9.22
Norway	1.71	1.55	1.49	1.85	2.58	2.96	5.60	4.01	3.97
Sweden	1.58	1.79	2.24	1.86	2.83	2.14	5.21	7.18	5.11

Table 4.A2 Male labor force participation rate (25–64 years of age)

	1960–64	1965–69	1970–1974	1975–79	1980–84	1985–89	1990–94	1995–99	2000–2004
Australia		79.29	78.91	78.39	89.87	87.46	88.11	86.87	85.18
Canada		..	..	..	90.99	89.16	88.37	85.78	86.00
Ireland		95.63	95.71	93.34	..	88.66	87.11	86.27	87.31
New Zealand		..	..	..	..	..	87.09	87.71	88.08
UK		..	..	..	..	89.67	89.62	86.91	86.21
US		93.20	93.21	90.63	89.87	89.14	89.33	87.75	87.65
Austria		..	..	..	..	..	..	84.56	83.40
Belgium		..	..	..	..	83.33	80.28	81.09	81.80
France		..	92.15	91.74	91.39	86.42	85.55	85.04	84.89
Germany		..	93.57	91.31	90.37	86.70	83.54	84.00	83.51
Greece		..	..	..	..	88.74	85.30	86.26	86.05
Italy		..	89.18	88.56	89.03	86.01	85.19	80.98	80.78
Netherlands		..	92.15	90.27	87.78	83.80	85.33	84.37	85.67
Portugal		..	..	91.24	90.17	88.35	88.63	86.73	86.99
Spain		..	..	93.13	91.46	88.68	87.47	85.50	87.20
Switzerland		..	..	..	..	..	..	95.49	93.39
Japan		51.07	95.67	95.79	95.31	94.26	94.53	94.72	94.17
Denmark		..	..	..	..	88.22	90.03	87.74	85.84
Finland		92.02	89.73	87.66	86.37	86.07	84.82	82.40	82.60
Norway		..	..	89.49	89.88	92.48	88.94	88.16	88.35
Sweden		94.31	92.56	92.14	91.65	91.18	91.12	88.04	86.83

Note: Beginning of period, initial value 1966.

Table 4.A3 Female labor force participation rate (25–64 years of age)

	1960–64	1965–69	1970–1974	1975-79	1980–84	1985–89	1990–94	1995–99	2000–2004
Australia		30.40	34.95	40.07	46.86	50.16	59.64	62.60	64.56
Canada		..	..	..	54.82	62.13	68.65	69.39	72.19
Ireland		22.29	..	24.95	..	33.76	40.86	49.05	58.69
New Zealand		..	..	..	..	..	62.66	66.61	69.41
UK		..	..	..	..	60.21	65.93	67.53	69.52
US		44.08	48.59	52.10	59.24	64.23	69.12	71.46	72.49
Austria		..	..	..	..	..	..	62.80	64.14
Belgium		..	..	..	..	46.15	49.27	56.51	61.98
France		..	47.69	53.51	59.08	60.40	64.02	68.34	70.17
Germany		..	42.29	46.73	50.47	50.52	55.15	63.19	66.17
Greece		..	..	..	..	42.99	44.55	47.30	53.20
Italy		..	26.50	28.83	37.55	40.14	45.05	44.43	48.81
Netherlands		..	..	25.63	32.21	38.10	50.83	58.08	64.24
Portugal		..	..	43.10	49.43	56.51	61.21	66.15	69.81
Spain		..	..	26.81	28.37	31.63	40.56	48.33	55.18
Switzerland		..	..	..	..	..	..	69.62	72.77
Japan		26.28	53.38	50.85	54.67	57.33	60.49	61.41	62.48
Denmark		..	..	..	..	75.30	79.66	74.29	77.41
Finland		64.97	64.85	70.91	74.46	78.21	77.32	76.29	76.99
Norway		..	..	52.71	64.17	70.77	74.47	76.48	79.44
Sweden		51.91	59.30	68.32	76.27	82.32	85.70	82.59	81.27

Note: Beginning of period, initial value 1966.

Table 4.A4 Male labor force participation rate (15–24 years of age)

	1960–64	1965–69	1970–1974	1975–79	1980–84	1985–89	1990–94	1995–99	2000–2004
Australia		78.93	76.54	74.65	78.08	75.58	75.27	73.82	72.26
Canada		..	..	..	73.15	71.09	72.41	64.90	65.93
Ireland		76.36	..	69.43	..	62.39	53.18	49.59	56.08
New Zealand		..	..	..	..	..	72.67	71.42	65.89
UK		..	..	..	..	..	..	65.05	70.55
US		..	..	..	..	82.84	83.47	74.37	73.65
Austria		..	..	..	..	..	..	64.39	61.28
Belgium		..	..	..	..	43.19	37.02	36.00	38.72
France		..	60.26	55.62	52.01	48.10	39.64	32.39	32.57
Germany		..	75.54	65.88	61.79	62.96	61.16	56.77	54.70
Greece		..	..	..	..	48.22	44.08	41.32	41.03
Italy		..	52.08	44.78	49.38	47.27	46.07	46.00	44.55
Netherlands		..	..	54.67	49.38	50.51	61.84	65.52	71.64
Portugal		..	..	51.89	65.07	64.31	63.91	57.99	67.47
Spain		..	..	78.76	78.46	72.83	66.53	49.30	50.81
Switzerland		71.70	67.03	72.38	72.46	66.85	69.49	52.87	53.40
Japan		58.98	57.68	50.23	42.87	42.56	43.40	48.01	47.41
Denmark		..	..	..	..	78.75	76.52	76.99	75.17
Finland		65.80	64.06	57.38	56.89	55.23	58.13	43.03	50.45
Norway		..	..	51.89	65.07	64.31	63.91	57.99	67.47
Sweden		..	..	71.87	70.47	65.21	61.83	52.79	53.59

Note: Beginning of period, initial value 1966.

Table 4.A5 *Female labor force participation rate (15–24 years of age)*

	1960–64	1965–69	1970–1974	1975–79	1980–84	1985–89	1990–94	1995–99	2000–2004
Australia		60.83	59.73	61.23	66.18	66.75	68.86	69.78	68.90
Canada		..	..	..	63.89	65.56	67.35	61.35	62.82
Ireland		62.28	..	54.06	..	54.35	47.25	42.37	46.89
New Zealand		..	..	..	..	..	64.93	63.45	59.85
UK		..	..	..	..	69.79	72.38	64.82	65.69
US		43.63	51.29	57.17	61.90	63.71	62.86	62.31	63.00
Austria		..	..	..	..	..	..	56.20	50.29
Belgium		..	..	..	..	41.45	34.08	31.68	32.64
France		..	47.20	45.50	42.89	39.65	33.13	26.46	25.96
Germany		..	64.85	60.13	56.44	56.45	56.83	49.93	48.20
Greece		..	..	..	..	34.01	35.25	32.51	35.35
Italy		..	35.55	31.63	41.20	40.37	40.78	34.09	34.28
Netherlands		..	..	48.74	47.34	49.13	60.85	63.54	69.96
Portugal		..	..	63.10	61.39	55.98	54.43	39.69	41.00
Spain		..	..	52.09	47.84	44.28	47.68	42.95	43.28
Switzerland		..	..	..	..	..	..	62.09	66.26
Japan		51.81	53.45	45.63	43.87	43.18	44.79	47.24	46.64
Denmark		..	..	..	..	72.19	70.35	69.44	68.76
Finland		54.70	55.06	53.50	52.41	54.90	56.92	39.48	51.08
Norway		..	..	48.35	55.15	57.39	56.94	53.67	61.76
Sweden		60.55	59.41	66.12	71.02	67.18	69.05	52.69	51.22

Note: Beginning of period, initial value 1966.

Table 4.A6 Male labor force participation rate (65+ years of age)

	1960–64	1965–69	1970–1974	1975–79	1980–84	1985–89	1990–94	1995–99	2000–2004
Australia		..	..	..	11.22	9.12	9.17	9.62	10.04
Canada		..	..	15.37	13.19	11.76	10.80	9.94	9.50
Ireland		48.43	..	28.20	..	16.34	16.45	15.25	14.73
New Zealand		..	..	..	..	..	10.41	9.85	11.76
UK		..	..	..	..	8.54	8.81	8.21	7.85
US		27.28	26.75	21.64	18.97	15.80	16.33	16.76	17.73
Austria		..	..	..	..	..	..	5.46	4.25
Belgium		..	..	..	..	2.58	1.92	2.28	2.21
France		..	19.48	14.03	8.37	5.28	3.74	2.53	1.89
Germany		..	17.20	10.58	6.84	5.11	4.65	4.23	4.42
Greece		..	..	..	..	14.98	11.81	11.69	8.43
Italy		..	12.90	10.40	12.62	8.40	7.13	6.41	5.83
Netherlands		..	11.33	7.98	4.77	3.47	..	5.38	5.51
Portugal		..	..	37.75	28.05	20.18	19.81	23.60	25.02
Spain		..	..	18.75	12.71	6.06	3.81	2.98	2.55
Switzerland		..	..	..	..	..	..	20.15	20.32
Japan		56.25	49.38	44.36	40.98	36.96	36.47	37.32	34.10
Denmark		..	..	..	..	13.15	13.00	4.68	3.91
Finland		18.00	41.03	29.41	17.01	10.64	9.21	5.56	6.25
Norway		..	..	37.58	34.34	26.40	25.00	15.29	14.19
Sweden		37.73	28.91	19.90	14.29	11.17	12.60	13.90	14.99

Note: Beginning of period, initial value 1966.

Table 4.A7 Female labor force participation rate (65+ years of age)

	1960–64	1965–69	1970–1974	1975–79	1980–84	1985–89	1990–94	1995–99	2000–2004
Australia		..	..	..	2.82	2.14	2.42	2.61	3.07
Canada		..	..	..	3.88	4.06	3.60	3.35	3.31
Ireland		13.23	11.33	7.20	4.76	3.87	3.40	3.00	2.94
New Zealand		..	..	..	..	4.50	3.63	2.96	4.40
UK		..	..	..	..	3.03	3.38	3.19	3.39
US		9.74	9.68	8.24	8.07	7.27	8.63	8.83	9.38
Austria		..	..	..	..	..	..	2.36	1.61
Belgium		..	..	..	..	0.86	0.57	0.97	1.14
France		..	8.60	5.83	3.43	2.19	1.52	1.19	0.92
Germany		..	6.10	4.62	3.21	2.30	2.21	1.55	1.49
Greece		..	..	..	..	5.42	4.54	3.71	2.73
Italy		..	2.60	2.10	3.48	2.07	2.21	1.76	1.56
Netherlands		..	2.23	1.77	0.94	0.65	..	0.91	1.46
Portugal		..	..	10.67	8.59	7.81	7.66	11.32	13.25
Spain		..	..	6.29	4.01	2.29	1.71	1.41	0.97
Switzerland		..	..	..	..	..	..	9.97	9.67
Japan		21.61	17.94	15.26	15.55	15.54	16.16	15.64	14.40
Denmark		..	..	..	..	3.24	3.35	0.95	1.60
Finland		3.85	10.99	8.49	5.58	4.82	3.40	2.01	1.64
Norway		..	..	12.11	12.69	13.55	11.98	9.00	8.47
Sweden		11.59	8.74	6.08	3.82	2.91	5.09	5.28	6.27

Note: Beginning of period, initial value 1966.

Table 4.A8 Hourly productivity relative to US levels

	1960–64	1965–69	1970–1974	1975–79	1980–84	1985–89	1990–94	1995–99	2000–2004
Australia			0.82	0.81	0.83	0.84	0.82	0.86	0.86
Canada			0.85	0.87	0.87	0.86	0.84	0.85	0.84
Ireland			0.48	0.56	0.65	0.70	0.80	0.91	1.03
New Zealand			0.70	0.67	0.63	0.64	0.65	0.64	0.62
UK			0.70	0.72	0.79	0.80	0.81	0.86	0.86
US			1.00	1.00	1.00	1.00	1.00	1.00	1.00
Austria			–	–	–	–	–	0.91	0.89
Belgium			0.84	0.94	1.05	1.09	1.15	1.18	1.14
France			0.73	0.80	0.89	0.96	1.02	1.05	1.05
Germany			0.70	0.78	0.85	0.87	0.94	1.00	0.98
Greece			–	–	0.67	0.68	0.67	0.66	0.69
Italy			0.66	0.73	0.81	0.84	0.86	0.90	0.84
Netherlands			0.88	1.03	1.08	1.12	1.13	1.16	1.11
Portugal			–	–	–	0.46	0.50	0.54	0.54
Spain			0.59	0.67	0.79	0.88	0.88	0.90	0.82
Switzerland			–	–	–	–	0.88	0.89	0.85
Japan			0.47	0.52	0.58	0.61	0.70	0.73	0.72
Denmark			0.73	0.79	0.85	0.88	0.92	0.98	0.91
Finland			0.53	0.58	0.64	0.69	0.75	0.82	0.83
Norway			0.89	1.01	1.12	1.19	1.26	1.38	1.39
Sweden			0.80	0.82	0.84	0.84	0.83	0.87	0.87

Table 4.A9 Real GDP per capita relative to US levels

	1960–64	1965–69	1970–1974	1975–79	1980–84	1985–89	1990–94	1995–99	2000–2004
Australia	84.63	80.56	84.65	84.19	82.11	77.7	76.01	77.17	75.18
Canada	81.08	80.75	79.20	87.90	89.13	83.16	81.36	77.01	78.05
Ireland	40.69	40.69	44.55	46.75	47.92	46.39	51.82	57.32	72.60
New Zealand	91.85	90.81	79.10	78.91	69.37	67.08	63.28	63.77	59.43
UK	76.62	72.14	72.12	71.63	71.38	69.02	72.55	71.64	71.78
US	100	100	100	100	100	100	100	100	100
Austria	65.48	65.62	74.06	81.50	84.61	80.33	83.72	81.96	78.57
Belgium	61.97	64.14	72.20	77.07	79.05	70.39	77.60	77.08	71.77
France	66.40	69.19	77.52	80.62	80.99	75.45	79.43	75.70	72.88
Germany	–	–	77.53	77.88	80.80	73.60	79.22	79.90	72.93
Greece	31.38	37.59	46.40	52.14	53.36	45.17	43.20	41.56	40.69
Italy	55.47	57.50	67.35	67.31	71.74	68.59	73.65	70.94	65.44
Netherlands	81.53	80.35	87.67	88.85	85.58	77.50	79.32	77.70	76.51
Portugal	27.48	30.06	38.81	40.81	43.06	39.03	48.91	50.61	50.41
Spain	37.49	44.71	52.48	58.84	54.24	49.55	56.96	56.10	56.85
Switzerland	117.47	113.93	116.80	108.72	108.02	100.91	101.07	94.43	83.90
Japan	35.91	45.12	66.76	70.04	72.35	72.73	81.84	79.78	69.75
Denmark	85.73	89.74	93.01	88.94	85.73	83.11	82.04	83.45	80.98
Finland	60.31	62.14	68.22	74.32	74.36	72.03	75.85	64.48	66.17
Norway	73.14	74.20	78.36	85.47	95.11	93.72	82.46	85.74	96.30
Sweden	86.89	88.61	92.68	94.75	85.82	81.13	82.78	76.24	73.42

APPENDIX 4.2: ESTIMATION OF EQUATION (4.3)

Table 4.A10 Estimated happiness equation (4.3)

Dependent variable: happiness									
Constant	**Log(GDP)**	**Freedom**	**Open**	**Trust**	**Conf. civil s.**	**PC1**	**PC2**	**PC3**	**R^2**
−488.76	38.13	0.76	0.08	0.06	0.36	−2.94	−2.28	2.59	0.86
(4.40)	(4.30)*	(3.07)*	(2.31)*	(0.60)	(1.08)	(2.65)*	(2.68)*	(2.69)*	

Note: White heteroskedasticity-consistent standard error & covariances. Significance at 5% level indicated by a star.

5. Entrepreneurship and the city

Edward L. Glaeser

INTRODUCTION

In 1961, Benjamin Chinitz described Pittsburgh and New York City as 'contrasts in agglomeration'. While New York City appeared to be full of independent entrepreneurs, Pittsburgh was dominated by a small number of large, vertically integrated firms. Thirty years later, Annalee Saxenian (1994) described a similar contrast between the highly entrepreneurial computer industry in Silicon Valley and its much more corporate counterpart in Boston's Route 128. Today, measures of entrepreneurship, like the self-employment rate, continue to show sizable differences across metropolitan areas. One in every ten workers in the West Palm Beach metropolitan area is self-employed; the comparable number for Dayton, Ohio, is less than one in thirty.

Why are some cities so much more entrepreneurial than others? This chapter attempts to analyze some basic facts about entrepreneurship across urban areas. In Section II, I discuss two widely available measures of entrepreneurship: the self-employment rate and average firm size. Both of these measures are quite imperfect attempts to capture the number of entrepreneurs relative to the overall amount of employment in an industry. Though it has a long history of being used to study entrepreneurship, the self-employment rate is particularly oriented towards the smallest entrepreneurs and makes little distinction between Michael Bloomberg and a hot dog vendor outside of city hall (Evans and Jovanovic, 1989; Blanchflower and Oswald, 1998). Conversely, the number of workers per firm is more likely to capture the presence of larger scale entrepreneurs. One problem with either measure is that when entrepreneurs are successful, they will hire more workers, and this will cause the self-employment rate in the industry to fall and the number of firms per worker to decline. The problems with both measures push towards using more dynamic measures, such as new establishment creation, but these measures require the use of restricted datasets such as the Longitudinal Research Database (LRD), which I will discuss at the end of the chapter.

In Section II, I examine the patterns of entrepreneurial activity within individual industries as well. Generally, the correlations across metropolitan areas between self-employment rates across industry groups are fairly high, except for the self-employment rate in high-skilled manufacturing. For instance, West Palm Beach is among the five most entrepreneurial places in the retail trade, wholesale trade and transportation, education, health and social services, low skilled manufacturing, and other services. The correlations of self-employment rates across income categories within a metropolitan area are also quite positive, although somewhat less strong. The self-employment rates are also related to the firm size-based measures of entrepreneurship.

Section II concludes by looking at the correlation between these entrepreneurship measures and city growth. Glaeser *et al.* (1992) and Miracky (1994) both found a connection between small firm size and employment growth. I duplicate this result, and find that an abundance of small firms is strongly correlated to later employment growth in a city industry. I also find that the self-employment rate at the city level in 1970 predicts growth in population and income over the next 30 years. While these finding are far from conclusive, they do suggest that local entrepreneurship helps explain why some cities grow faster than others.

Section III describes four theories that explain why entrepreneurship differs so much across space. The simplest theory holds that entrepreneurship reflects a supply of potential entrepreneurs with plenty of either general human capital or human capital that is particularly valuable for entrepreneurs. According to this view, cities differ in their human capital base for historical reasons, and these initial differences drive the level of entrepreneurship today. A second theory emphasizes a local 'culture of entrepreneurship'. This theory predicts that exogenous variables that cause an increase in entrepreneurship in one sector of the economy will also increase the level of entrepreneurship in other sectors of the economy.

A third theory emphasizes the presence of inputs to entrepreneurship such as capital, labor and goods. A variant of this theory, following from Chinitz (1961), emphasizes the presence of small, independent input suppliers. A fourth theory emphasizes the presence of a large customer base.

In Section IV, I evaluate these four hypotheses using data on self-employment, firm size and employment growth due to unaffiliated plant formation. Self-employment is strongly connected to age, education and industry. These variables can explain roughly 50 per cent of the variation in self-employment rates across metropolitan areas, and this fact supports the view that entrepreneurial people explain a fair amount of why some places are more entrepreneurial than others. Using firm size data, I also find that basic demographic variables can explain about one-third of the variation in firm sizes across metropolitan areas.

By contrast, the evidence for the 'culture of entrepreneurship' hypothesis is much weaker. There is a tendency for people who live in metropolitan areas filled with more entrepreneurial industries to be more entrepreneurial, holding their industry constant. This is the only positive evidence for a culture of entrepreneurship, and it could be explained by many theories, such as the tendency of more entrepreneurial industries to locate in places with more entrepreneurial people. When I look at industry clusters within metropolitan areas, there is no correlation between entrepreneurial industries and individual entrepreneurship, again holding the individual industry constant. The firm size evidence also points against the culture of entrepreneurship theory.

Both the self-employment and firm size data show that the entrepreneurship levels are higher when industry employment is lower. One explanation for this phenomenon is that if the number of entrepreneurs is relatively constant over space, but the success of entrepreneurs differs, then we should expect to see more employment in areas where entrepreneurs are more successful, and that higher level of employment then causes the entrepreneurship rate to look lower.

The self-employment rate is correlated with the presence of input suppliers. It is not correlated with the presence of customers, appropriate labor supply, venture capitalists or small firms that supply inputs. The self-employment level in retail industries does rise in big cities, but this is the only demand-side effect that is readily apparent.

Average firm size tends to decrease with the availability of inputs, and the presence of many small input suppliers is also highly indicative of a large number of small firms, just as Chinitz suggests. Firm size is also weakly associated with demand, but the presence of the appropriate labor force seems to be the most important variable for explaining an abundance of small firms. The entrepreneurs seem to be in areas where there are lots of workers, either because they are attracted by those workers or because these workers provide the pool of potential entrepreneurs.

The regressions taken from Dumais, Ellison and Glaeser (1997) confirm the importance of labor supply. New plant growth is associated with input suppliers and customers, but the impact of workers is far more important. We also find that intellectual connections across industries are important.

Section V concludes and emphasizes that these results should be seen as a tentative first step in the task of explaining the variation in entrepreneurship across metropolitan areas. My limited evidence suggests that local entrepreneurship depends mainly on having the right kind of people. Older, skilled workers are more likely to be entrepreneurs, and entrepreneurship in an industry depends strongly on the presence of workers who both provide the pool of labor for entrepreneurs and are themselves the source of new entrepreneurship.

THE MEASUREMENT OF ENTREPRENEURSHIP

In this section, I discuss the measurement of entrepreneurship across space. Perhaps the most natural individual measure of entrepreneurship is the self-employment rate, which captures the share of people who lead their own enterprise. Since self-employment rates are easy to measure, they have been the standard for much of the empirical work in this area (Evans and Jovanovic, 1989; Blanchflower and Oswald, 1998). The downside of using self-employment rates is that the raw measure is extremely coarse. There were over 8.5 million self-employed Americans in the 2000 Census, and that group includes both many of the richest and many of the poorest people in the country. Since I am interested not only in the amount of entrepreneurial activity, but also in the amount of successful entrepreneurial activity, I will examine both the total amount of self-employment and the amount of self-employment in different income categories.

Income categories offer one way of dividing up self-employment rates; industry grouping represents a second means of doing so. Since self-employment information comes from the Census, respondents are identified by their industry group using the North American Industrial Classification System (NAICS). This system offers finely detailed industry groupings, which I will use in later analysis in this chapter. For the purposes of this preliminary data description, I divide the overall population into ten groups based on one- and two-digit NAICS codes.

The essential division is along one-digit lines. Within the initial nine different one-digit codes, I eliminate all of the workers in agriculture, since my focus is on urban areas, and in public administration and the military, since my focus is on the private sector. This leaves me with seven one-digit codes. I then divide each of the three largest one-digit codes – manufacturing (NAICS code 3), trade (NAICS code 4) and information-related services (NAICS code 5) – into two groups. Manufacturing and information-related services are divided on the basis of the average education level in the two-digit NAICS code, separating the self-employed in the more-educated two-digit industry codes from those in the less-educated two-digit codes. Since education is correlated with both technology and income, it provides a reasonable dividing line. I also divide the trade-related industries into a retail trade category and a wholesale trade, transportation and warehousing category. This division is based on the fact that entrepreneurship in retail trade is likely to be correlated with ordinary consumers in a way that is less true for the other trade industries.

Table 5.1 shows the distribution of the non-agricultural, non-governmental workforce across these ten groupings. The first column shows the overall share of employment in each one of the industry categories. The second column shows the share of the total overall self-employment in each of these industry categories, and the third column gives the self-employment rate within each industry category.

The first category, mining, utilities and construction, has only 8 per cent of total employment in the United States, but it accounts for more than 15 per cent of the total self-employment in the United States. The self-employment rate in this category is the highest across all industry groupings at almost 10 per cent, and this mainly reflects the high self-employment rates in construction. The home building business is populated by thousands of independent contractors, and is in many ways one of the most entrepreneurial sectors of the economy.

The next two rows in the table show the results for high- and low-skilled manufacturing. As there tend to be large economies of scale in these industries, self-employment rates are low. High-skilled manufacturing is an area where less than one per cent of its labor force is self-employed. This fact clearly illustrates the mismatch between the number of people who are self-employed and the importance of entrepreneurship within an industry. Certainly, some of the country's most important entrepreneurs are in high-skilled manufacturing, but there are very few of them relative to the overall workforce in those industries. This fact is a warning against treating the self-employment rate as any kind of definitive measure of entrepreneurship.

Both retail trade and wholesale trade and transportation have self-employment rates of around 5 per cent. The share of self-employed workers in the less skilled information services is similar. The self-employment rate in high-skilled information services is over 8 per cent. While the more skilled manufacturing industries have less self-employment, the more skilled information services have more self-employment. This reflects both the lower capital requirements and the general entrepreneurial nature of many information services such as accounting, management consulting and law.

The self-employment rate in education, health and social services is quite low. Non-profit firms figure prominently in this sector and many of them are extremely large. The self-employment rate in entertainment, accommodation and food services is over 5 per cent. Given the large number of independent food salesmen, it makes sense that this number is rather high. The final grouping is 'other services', which includes a hodgepodge of service

Table 5.1 Share of U.S. employment by industry

	Share of Total US Employment (%)	Share of Total US Self-Employment (%)	Employees Self Employed Within the Industry (%)
Mining, Utilities, and Construction	8.28	15.36	9.81
Low-Skilled Manufacturing	11.45	5.54	2.56
High-Skilled Manufacturing	7.14	1.16	0.86
Wholesale Trade and Transportation	9.94	9.77	5.20
Retail Trade	11.05	11.58	5.54
Low-Skilled Information Services	14.90	13.35	4.74
High-Skilled Information Services	12.54	19.56	8.25
Education, Health, and Social Services	13.77	9.89	3.80
Entertainment, Accommodation and Food Services	6.22	6.71	5.70
Other Services	4.71	7.08	7.96
Total	100.00	100.00	

Notes:

1. Share of Total US Employment = (Number Employed in Industry)/(Total Employed)
2. Share of Total US Self-Employment = (Number Self Employment in Industry)/(Total Self Employed)
3. Percentage of Employees Self Employed Within the Industry = (Number Self Employed in Industry)/(Number Employed in Industry)
4. Data is microlevel 2000 Census data, from the Integrated Public Use Microdata Series (IPUMS) at http://usa.ipums.org/usa/. Steven Ruggles, Matthew Sobek, Trent Alexander, Catherine A. Fitch, Ronald Goeken, Patricia Kelly Hall, Miriam King and Chad Ronnander. *Integrated Public Use Microdata Series: Version 3.0* [Machine-readable database]. Minneapolis, MN: Minnesota Population Center [producer and distributor], 2004.
5. Industry divisions are taken using the divisions presented on the IPUMS website at http://usa.ipums.org/usa/volii/indcross.shtml, based on each establishment's 1997 NAICS code. Certain categories are aggregated, dropped or divided as described in notes (6), (7) and (8).
6. Wholesale trade and transportation is made up of those codes of the form 42-- or 48--. Mining, utilities, and construction corresponds to the codes 21--, 22--, and 23--. Information services covers the NAICS codes that begin with 51–56 and includes Information and Communications: Finance, Insurance, Real Estate, Rental and Leasing; Professional, Scientific, Management, Administrative, and Waste Management Services.
7. Observations for agriculture, forestry, fishing, and hunting (NAICS code 11-), public administration, and active duty military (NAICS codes 9---) are dropped during the analysis. The unemployed are also are also dropped.

Table 5.1 (continued)

8. The Manufacturing category is divided by skill level in the following way. The level of skill within the broad Manufacturing industry is determined first by calculating the mean percentage of workers with a bachelor's degree or higher over the entire industry. Then, the mean percentage of workers with a bachelor's degree is calculated for each detailed sub-industry within the broad Manufacturing industry category. If a sub-industry of Manufacturing has a higher mean level of bachelor degrees than the average over the entire Manufacturing industry, then it is classified as a High-Skilled Manufacturing industry. If it has a lower mean level of bachelor degrees, it is classified as Low-Skilled Manufacturing. The same procedure is used to create the High-Skilled and Low-Skilled Information Services categories.

industries ranging from 'repair and maintenance services' to 'personal and laundry services' to 'religious services'. The self-employment rate in this sector is almost 8 per cent, and it is the third most entrepreneurial of these industry groupings.

Entrepreneurs differ in the industries they choose, and they also differ in the degree of their financial success. When I turn to the cross-metropolitan statistical area data, I will be interested in examining both the correlates of self-employment and the correlates of being prosperous and self-employed. Table 5.2 shows the distribution of prosperity among the self-employed across the ten industry groups.

The columns of the table represent five different financial groupings. The lowest group includes people earning less than 23000 dollars, who are in the bottom quartile of the income distribution. The second group includes people earning between 23000 and 53000 dollars, who are in the middle two quartiles of the income distribution. The third group includes people earning between 53000 and 110000 dollars, who are in the top quartile of the income distribution, but outside the top 5 per cent. The fourth group earns between 110000 and 175000 dollars, which means that they earn more than 95 per cent of the employed workers in the Census, but that they are not among the elite group of workers whose income has been top-coded. The fifth and final group includes only those whose incomes have been top-coded.

The industry groups are ranked by mean earnings, with high-skilled information services at the top of the table and entertainment, accommodation and food services at the bottom. The average income for that top group is more than double the average income in the bottom group. The matrix gives two entries in every cell. The top entry is the ratio of the number of people in that particular industry group and in that particular earnings category who are self-employed, in relation to the total number of people in that particular industry group who are self-employed. The bottom entry is the ratio of the number of people in that particular industry

Table 5.2 Self-employment by income and industry

	Average Income in Industry ($)	Earnings Category					
		Bottom 25th Percentile	25th to 75th Percentile	75th to 95th Percentile	95th Percentile to Top Codes	Top Codes	
High-Skilled Information Services							
Share of Total S.E. in Industry = Total S.E. in Industry & Earnings Category/Total S.E. in Industry	68 577	14.74%	28.96%	31.59%	12.10%	12.61%	100%
Share of Total S.E. in Earnings Category = Total S.E. in Industry & Earnings Category/Total S.E. in Earnings Category		13.75%	15.21%	23.98%	31.01%	29.39%	
High-Skilled Manufacturing							
Share of Total S.E. in Industry = Total S.E. in Industry & Earnings Category/Total S.E. in Industry	57 000	16.47%	32.62%	35.58%	7.15%	8.18%	100%
Share of Total S.E. in Earnings Category = Total S.E. in Industry & Earnings Category/Total S.E. in Earnings Category		0.91%	1.02%	1.60%	1.09%	1.13%	
Low-Skilled Information Services							
Share of Total S.E. in Industry = Total S.E. in Industry & Earnings Category/Total S.E. in Industry	47 444	20.83%	39.64%	25.36%	7.53%	6.64%	100%
Share of Total S.E. in Earnings Category = Total S.E. in Industry & Earnings Category/Total S.E. in Earnings Category		13.27%	14.21%	13.14%	13.18%	10.56%	

Mining, Utilities, and Construction							
Share of Total S.E. in Industry = Total S.E. in Industry & Earnings Category/Total S.E. in Industry	45 509	18.46%	44.40%	27.08%	4.82%	5.25%	100%
Share of Total S.E. in Earnings Category = Total S.E. in Industry & Earnings Category/Total S.E. in Earnings Category		13.52%	18.30%	16.14%	9.69%	9.60%	
Wholesale Trade and Transportation							
Share of Total S.E. in Industry = Total S.E. in Industry & Earnings Category/Total S.E. in Industry	45 053	20.23%	40.50%	26.20%	7.14%	5.93%	100%
Share of Total S.E. in Earnings Category = Total S.E. in Industry & Earnings Category/Total S.E. in Earnings Category		9.43%	10.62%	9.93%	9.14%	6.90%	
Education, Health, and Social Services							
Share of Total S.E. in Industry = Total S.E. in Industry & Earnings Category/Total S.E. in Industry	44 276	21.72%	21.36%	21.12%	12.99%	22.81%	100%
Share of Total S.E. in Earnings Category = Total S.E. in Industry & Earnings Category/Total S.E. in Earnings Category		10.25%	5.67%	8.11%	16.84%	26.88%	
Low-Skilled Manufacturing							
Share of Total S.E. in Industry = Total S.E. in Industry & Earnings Category/Total S.E. in Industry	42 463	17.93%	37.85%	30.66%	6.08%	7.48%	100%
Share of Total S.E. in Earnings Category = Total S.E. in Industry & Earnings Category/Total S.E. in Earnings Category		4.74%	5.63%	6.59%	4.41%	4.94%	
Retail Trade							
Share of Total S.E. in Industry = Total S.E. in Industry & Earnings Category/Total S.E. in Industry	39 716	23.72%	42.15%	23.51%	6.13%	4.49%	100%

Table 5.2 (continued)

	Average Income in Industry ($)	Earnings Category					
		Bottom 25th Percentile	25th to 75 Percentile	75th to 95th Percentile	95th Percentile to Top Codes	Top Codes	
Share of Total S.E. in Earnings Category = Total S.E. in Industry & Earnings Category/Total S.E. in Earnings Category		13.10%	13.11%	10.57%	9.30%	6.19%	
Other Services							
Share of Total S.E. in Industry = Total S.E. in Industry & Earnings Category/Total S.E. in Industry	34 844	33.82%	44.13%	18.19%	2.19%	1.67%	100%
Share of Total S.E. in Earnings Category = Total S.E. in Industry & Earnings Category/Total S.E. in Earnings Category		11.43%	8.39%	5.00%	2.03%	1.41%	
Entertainment, Accommodation and Food Services							
Share of Total S.E. in Industry = Total S.E. in Industry & Earnings Category/Total S.E. in Industry	31 265	30.02%	43.54%	18.93%	3.77%	3.74%	100%
Share of Total S.E. in Earnings Category = Total S.E. in Industry & Earnings Category/Total S.E. in Earnings Category		9.60%	7.84%	4.93%	3.31%	2.99%	
		100%	100%	100%	100%	100%	

Notes:

1. Data is microlevel 2000 Census data, from the Integrated Public Use Microdata Series (IPUMS) at http://usa.ipums.org/usa/. Steven Ruggles, Matthew Sobek, Trent Alexander, Catherine A. Fitch, Ronald Goeken, Patricia Kelly Hall, Miriam King, and Chad Romander, *Integrated Public Use Microdata Series Version 3.0* [Machine-readable database]. Minneapolis, MN: Minnesota Population Center [producer and distributor], 2004.
2. Industry divisions are taken using the divisions presented on the IPUMS website at http://usa.ipums.org/usa/volii/indcross.shtml, based on each establishment's 1997 NAICS code. Certain categories are aggregated, dropped or divided as described in notes (3), (4) and (5).
3. Wholesale trade and transportation is made up of those codes of the form 42-- or 48--. Mining, utilities, and construction corresponds to the codes 21--, 22--, and 23--. Information services covers the NAICS codes that begin with 51–56 and includes Information and Communications; Finance, Insurance, Real Estate, Rental and Leasing; Professional, Scientific, Management, Administrative, and Waste Management Services.
4. Observations for agriculture, forestry, fishing, and hunting (*NAICS code 11-*), public administration and active duty military (NAICS codes 9---) are dropped during the analysis. The unemployed are also dropped.
5. The Manufacturing category is divided by skill level in the following way. The level of skill within the broad Manufacturing industry is determined first by calculating the mean percentage of workers with a bachelor's degree or higher over the entire industry. Then, the mean percentage of workers with a bachelor's degree is calculated for each detailed sub-industry within the broad Manufacturing industry category. If a sub-industry of Manufacturing has a higher mean level of bachelor degrees than the average over the entire Manufacturing industry, then it is classified as a High-Skilled Manufacturing industry. If it has a lower mean level of bachelor degrees, it is classified as Low-Skilled Manufacturing. The same procedure is used to create the High-Skilled and Low-Skilled Information Services categories.

group and particular earnings category who are self-employed, in relation to the total number of people in that particular earnings category who are self-employed. The top numbers sum horizontally to equal 100 per cent; the bottom numbers sum vertically to equal 100 per cent. The top figures give a sense of the income distribution of the industry; the bottom numbers tell us what share of all self-employed people earning a certain amount work for a particular industry group.

For example, the top row indicates that 14.74 per cent of the self-employed in high-skilled information services are in the bottom quartile of the income distribution while 12.61 per cent of them are in the top coded category. Of all self-employed people in the top coded category, 29.39 per cent are in high-skilled information services. This industry group is the largest repository of highly paid entrepreneurs. The second largest repository is in education, health and social services, which has 26.88 per cent of the top coded self-employed workers. There is much truth to the view that doctors and lawyers provide a large share of the most successful self-employed people. Interestingly, the education, health and social services group is particularly unequal, and overall has a relatively low average income grouping. Together, the high-skilled information services and the education, health and social services industry groups contain approximately 56 per cent of the top coded self-employed workers, and almost 50 per cent of the self-employed people in the top 5 per cent of the income distribution.

The poorest industry groups are entertainment, accommodation and food services and 'other services', which includes industries such as 'repair and maintenance services' and 'personal and laundry services'. More than 70 per cent of the self-employed people in these areas are in the bottom three-quarters of the income distribution. Of course, they are not particularly poorer than the US population as a whole, but they are not particularly richer as a group either. Retail trade and low-skilled manufacturing are the other groups that have an income distribution that is closest to the overall US income distribution. However, these people are still vastly over-represented among the top-coded earners, which suggests that even in these industry groups there is some chance of doing quite well.

The earnings distributions for low-skilled information services, wholesale trade and transportation, and mining, utilities and construction are all quite similar. Average earnings in these sectors are clustered around 45000 dollars, and between 5 and 7 per cent of their populations are in the top-coded category. High-skilled manufacturing has average earnings that are higher than any of these groups, and more than 8 per cent of its entrepreneurs have top-coded income levels.

One issue with comparing the earnings of self-employed workers with the US population as a whole is that the earnings of the self-employed typically include both the returns to their labor and the returns to any capital that they have invested. The earnings of most workers do not include any returns to capital. As a result, the high incomes of some self-employed workers surely overstate their labor income.

I now turn to the heterogeneity of self-employment rates across metropolitan areas. To get a sense of the range of self-employment rates, Table 5.3 presents the five metropolitan areas with the highest and lowest self-employment rates overall and in each of the ten industry groups. The top panel of the table shows that the heterogeneity in the overall self-employment rate is significant but not extreme. All but eight of the country's metropolitan areas have overall self-employment rates, across all industries, between 3.20 and 7.76 per cent. This top panel shows some outliers, like West Palm Beach and Honolulu, and these Metropolitan Statistical Areas (MSAs) reappear in Table 5.3 in some of the other panels representing our ten different industry groups. The problems with this overall measure are well illustrated by the fact that San Jose, CA, has among the lowest self-employment rates in the country. Despite all those Silicon Valley entrepreneurs who have changed the world, their region has, on a per capita basis, far fewer entrepreneurs than all but four other areas.

The remaining panels give us the top and bottom five metropolitan areas ranked by the self-employment rate within each MSA. The self-employment rate is defined as the share of workers in that industry group who are self-employed. In these areas, the heterogeneity can be striking. The self-employment rate in mining, utilities and construction is more than 20 per cent in Fort Wayne, Indiana, but less than 2 per cent in Modesto, California. In high-skilled information services, the self-employment rate in Spokane, Washington, is 16 per cent, while the self-employment rate in Bakersfield, California is 3.13 per cent.

In some cases, these differences are driven by industrial differences within the categories. Construction has a high self-employment rate, while mining and utilities do not. As such, MSAs that have a large portion of their labor force employed in mining will probably have low overall self-employment rates within the aggregated mining, utilities and construction industry group, because the very low self-employment rates in mining will offset any high self-employment rates in construction in those areas. Thus, it is clear that controlling for very finely detailed industry groups will be important for any further work on the local determinants of entrepreneurship.

Still, the continuing reappearance of some metropolitan areas in a wide range of different categories makes it clear that industrial differences cannot be entirely responsible for the variation across metropolitan areas. For example, West Palm Beach ranks in the top five for five of the ten industry

Table 5.3 Shares of self-employment by Metropolitan Statistical Area (%)

	All Industries	
Highest Share Self-Employed	West Palm Beach–Boca Raton–Delray Beach, FL	10.81
	Miami–Hialeah, FL	8.69
	Fort Lauderdale–Hollywood–Pompano Beach, FL	8.48
	Sarasota, FL	8.00
	Honolulu, HI	7.76
Lowest Share Self-Employed	Dayton–Springfield, OH	2.91
	Springfield–Holyoke–Chicopee, MA	2.97
	Memphis, TN/AR/MS	3.00
	Lancaster, PA	3.10
	San Jose, CA	3.20
	Mining, Utilities, and Construction	
Highest Share Self-Employed	Providence–Fall River–Pawtucket, MA/RI	20.49
	Fort Wayne, IN	20.17
	Honolulu, HI	19.29
	Rochester, NY	18.73
	Youngstown–Warren, OH/PA	17.77
Lowest Share Self-Employed	Modesto, CA	1.64
	Las Vegas, NV	2.20
	McAllen–Edinburg–Pharr–Mission, TX	3.35
	Stockton, CA	3.75
	Allentown–Bethlehem–Easton, PA/NJ	3.93
	Low-Skilled Manufacturing	
Highest Share Self-Employed	Honolulu, HI	14.41
	West Palm Beach–Boca Raton–Delray Beach, FL	12.19
	Pensacola, FL	8.86
	Fort Lauderdale–Hollywood–Pompano Beach, FL	7.77
	Miami–Hialeah, FL	7.09
Lowest Share Self-Employed	Cincinnati–Hamilton, OH/KY/IN	0.51
	Lancaster, PA	0.60
	Wichita, KS	0.64
	Ventura–Oxnard–Simi Valley, CA	0.67
	Hartford–Bristol–Middleton–New Britain, CT	0.73
	High-Skilled Manufacturing	
Highest Share Self-Employed	Fresno, CA	6.70
	Little Rock–North Little Rock, AR	4.83
	Honolulu, HI	3.72
	Sarasota, FL	3.60
	Lakeland–Winterhaven, FL	3.49

Table 5.3 (continued)

Lowest Share Self-Employed	Portland, OR/WA	0.25
	Philadelphia, PA/NJ	0.28
	Charlotte–Gastonia–Rock Hill, NC/SC	0.29
	Cincinnati–Hamilton, OH/KL/IN	0.34
	San Jose, CA	0.35
	Wholesale Trade and Transportation	
Highest Share Self-Employed	Sarasota, FL	14.05
	Melbourne–Titusville–Cocoa–Palm Bay, FL	12.44
	West Palm Beach–Boca Raton–Delray Beach, FL	11.65
	Hartford–Bristol–Middleton–New Britain, CT	10.70
	Fort Lauderdale–Hollywood–Pompano Beach, FL	9.80
Lowest Share Self-Employed	Memphis, TN/AR/MS	0.75
	Pensacola, FL	0.77
	Harrisburg–Lebanon–Carlisle, PA	0.95
	Modesto, CA	0.96
	Fort Wayne, IN	1.11
	Retail Trade	
Highest Share Self-Employed	Bakersfield, CA	16.75
	McAllen–Edinburg–Pharr–Mission, TX	11.41
	Miami–Hialeah, FL	10.23
	Baton Rouge, LA	9.43
	West Palm Beach–Boca Raton–Delray Beach, FL	9.36
Lowest Share Self-Employed	Jackson, MS	0.96
	Wichita, KS	0.97
	Tucson, AZ	1.25
	Lancaster, PA	1.30
	Stockton, CA	1.44
	Low-Skilled Information Services	
Highest Share Self-Employed	Sarasota, FL	9.22
	Canton, OH	9.17
	Charleston–N. Charleston, SC	9.07
	Colorado Springs, CO	8.97
	Melbourne–Titusville–Cocoa–Palm Bay, FL	8.83
Lowest Share Self-Employed	Allentown–Bethlehem–Easton, PA/NJ	0.89
	Scranton–Wilkes–Barre, PA	1.38
	Sacramento, CA	2.00
	Grand Rapids, MI	2.25
	Baton Rouge, LA	2.36

Table 5.3 (continued)

	High-Skilled Information Services	
Highest Share Self-Employed	West Palm Beach–Boca Raton–Delray Beach, FL	18.56
	New Orleans, LA	18.07
	Jackson, MS	17.13
	Spokane, WA	16.07
	McAllen–Edinburg–Pharr–Mission, TX	15.74
Lowest Share Self-Employed	Youngstown–Warren, OH/PA	1.63
	Dayton–Springfield, OH	2.02
	Springfield–Holyoke–Chicopee, MA	2.74
	Bakersfield, CA	3.13
	Stockton, CA	4.06
	Education, Health and Social Services	
Highest Share Self-Employed	West Palm Beach–Boca Raton–Delray Beach, FL	7.60
	Stockton, CA	7.12
	Sarasota, FL	6.50
	Bakersfield, CA	6.38
	Melbourne–Titusville–Cocoa–Palm Bay, FL	6.08
Lowest Share Self-Employed	Modesto, CA	0.60
	Dayton–Springfield, OH	0.81
	Springfield–Holyoke–Chicopee, MA	1.30
	Canton, OH	1.33
	Syracuse, NY	1.43
	Entertainment, Accommodation and Food Services	
Highest Share Self-Employed	Omaha, NE/IA	15.27
	Boise City, ID	15.10
	Providence–Fall River–Pawtucket, MA/RI	14.64
	Scranton–Wilkes–Barre, PA	13.54
	Tulsa, OK	13.10
Lowest Share Self-Employed	Fresno, CA	0.80
	Las Vegas, NV	0.97
	Lakeland–Winterhaven, FL	1.63
	Orlando, FL	1.63
	Lancaster, PA	1.70
	Other Services	
Highest Share Self-Employed	Rochester, NY	25.86
	West Palm Beach–Boca Raton–Delray Beach, FL	18.23
	Fort Lauderdale–Hollywood–Pompano Beach, FL	17.12
	Tulsa, OK	16.05
	Orlando, FL	16.04

Table 5.3 (continued)

Lowest Share Self-Employed	Lancaster, PA	1.28
	Omaha, NE/IA	1.77
	Columbus, OH	1.77
	Fresno, CA	2.16
	Springfield–Holyoke–Chicopee, MA	2.86

Notes:
1. Total Share Self Employed (by MSA) = (Number Self-Employed in MSA)/(Number Employed in MSA)
2. Share Self Employed (by MSA and industry) = (Number Self-Employed in MSA and Industry)/(Number Employed in MSA and Industry)
3. Data is microlevel 2000 Census data, from the Integrated Public Use Microdata Series (IPUMS) at http://usa.ipums.org/usa/. Steven Ruggles, Matthew Sobek, Trent Alexander, Catherine A. Fitch, Ronald Goeken, Patricia Kelly Hall, Miriam King and Chad Ronnander. *Integrated Public Use Microdata Series: Version 3.0* [Machine-readable database]. Minneapolis, MN: Minnesota Population Center [producer and distributor], 2004.
4. Industry divisions are taken using the divisions presented on the IPUMS website at http://usa.ipums.org/usa/volii/indcross.shtml, based on each establishment's 1997 NAICS code. Certain categories are aggregated, dropped or divided as described in notes (5), (6) and (7).
5. Wholesale trade and transportation is made up of those codes of the form 42-- or 48--. Mining, utilities, and construction corresponds to the codes 21--, 22-- and 23--. Information services covers the NAICS codes that begin with 51–56 and includes Information and Communications: Finance, Insurance, Real Estate, Rental and Leasing; Professional, Scientific, Management, Administrative, and Waste Management Services.
6. Observations for agriculture, forestry, fishing, and hunting (NAICS code 11-) and public administration, and active duty military (NAICS codes 9---) are dropped during the analysis. The unemployed are also dropped.
7. The Manufacturing category is divided by skill level in the following way. The level of skill within the broad Manufacturing industry is determined first by calculating the mean percentage of workers with a bachelor's degree or higher over the entire industry. Then, the mean percentage of workers with a bachelor's degree is calculated for each detailed sub-industry within the broad Manufacturing industry category. If a sub-industry of Manufacturing has a higher mean level of bachelor degrees than the average over the entire Manufacturing industry, then it is classified as a High-Skilled Manufacturing industry. If it has a lower mean level of bachelor degrees, it is classified as Low-Skilled Manufacturing. The same procedure is used to create the High-Skilled and Low-Skilled Information Services categories.

groups (low-skilled manufacturing; retail trade; high-skilled information services; education, health and social services; and other services). Honolulu is in the top five for three different industry groups, and Springfield, Massachusetts, is in the bottom five for three different industry groups.

The heavy representation of Florida's cities in so many of the top five lists is quite striking. This might represent a preponderance of older citizens who have enough human capital to operate independently and who prefer the control that comes from working on their own. Alternatively, it might represent a response to the physical distance of Florida from the locations of many of the larger corporations in America.

Table 5.4 presents an overview of the degree to which self-employment rates across these industrial categories are correlated with the overall self-employment rate. The first column gives the correlation of the overall self-employment rate in an MSA with the self-employment rate within each industry group in an MSA, which is calculated as the number of self-employed workers in the industry group divided by total employment in the industry group. The second column gives the correlation between the overall self-employment rate in an MSA with the share of the metropolitan area's workers that are self-employed in each of the industry groups, which is calculated by dividing the number of self-employed workers in an industry group by the total number of self-employed workers in all industries in the MSA. The third column shows correlations of the same self-employment rates using a smaller sample of people earning over 75 000 dollars a year.

The correlations shown in the first column can be separated into three groups. Five of the industries have self-employment rates that have a correlation with the overall self-employment rate between 61 and 66 per cent. These five are both information services groups, both types of trade, and mining, utilities and construction. The second column shows that the overall self-employment rate is also quite well correlated with the share of the overall city's workforce that is self-employed in those industry groups. Figure 5.1 shows the correlation across MSAs between the overall self-employment rate and the share of the workforce that is self-employed in the retail trade.

The second group includes four industries with self-employment rates that have a correlation with the overall self-employment rate ranging from 35 per cent (low-skilled manufacturing) to 50 per cent (other services). The other two industry groups in this set are education, health and social services, and entertainment, accommodation and food services.

The final industry group is high-skilled manufacturing, which has an insignificant and negative correlation with the overall self-employment rate. The correlation between the self-employment rate in this MSA-industry group and the overall self-employment rate in this MSA is shown in Figure 5.2. While self-employment in most of the industry groups shares some degree of connection with self-employment in the metropolitan area as a whole, self-employment in high-skilled manufacturing is something unto itself and is unrelated to self-employment in any of the other industries.

My second measure of entrepreneurship for the metropolitan area is average firm size. When the same amount of employment is spread over more firms, there must be more firm leaders or entrepreneurs per worker. My firm

Table 5.4 Shares of self-employment by industry: correlations

	(1)	(2)	(3)	(4)
	Share of Overall Self-Employment (All Industries) Correlated With:		Share of Overall Self-Employment (All Industries) Correlated With Self-Employment by Industry >$75 000 Salaries)	Firm Size Correlated With Self-Employment Rate by Industry
	Self-Employment Rate by Industry	Share of Total Self-Employed in Industry		
Education, Health, and Social Services	0.4179	−0.1828	0.3137	−0.5175
Entertainment, Accommodation and Food Services	0.3707	−0.1732	0.1904	−0.4080
High-Skilled Manufacturing	−0.0374	−0.2836	0.2553	
Low-Skilled Manufacturing	0.3501	−0.1343	0.2789	−0.5849
High-Skilled Information Services	0.6118	0.0802	0.6055	
Low-Skilled Information Services	0.6607	0.0508	0.4984	−0.5842
Mining, Utilities and Construction	0.6253	0.0142	0.2907	−0.4839
Other Services	0.5032	−0.0765	−0.2071	−0.1993
Retail Trade	0.6377	0.1437	0.4986	−0.3861
Wholesale Trade and Transportation	0.6480	0.1722	0.4362	−0.6832

Table 5.4 (continued)

Notes:

1. Column (1) is correlation of (Self Employed in Industry x)/(Total Employment in Industry x) and (Self Employed All Industries)/(Total Employment All Industries)
2. Column (2) is correlation of (Self Employed in Industry x)/(Total Self Employment) and (Self Employed All Industries)/(Total Employment All Industries)
3. Column (3) is correlation of (Self Employed in Industry x with Salary Over $75 000)/(Total Employment in Industry x with Salary Over $75 000) and (Self Employed with Salary Over $75 000 All Industries)/(Total Employment with Salary Over $75 000 All Industries)
4. Column (4) is correlation of (Self Employed in Industry x)/(Total Employment in Industry x) and Average Firm Size in 2000.
5. Self Employment data is from the 2000 Census microdata, found in the Integrated Public Use Microdata Series (IPUMS) at http://usa.ipums.org/usa/. Steven Ruggles, Matthew Sobek, Trent Alexander, Catherine A. Fitch, Ronald Goeken, Patricia Kelly Hall, Miriam King and Chad Ronnander. *Integrated Public Use Microdata Series: Version 3.0* [Machine-readable database]. Minneapolis, MN: Minnesota Population Center [producer and distributor], 2004.
6. For the self-employment data, industry divisions are taken using the divisions presented on the IPUMS website at http://usa.ipums.org/usa/volii/indcross.shtml, based on each establishment's 1997 NAICS code. Certain categories are aggregated, dropped or divided as described in notes (7), (8) and (9).
7. For the self-employment data, wholesale trade and transportation is made up of those codes of the form 42-- or 48--. Mining, utilities, and construction corresponds to the codes 21--, 22-- and 23--. Information services covers the NAICS codes that begin with 51–56 and includes Information and Communications: Finance, Insurance, Real Estate, Rental and Leasing; Professional, Scientific, Management, Administrative and Waste Management Services.
8. For the self-employment data, observations for agriculture, forestry, fishing, and hunting (*NAICS* code 11-) and public administration and active duty military (NAICS codes 9---) are dropped during the analysis. The unemployed are also dropped.
9. For the self-employment data the Manufacturing category is divided by skill level in the following way. The level of skill within the broad Manufacturing industry is determined first by calculating the mean percentage of workers with a bachelor's degree or higher over the entire industry. Then, the mean percentage of workers with a bachelor's degree is calculated for each detailed sub-industry within the broad Manufacturing industry category. If a sub-industry of Manufacturing has a higher mean level of bachelor degrees than the average over the entire Manufacturing industry, then it is classified as a High-Skilled Manufacturing industry. If it has a lower mean level of bachelor degrees, it is classified as Low-Skilled Manufacturing. The same procedure is used to create the High-Skilled and Low-Skilled Information Services categories.
10. Firm Size data is calculated using the 2000 County Business Patterns at http://www.census.gov/epcd/cbp/index.html.

Notes:
1. Share Self-Employment Retail Trade=(Self-Employed Retail Trade)/(Total Employment Retail Trade)
2. Share Self-Employment Total=(Self-Employed All Industries)/(Total Employment All Industries)
3. Self-Employment data is from the 2000 Census microdata, from the Integrated Public Use Microdata Series (IPUMS) at http://usa.ipums.org/usa/. Steven Ruggles, Matthew Sobek, Trent Alexander, Catherine A. Fitch, Ronald Goeken, Patricia Kelly Hall, Miriam King, and Chad Ronnander. *Integrated Public Use Microdata Series: Version 3.0* [Machine-readable database]. Minneapolis, MN: Minnesota Population Center [producer and distributor], 2004.
4. See notes to Table 5.4 for further description of the industry categories.

Figure 5.1 Self-Employment – Retail Trade vs. Total

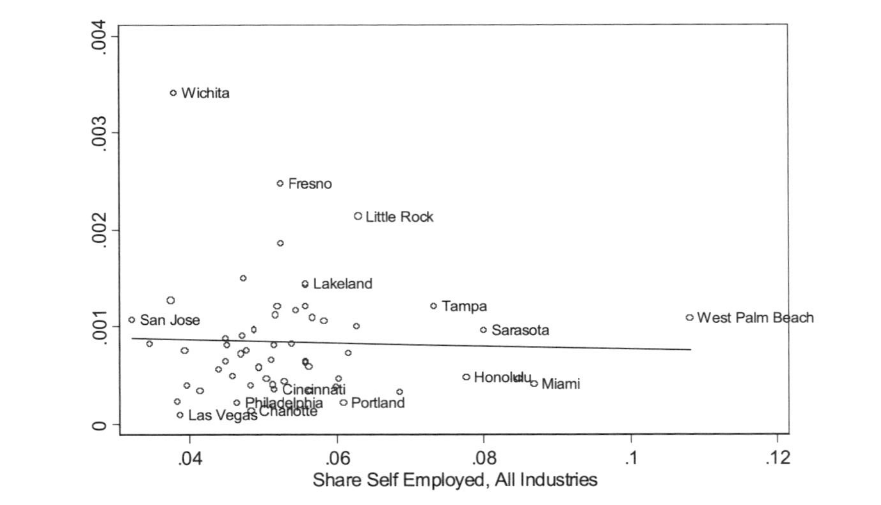

Notes:

1. Share Self-Employment High-Skilled Manufacturing=(Self-Employed High-Skilled Manufacturing)/(Total Employment High-Skilled Manufacturing)
2. Share Self-Employment Total=(Self-Employed All Industries)/(Total Employment All Industries)
3. Self-Employment data is from the 2000 Census microdata, from the Integrated Public Use Microdata Series (IPUMS) at http://usa.ipums.org/usa/. Steven Ruggles, Matthew Sobek, Trent Alexander, Catherine A. Fitch, Ronald Goeken, Patricia Kelly Hall, Miriam King, and Chad Ronnander. *Integrated Public Use Microdata Series: Version 3.0* [Machine-readable database]. Minneapolis, MN: Minnesota Population Center [producer and distributor], 2004.
4. See notes to Table 5.4 for further description of the industry categories.

Figure 5.2 Self-Employment – High-Skilled Manufacturing vs. Total

size data is taken from County Business Patterns and it is also available for a wide range of industries. In principle, this measure would not need to be all that highly correlated with self-employment, especially if self-employed people work overwhelmingly on their own, because self-employed individuals are specifically excluded from County Business Patterns reporting.

The fourth column of Table 5.4 shows the correlation between average firm size within each industry group and the self-employment rate within that group. Overall, there is a robust −67.6 per cent correlation between average firm size and the self-employment rate, which is shown in Figure 5.3. This figure shows that West Palm Beach has among the lowest number of workers per firm. There is considerable heterogeneity across the industry groups. In the County Business Patterns data, I did not separate manufacturing or information services into high- and low-skilled categories. Therefore, the table reports the correlation with firm size in all manufacturing and all information services.

The correlations are generally quite significantly negative: larger average firm sizes are highly correlated with lower self-employment rates. The strongest correlation is in wholesale trade and transportation, and five of the correlations are stronger than −48 per cent. The correlations for the two more consumer-oriented industries – retail trade and entertainment, accommodation and food services – are close to −40 per cent. The weakest correlation is in other services, which is nearly −20 per cent. This correlation is shown in Figure 5.4.

In the later empirical work, I will use both measures of entrepreneurship. The primary advantage of the self-employment rate is that I am able to control for individual-level characteristics. With the firm size data, I will only be able to control for aggregate statistics at the metropolitan area level and the industrial composition of the metropolitan area. Both measures are quite imperfect, but they are convenient and surely at least correlated with some aspects of local entrepreneurship.

Entrepreneurship and city growth

I now turn to the correlation between the entrepreneurship measures and metropolitan growth. Glaeser *et al.* (1992) found a significant correlation between average firm size and employment growth at the city-industry level, and Miracky (1994) confirmed this result for a larger sample. Using data from the 1977 and 2000 County Business Patterns, I can relate employment growth within each metropolitan area-industry cell to the logarithm of the average firm size in the metropolitan area. In this case, in part because of a desire to avoid suppressed data, I use the following, quite coarse, industry groupings: 'manufacturing', 'services', 'finance, insurance

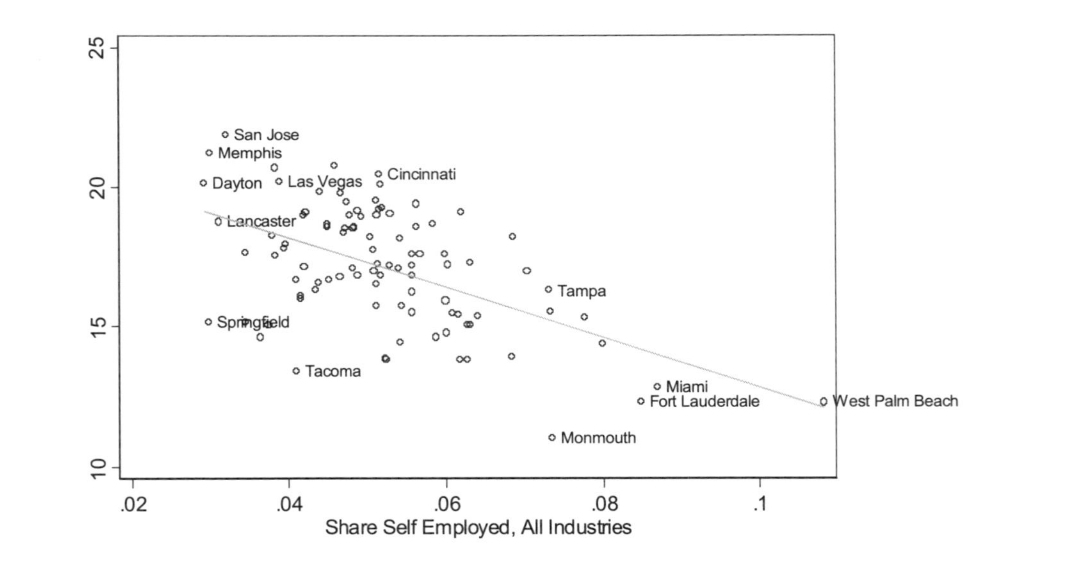

Notes:
1. Share Self-Employment Total=(Self-Employed All Industries)/(Total Employment All Industries)
2. Self-Employment data is from the 2000 Census microdata, from the Integrated Public Use Microdata Series (IPUMS) at http://usa.ipums.org/usa/. Steven Ruggles, Matthew Sobek, Trent Alexander, Catherine A. Fitch, Ronald Goeken, Patricia Kelly Hall, Miriam King, and Chad Ronnander. *Integrated Public Use Microdata Series: Version 3.0* [Machine-readable database]. Minneapolis, MN: Minnesota Population Center [producer and distributor], 2004.
3. 'Firm Size' is the average firm size across all industries. Firm size data is from the 2000 County Business Patterns.
4. See notes to Table 5.4 for further description of these variables.

Figure 5.3 Average Firm Size and Self-Employment – All Industries

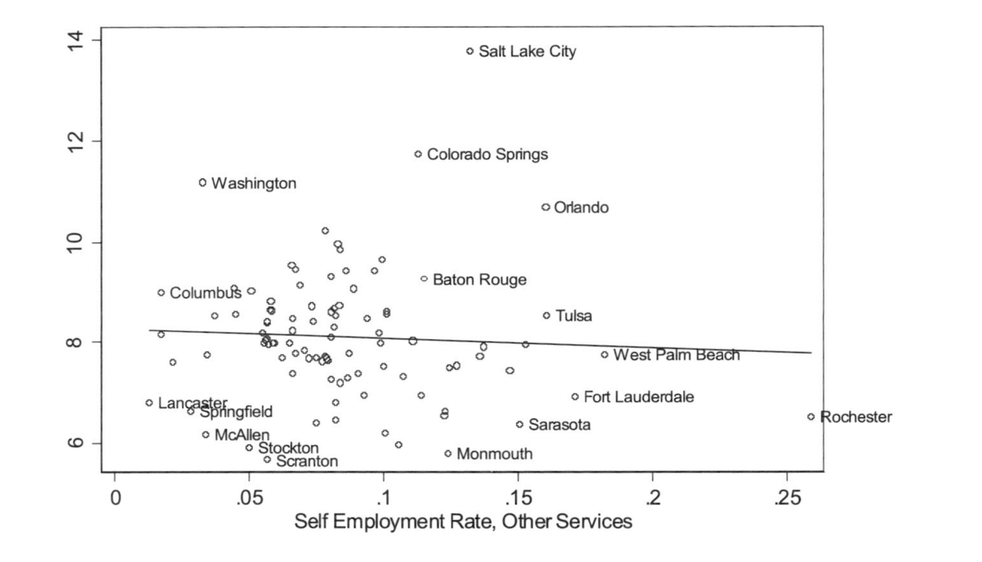

Notes:

1. Share Self-Employment Rate=(Self-Employed Other Services)/(Total Employment Other Services)
2. Self-Employment data is from the 2000 Census microdata, from the Integrated Public Use Microdata Series (IPUMS) at http://usa.ipums.org/usa/. Steven Ruggles, Matthew Sobek, Trent Alexander, Catherine A. Fitch, Ronald Goeken, Patricia Kelly Hall, Miriam King, and Chad Ronnander. *Integrated Public Use Microdata Series: Version 3.0* [Machine-readable database]. Minneapolis, MN: Minnesota Population Center [producer and distributor], 2004.
3. "Firm Size" is the average firm size for Other Services. Firm size data is from the 2000 County Business Patterns.
4. See notes to Table 5.4 for further description of these variables.

Figure 5.4 Average Firm Size and Self-Employment – Other Services

and real estate', 'retail trade', 'wholesale trade', 'construction', 'mining' and 'transportation, warehousing and utilities'.

Using these measures, I estimate the regression:

$$Log\left(\frac{Emp_{2000}}{Emp_{1977}}\right) = -\underset{(.04)}{.60}Log\left(\frac{Firms_{1977}}{Emp_{1977}}\right) + \underset{(.01)}{.04}Log(Emp_{1977}) + MSA\ and\ Industry\ Dummies \qquad (5.1)$$

Standard errors are in parentheses and clustered at the metropolitan area level. There are 2735 observations. A 0.1 log point increase in average firm size is associated with a 0.06 decrease in industry employment growth over the period 1977–2000. This effect has a t-statistic of 15 and is quite statistically significant.

If these regressions are run independently for each of the seven broad industry groups (obviously without metropolitan area dummies), the effect of firm size is negative and significant in each one of the groups, and ranges from −0.31 in retail trade to −0.86 in wholesale trade.

If I estimate this relationship at the metropolitan area level, I find

$$Log\left(\frac{Emp_{2000}}{Emp_{1977}}\right) = -\underset{(.10)}{.88}Log\left(\frac{Firms_{1977}}{Emp_{1977}}\right) + \underset{(.02)}{.02}Log(Emp_{1977}) \qquad (5.2)$$

There are 353 observations in this regression. Again the result is statistically significant and even larger economically. Figure 5.5 shows the univariate relationship between employment growth and average firm size at the metropolitan area level.

The firm size effect is quite robust, but it is less clear what this effect means. It could indeed be measuring entrepreneurship, but it could also measure competition (as suggested by Glaeser *et al.*, 1992) or perhaps even the timing in the firm cycle (as suggested by Miracky, 1994). I now turn to the other measure of entrepreneurship: the self-employment rate.

At the metropolitan area level, self-employment does predict metropolitan area growth. In this case, I estimate:

$$Log\left(\frac{Pop_{2000}}{Pop_{1970}}\right) = \underset{(4.8)}{10.4}\ Self\text{-}Employment\ Rate - \underset{(.06)}{.15}\ Log(Pop_{1970}) \qquad (5.3)$$

However, the self-employment rate does not predict growth within industries. Still, the results of firm size and self-employment at the metropolitan area level help to motivate the analysis of the causes of heterogeneity in these variables across space.

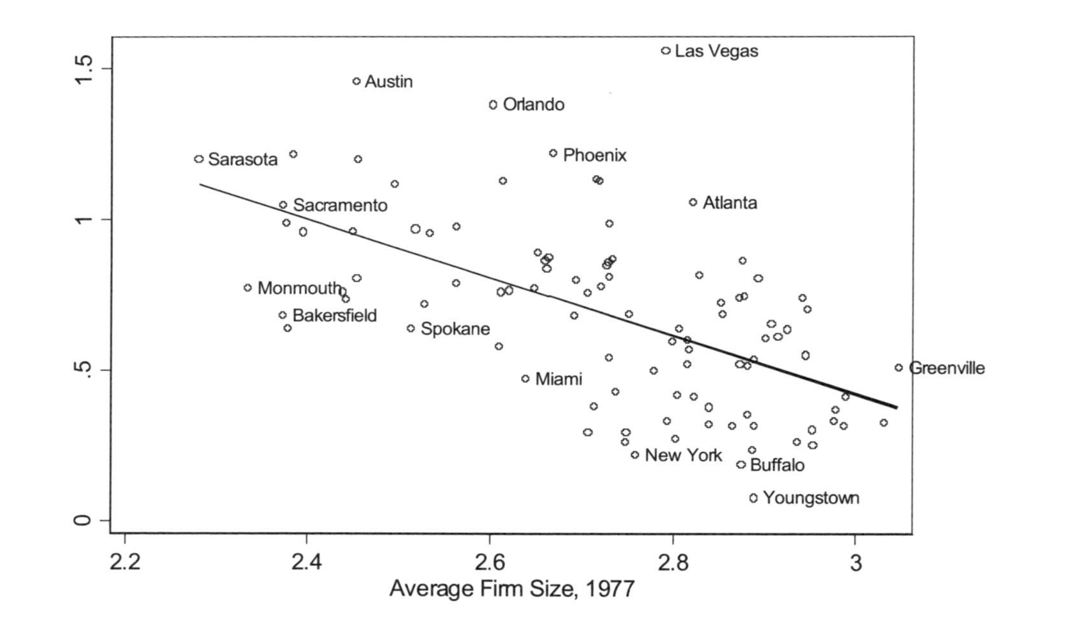

Notes:

1. Data on Firm Size and Employment Growth from the 1977 and 2000 County Business Patterns
2. County Business Patterns for 2000 from www.census.gov
3. County Business Patterns for 1977 from United States Department of Commerce, Bureau of the Census, 1986-04-28, *County Business Patterns, 1977 [United States]: U.S. Summary, State, and County Data*, hdl:1902.2/08464 http://id.thedata.org/hdl%3A1902.2%2F08464 Inter-university Consortium for Political and Social Research [distributor(DDI)].

Figure 5.5 Employment Growth and Average Firm Size

WHY DOES ENTREPRENEURSHIP DIFFER ACROSS CITIES?

In this section, I discuss the four different theories that can explain the heterogeneity of entrepreneurship. I will test these four theories empirically in the next section.

Hypothesis # 1: Supply of Entrepreneurs

Perhaps the simplest hypothesis about the heterogeneity of entrepreneurship across space is that some people are inherently more entrepreneurial than others because of their education levels, ages or industry of choice. Better educated people could easily have more skills to succeed as entrepreneurs. Older people might have accumulated more capital or experience that might make entrepreneurship more attractive. Finally, some industries inherently have lower capital requirements, and this might make entrepreneurship easier.

This hypothesis suggests that controlling for individual characteristics and the industry mix of a metropolitan area will explain a significant amount of the variation in entrepreneurship rates across metropolitan areas. Perhaps the most intuitive means of testing this hypothesis is to look at raw entrepreneurship rates at the metropolitan area level, and then to compare those rates with rates that are calculated as the residuals from individual-level regressions that control for individual characteristics and industries. If this hypothesis is correct, the variance of metropolitan area self-employment rates should decline substantially by controlling for the industry mix in the metropolitan area. I can also test this hypothesis by looking at the extent to which area-level demographic variables can explain the average firm size at the metropolitan area level.

This hypothesis does not seek to explain why the education level or age characteristics differ across metropolitan areas. Presumably these variables are themselves a function of historical variables (like the existence of universities before 1940 as in Moretti, 2004) or temperature. If demographics are found to be important, then future work can use more exogenous variables as instruments for demographics.

Hypothesis # 2: A Culture of Entrepreneurship

A second hypothesis is that cities tend to have an entrepreneurial zeitgeist that then infects their citizenry. According to this view, there are some places that are intrinsically full of new ideas and a spirit of change. Alternatively, there are other places where tradition and old social structures rule.

In a sense, this model argues that there are positive social spillovers from entrepreneurship that generate high degrees of variation across space (as in Glaeser *et al.* 1992). If one person's decision to start a new firm makes it more likely that his neighbor will also become an entrepreneur, this could create a cascade within the city and variation across cities. In some cases, these complementarities may work through easy-to-understand economic processes. If there are fixed costs in the provision of venture capital or inputs, then the positive spillover may work through inducing more of these needed inputs. In other cases, the positive complementarity may work through more ephemeral channels.

One critical issue is the extent to which this positive spillover works across industries. If we believe that there is a general urban tendency towards entrepreneurship, then this can be tested by looking at the impact of being around other entrepreneurial industries in the city. To measure this, I create a predicted entrepreneurship measure by using a measure

$$\sum_{j \neq i} \frac{Emp_{j,MSA} * Entrepreneurship_{j,USA}}{Emp_{MSA} * Entrepreneurship_{USA}},$$

where $Emp_{j,MSA}$ is the employment in industry j in the MSA, Emp_{MSA} is the total employment in the MSA, $Entrepreneurship_{j,USA}$ is an entrepreneurship measure (either the self-employment rate or average firm size) for industry j across the entire US and $Entrepreneurship_{USA}$ is the same entrepreneurship measure across all industries in the country.

This measure takes the average of the entrepreneurship measures weighted by the industrial employment outside of the industry in question. In other words, it is the predicted level of entrepreneurship based on the industry mix in the city and the entrepreneurship measure for that industry in the country as a whole. I will use both the self-employment measure and the average firm size measure for this input.

As there is some question about whether or not this 'spirit of entrepreneurship' travels far across industrial borders, I will calculate this measure both for the country as a whole and within specific industry groups, that is, one-digit NAICS industries. I will also estimate this spirit of entrepreneurship using both the self-employment rate and average firm size data.

Hypothesis # 3: Inputs for New Firms

A third hypothesis is that different metropolitan areas are endowed with the inputs that are needed to produce new firms. Chinitz himself emphasized the importance of decentralized inputs in making things easier for entrepreneurship. I will focus on three inputs that are needed by new firms forming in particular industries.

One of the inputs into entrepreneurship that has received the most attention is venture capital. These high-risk lenders have certainly played a major role in a large number of new start-ups. Naturally, one can question the extent to which geographic distance makes it difficult to get financing. Venture capitalists have been known to get on airplanes. As a result, I think that while there is no question that venture capital matters to new start-ups, there is a question about whether local venture capital is needed for local entrepreneurship.

Unfortunately, finding exogenous variation in venture capital is far from easy. I will take the easier step of just looking at whether measures of venture capital[1] correlate with self-employment and firm size at the metropolitan area level. I will also ask whether this financing has more of an effect for manufacturing industries with more capital requirement.

While venture capital is a particularly obvious input, firms also purchase inputs and hire labor, and supplies of inputs and labor also differ across metropolitan areas. Dumais, Ellison and Glaeser (1997) look at the connection between measures of input, labor supply and new firm births. Our input measure is

$$Input_{i,MSA} = \sum_{j \neq i} \frac{Emp_{j,MSA}}{Emp_{MSA}} Input_{ji}$$

where $Input_{ji}$ describes the share of industry i's inputs that are bought from industry j.

Chinitz (1961) emphasized the role of small decentralized input suppliers, rather than large centralized firms. He argued that the overall level of entrepreneurship depended on the presence of many small firms that can readily supply new start-ups. To capture this, I use an alternative input measure

$$Chinitz_{i,MSA} = \sum_{j \neq i} \frac{Firms_{j,MSA}}{Emp_{j,MSA}} \frac{Emp_{j,MSA}}{Emp_{MSA}} Input_{ji} = \sum_{j \neq i} \frac{Firms_{j,MSA}}{Emp_{MSA}} Input_{ji}$$

This measure captures the number of firms that supply this industry's needs in this metropolitan area.

My third measure of inputs focuses on the labor supply. In this case, I start with$Share_{oi}$, which is the share of industry i in occupation o. I then use the distribution of occupations within the metropolitan area to define

$$LaborMix_{i,MSA} = \sum_{o} \frac{Emp_{o,MSA}}{Emp_{MSA}} Share_{oj}$$

which represents the preponderance of employment in occupation o in this particular metropolitan area.

In all cases, these measures are endogenous to the level of entrepreneurship. I believe that this problem is less severe when looking at our entrepreneurship measure than it would be if I was examining the overall employment in the industry. Nonetheless, if these factors do matter, endogeneity would generally mean that the estimated coefficients may be biased upwards.

Hypothesis # 4: Customers

A final hypothesis is that entrepreneurship is driven by local customer needs. There are at least three reasons why customers would tend to increase the overall amount of entrepreneurship. First, the entrepreneurs may start firms to cater to this customer base. This is surely the most natural reason for a connection between entrepreneurship and customer base. I suspect that this is particularly important for industries like health services. There are surely more doctors in West Palm Beach because of their retiree customers.

A second reason why customers might matter for entrepreneurship is that innovators often learn by connecting with their customer base. Porter (1990) emphasizes this connection in the Sassuolo ceramics industry. There is also evidence that this chain of information flow operates in the software industry as well (Saxenian, 1994). A third reason why customers might matter is that erstwhile customers may have eventually become entrepreneurs themselves.

The most basic demand side measure is

$$Demand_{i,MSA} = \sum_{j \neq i} \frac{Emp_{j,MSA}}{Emp_{MSA}} Output_{ij},$$

where $Output_{ij}$ represents the share of output in industry i that is sold to industry j. This is the measure used by Dumais, Ellison and Glaeser (1997) and it represents the extent to which employment in this area is skewed towards the industry to which industry i generally sells its goods.

I will also consider two alternative measures of consumer demand. First, I will use an interaction of population and retail trade to examine whether industries that sell directly to the public have more entrepreneurship in cities that are bigger, relative to sectors that don't sell directly to the public. Second, I will specifically look at whether entrepreneurs who take care of the elderly specifically locate in places with an older population.

THE CORRELATES OF ENTREPRENEURSHIP ACROSS METROPOLITAN AREAS

I now turn to three empirical exercises which are meant to assess the relative importance of these different theories in explaining the level of entrepreneurial activity across American cities. I first look at self-employment rates using individual data from the 2000 Census. I then turn to average firm size. Finally, I reproduce results from Dumais, Ellison and Glaeser (1997) on growth in new establishments using the Longitudinal Research Database.

Self-Employment Evidence

Table 5.5 includes regressions where self-employment is regressed on individual characteristics, including dummies for gender, eight age categories and five education categories. The data include only employed adults between 25 and 65. The regression also includes industry dummies in all regressions, and the standard errors are clustered at the metropolitan area level. The results are from a linear probability model. The coefficients are quite similar if a Probit model is used instead; the linear probability model is used to facilitate correcting the standard errors.

The first regression (1) includes only the industry dummies and the individual demographic controls. Men are about 3.7 per cent more likely to be self-employed than women. Self-employment rates rise steadily with age, where 60–65 year olds are 8.1 per cent more likely to be self-employed than 25–30 year olds. The relationship with education is also monotonic. High school dropouts are 6.9 per cent less likely to be self-employed than college graduates. Education and age are associated with both human capital and assets, both of which are useful inputs when starting your own business.

How well can individual characteristics and industries explain the self-employment rates across space? The overall r-squared of the regression is 7 per cent, which means that these characteristics can only explain 7 per cent of the individual variation in self-employment. To calculate the extent to which metropolitan area variation in self-employment can be explained by individual characteristics, I compare the raw standard deviation of self-employment rates across areas with the self-employment rates correcting for individual characteristics. I form these corrected rates by taking the residuals of the first regression and averaging them at the metropolitan area level.

The raw standard deviation of self-employment rates is 0.013. The standard deviation of the averaged residual is 0.009. Squaring these standard deviations to get variances, I find that the variance of the

Table 5.5 Self-employment regressions

	Dependent Variable: Self-Employment Indicator (0 or 1)							
	(1)	(2)	(3)	(4)	(5)	(6)	(7)	(8)
Predicted Self-Employed – 1		0.909						
		(0.145)						
Log of Venture Capital per		−0.003						
Capita (State Level)		(0.000)						
Log of Population in the MSA		0.009						
		(0.001)						
Predicted Self-Employed – 2			−0.445					
			(0.133)					
Log of VC/capita Interacted				−0.004				
with High-Skilled Info Services				(0.001)				
Input Measure				0.422				0.470
				(0.054)				(0.058)
Chinitz Measure					0.0154			0.012
					(0.070)			(0.069)
Labor Mix Measure						−0.018		−0.018
						(0.004)		(0.004)
Demand							−0.59	−0.301
							(0.078)	(0.084)
Log of Population Interacted							0.004	0.003
with Retail Trade							(0.001)	(0.001)
Share of Population over 65							−0.112	−0.102
Interacted with Health Services							(0.028)	(0.028)

Table 5.5 (continued)

	Dependent Variable: Self-Employment Indicator (0 or 1)							
	(1)	**(2)**	**(3)**	**(4)**	**(5)**	**(6)**	**(7)**	**(8)**
Log Employment in Industry in		−0.008	−0.008	−0.01	−0.008	−0.007	−0.008	−0.009
MSA		(0.001)	(0.001)	(0.001)	(0.001)	(0.001)	(0.001)	(0.001)
Male	0.037	0.037	0.037	0.036	0.037	0.037	0.036	0.036
	(0.001)	(0.001)	(0.001)	(0.001)	(0.001)	(0.001)	(0.001)	(0.001)
30 to 34	0.014	0.014	0.014	0.014	0.014	0.014	0.014	0.014
	(0.001)	(0.001)	(0.001)	(0.001)	(0.001)	(0.001)	(0.001)	(0.001)
35 to 39	0.033	0.033	0.033	0.033	0.033	0.033	0.033	0.033
	(0.001)	(0.001)	(0.001)	(0.001)	(0.001)	(0.001)	(0.001)	(0.001)
40 to 44	0.046	0.046	0.046	0.046	0.046	0.046	0.046	0.046
	(0.001)	(0.001)	(0.001)	(0.001)	(0.001)	(0.001)	(0.001)	(0.001)
45 to 49	0.055	0.055	0.055	0.055	0.055	0.055	0.055	0.055
	(0.001)	(0.001)	(0.001)	(0.001)	(0.001)	(0.001)	(0.001)	(0.001)
50 to 54	0.063	0.063	0.063	0.062	0.063	0.063	0.062	0.062
	(0.001)	(0.001)	(0.001)	(0.001)	(0.001)	(0.001)	(0.001)	(0.001)
55 to 60	0.073	0.073	0.073	0.072	0.073	0.073	0.072	0.071
	(0.002)	(0.002)	(0.002)	(0.002)	(0.002)	(0.002)	(0.002)	(0.002)
60 to 65	0.081	0.081	0.08	0.08	0.081	0.08	0.079	0.08
	(0.002)	(0.002)	(0.002)	(0.002)	(0.002)	(0.002)	(0.002)	(0.002)
No High School	−0.069	−0.069	−0.07	−0.068	−0.07	−0.07	−0.067	−0.043
	(0.002)	(0.002)	(0.002)	(0.002)	(0.002)	(0.002)	(0.002)	(0.001)
Some High School	−0.058	−0.059	−0.059	−0.056	−0.059	−0.059	−0.056	−0.068
	(0.002)	(0.002)	(0.002)	(0.002)	(0.002)	(0.002)	(0.002)	(0.002)
High School Graduate	−0.045	−0.045	−0.046	−0.044	−0.045	−0.046	−0.044	−0.028
	(0.001)	(0.001)	(0.001)	(0.001)	(0.001)	(0.001)	(0.001)	(0.001)

Some College	−0.029	−0.029	−0.029	−0.028	−0.029	−0.029	−0.028	−0.056
	(0.001)	(0.001)	(0.001)	(0.001)	(0.001)	(0.001)	(0.001)	(0.002)
Constant	−0.033	−0.108	0.059	0.033	0.023	0.02	0.024	0.026
	(0.016)	(0.018)	(0.021)	(0.018)	(0.019)	(0.018)	(0.018)	(0.019)
Observations	369 544	369 543	369 543	361 271	364 613	369 543	361 271	356 341
R-squared	0.07	0.07	0.08	0.07	0.08	0.08	0.07	0.08

Notes:

1. Standard errors in parenthesis. All regressions include detailed industry-fixed effects. Regressions (3)–(8) also include MSA-fixed effects. Standard errors are clustered at the MSA level.
2. Except for the venture capital measure, data is from 2000 Census microdata, found in the Integrated Public Use Microdata Series (IPUMS) at http://usa.ipums.org/usa/. Steven Ruggles, Matthew Sobek, Trent Alexander, Catherine A. Fitch, Ronald Goeken, Patricia Kelly Hall, Miriam King and Chad Ronnander. *Integrated Public Use Microdata Series: Version 3.0* [Machine-readable database]. Minneapolis, MN: Minnesota Population Center [producer and distributor], 2004; the 2000 County Business Patterns; and the Bureau of Economic Analysis Input-Output tables at http://www.bea-gov/industry/.
3. The "Predicted Self-Employed – 1" variable is test of the culture of entrepreneurship hypothesis, predicted self-employment rate in the city, outside of an individual's industry, based on the industrial mix of the city. The "Predicted Self-Employed – 2" is a similar measure calculated within an individual's one-digit industry. See text for a detailed description of how these variables were calculated.
4. The measure of venture capital used to calculate the "Log of Venture Captial per Capita (State Level)" variable and the "Log of VC/capita Interacted with High-Skilled Info Services" variable is found at https://www.pwc.moneytree.com/MTPublic/ns/index/jsp.
5. The "Input Measure" variable captures the share of an industry's inputs that are bought from other industries. See text for a detailed description of how this variable was calculated.
6. The "Chinitz Measure" variable is used to capture the number of firms that supply an industry's needs in this metropolitan area, based on Chinitz's argument that the overall level of entrepreneurship depended on the presence of many small firms that can readily supply new start-ups. See text for a detailed description of how this variable was calculated.
7. The "Labor Mix Measure" captures the labor mix of an area. See text for a detailed description of how this variable was calculated.
8. The "Demand" variable captures the demand of other industries for a particular industry's goods. See text for a detailed description of how this variable was calculated.
9. There are two measures of consumer demand, captured with "Log of Population Interacted with Retail Trade" variable and the "Share of Population over 65 Interacted with Health Services" variable. See text for a detailed description of how these variables were calculated.
10. The coefficient and standard error on the Chinitz Measure were multiplied by 100 for readability.

corrected rates is slightly less than one-half of the variance of the uncorrected rates. In other words, correcting for individual characteristics and industries explains one-half of the variation in self-employment rates across space. Nothing that I will do subsequently will have the same ability to explain the variation in self-employment rates across space. This means that the most important indicators of heterogeneity in self-employment rates across space are the industrial mix of the area and the tendency of some areas to have older people who are more likely to be self-employed.

The second regression (2) looks at the impact of area-level characteristics, including city size and the presence of venture capital. The regression shows that the self-employment rate rises significantly with the size of the metropolitan area, but the effect is modest. As the size of the metropolitan area increases by 10 per cent, the self-employment rate increases by 0.09 percentage points. Big cities seem to be moderately friendlier to entrepreneurs. The regression finds little connection between venture capital and the self-employment rate, perhaps because venture capital is targeted towards a small set of industries that have high returns, but don't account for a large share of the total self-employed population.

This regression includes the logarithm of overall employment in one's industry in the area. The coefficient on this variable is −0.008. This suggests that as one's industry becomes more prevalent, the self-employment rates declines by 0.08 percentage points. High self-employment rates are more prevalent in areas where industries are poorly represented rather than in areas where industries are more common. All subsequent regressions include this control.

This regression also presents a test of the culture of entrepreneurship hypothesis by adding the variable

$$\sum_{j \neq i} \frac{Emp_{j,MSA} * Self\text{–}Employment_{j,USA}}{Emp_{MSA} * Self\text{–}Employment_{USA}}.$$

This variable is a predicted self-employment rate in the city, outside of an individual's industry, based on the industrial mix of the city. In the regression, this measure has a coefficient of 0.91 and a standard error of 0.14. People who work in cities which have industries that are prone to be entrepreneurial are more likely to be entrepreneurial themselves.

The magnitude of the coefficient implies that as predicted entrepreneurship outside of one's own industry increases by 10 per cent, relative to the US self-employment rate, the probability of being self-employed increases by about 9 per cent. The biggest problem in interpreting this result is that the industrial mix of the area may not be endogenous. Areas that have attributes that make them friendlier to self-employment may attract industries that have higher self-employment rates. As a result, these findings may be compromised by an omitted variables bias, where the omitted variables create a spurious correlation between the predicted self-employment rate and the self-employment in one's own industry.

To address this issue, regression (3) includes metropolitan area fixed effects. Since the overall predicted self-employment rate variable does not differ significantly within the metropolitan area, I instead use the measure calculated within an individual's one-digit industry. This regression should be seen, therefore, as testing the hypothesis that people who are in one-digit industries that are particularly oriented towards high self-employment rate activities are more likely to be self-employed. In this case, the coefficient is −0.45 and the standard error is 0.13. People are less likely to be self-employed if the industry mix within their one-digit industry in the city favors self-employment. When I estimate regression (3) without metropolitan area fixed effects, the coefficient remains quite negative and significant.

Since regressions (2) and (3) give us such different results, it is hard to know how to interpret these findings. Regression (2) certainly suggests a strong connection between areas with industries that are oriented towards self-employment and individual self-employment. Regression (3) shows that this does not persist with metropolitan area fixed effects. One interpretation is that regression (2) is driven entirely by omitted area level characteristics. Another interpretation is that the culture of entrepreneurship is not particularly localized to one's own industry. Further work will be needed to differentiate between these two interpretations.

Regression (4) includes our first measures of inputs to entrepreneurship: the measure of presence of industry suppliers,

$$Input_{i,MSA} = \sum_{j \neq i} \frac{Emp_{j,MSA}}{Emp_{MSA}} Input_{ji}$$

and the interaction of venture capital with being a capital-intensive industry. The input measure has a strong and significant positive effect. As the value of this variable increases by 0.05, which could signal a transfer of 20 per cent of employment from an industry that provides no inputs for industry *i* to an industry that provides 25 per cent of industry *i*'s inputs, then the self-employment rate goes up by slightly over two per cent in that industry.

This regression also includes an interaction term between the venture capital measure and being in a high-skilled manufacturing industry. This interaction is testing the hypothesis that venture capital particularly matters in that capital-intensive sector. I find no evidence of this interaction. In general, the venture capital measures have little correlation with the self-employment rate, so I omit them from future regressions in this table.

Regression (5) includes our measure of input suppliers who are in small firms,

$$Chinitz_{i,MSA} = \sum_{j \neq i} \frac{Firms_{j,MSA}}{Emp_{MSA}} Input_{ji}.$$

In this case, there is no effect of this variable. Input suppliers seem to increase self-employment, but the size of these suppliers is not important. Regression (6) includes the labor mix variable

$$LaborMix_{i,MSA} = \sum_{o} \frac{Emp_{o,MSA}}{Emp_{MSA}} Share_{oj}.$$

In this case, more workers lead to less, not more, self-employment in the area.

Regression (7) looks at demand-side variables. The basic demand variable

$$Demand_{i,MSA} = \sum_{j \neq i} \frac{Emp_{j,MSA}}{Emp_{MSA}} Output_{ij}$$

has a negative effect. I also look at whether city population has a disproportionate impact on self-employment rates in those industries that cater directly to the public. I find that self-employment rates rise in big cities for retail trade in this regression with metropolitan area fixed effects. I also look at whether self-employment rates rise in the health services industry in those cities with a greater population over the age of 65. I find that the opposite is true and self-employment rates in the health services industry are actually lower in the cities with a more elderly population.

Regression (8) combines all of our major explanatory variables. The significant variables that are positively associated with self-employment are the input measure and the interaction between city size and retail trade. Beyond that, there is little evidence for the other hypotheses. Suppliers seem to matter, but consumers are less important apart from retail trade. There is certainly evidence (Ellison, Glaeser and Kerr, 2007) that the location of suppliers and workers matters for overall employment in an industry, but there is no evidence that the demand-side factors increase the rate of self-employment in the industry. I now turn to regressions on firm size.

Firm Size Correlations

Table 5.6 looks at the correlates of firm size across metropolitan areas. Regression (1) looks at average firm size in the metropolitan area as a dependent variable. Regressions (2)–(5) look at average firm size in a metropolitan area in a particular industry as a dependent variable.

In the first regression, I include the basic city demographics, the log of city population and the log of venture capital spending as explanatory variables. To correct for the industrial mix of the city, I include a control variable

$$\sum_j \frac{Emp_{j,MSA}}{Emp_{MSA}} \frac{Firms_{j,USA}}{Emp_{j,USA}},$$

which is average firm size in the industries in the metropolitan area, weighted by the employment share of each industry in the area. This measure is meant to control for the industrial mix of the metropolitan area.

The first regression shows the basic correlates of firm size in the city as a whole. The industry mix certainly does matter, but it tends to matter less than one-for-one. For every extra person per firm predicted by this measure, the city will have only one-quarter of an extra person per firm. This result actually also tends to reject the 'culture of entrepreneurship' hypothesis, which would predict that this coefficient would be greater than one because entrepreneurship in one industry should inspire more entrepreneurship in other industries. Under this hypothesis, this would create a social multiplier and a coefficient greater than one.

The demographic variables do not correspond well to the individual level facts about demographics and self-employment. Education is associated with bigger, not smaller, firms. An abundance of people under the age of 40 predicts smaller firms. Only the coefficient on people over the age of 60 supports the previous finding that older people are more entrepreneurial. City size also favors bigger firms. This finding runs in the opposite direction from the self-employment regressions. I do find that venture capital positively predicts small firms. The overall r-squared in this regression is 35 per cent. This supports the view that basic demographics can explain a significant amount of the variation across cities.

In the second regression, I turn to industry-specific measures. Since these regressions are performed at the MSA-industry level, I include both industry- and MSA-fixed effects. I also include the logarithm of employment in the industry in the MSA. Just as the logarithm of employment is associated with less self-employment, it is also associated with smaller average firm sizes.

Table 5.6 Firm size regressions

	(1)	(2)	(3)	(4)	(5)	(6)
	Dependent Variable					
	Average Firm Size in MSA	Average Firm Size in the Industry and MSA				
Predicted Firm Size	0.251					
	(0.007)					
Log Venture Capital per Capita (State Level)	−0.784					
	(0.007)					
Share of Population with BA – MSA	11.017					
	(0.201)					
Log of Population – MSA	0.747					
	(0.008)					
Share of Population under 40 – MSA	−33.010					
	(0.836)					
Share of Population over 60 – MSA	−46.770					
	(1.098)					
Log of VC/capita Interacted with High-Skilled Manufacturing		−1.098				
		(0.157)				
Input Measure		−0.032				−0.041
		(0.001)				(0.002)
Chintiz Measure			−0.297			0.326
			(0.012)			(0.023)

	(1)	(2)	(3)	(4)	(5)	(6)
Labor Mix Measure				−7.105		−6.911
				(0.126)		(0.126)
Demand					−0.037	−0.019
					(0.001)	(0.001)
Log of Population Interacted with Retail Trade					−0.287	
					(0.178)	
Share of Population over 65 Interacted with Health Services					−8.322	
					(8.301)	
Log of Employment in the Industry and MSA		23.094	22.306	24.038	22.683	25.365
		(0.134)	(0.131)	(0.135)	(0.134)	(0.138)
Constant	36.223	−181.509	−174.772	−230.495	−177.316	−244.399
	(0.676)	(4.342)	(4.348)	(1.566)	(4.385)	(1.596)
Observations	76119	141832	141832	137620	138351	137620
R-squared	0.35	0.68	0.67	0.70	0.67	0.71

Notes:

1. Regression (1) looks at average firm size in the metropolitan area as a dependent variable. Regressions (2)–(6) look at average firm size in a metropolitan area in a particular industry as a dependent variable. All regressions include industry-fixed effects. Regressions (2)–(6) also include MSA-fixed effects. Standard errors are in parentheses and are clustered at the MSA level.
2. MSA-level demographic data (education, population, age, employment) is from 2000 Census microdata, from the Integrated Public Use Microdata Series (IPUMS) at http://usa.ipums.org/usa/. Steven Ruggles, Matthew Sobek, Trent Alexander, Catherine A. Fitch, Ronald Goeken, Patricia Kelly Hall, Miriam King and Chad Ronnander. *Integrated Public Use Microdata Series: Version 3.0* [Machine-readable database]. Minneapolis, MN: Minnesota Population Center [producer and distributor], 2004.

Table 5.6 (continued)

3. Firm size data is from the 2000 County Business Patterns, and the Input-Output data is from the tables at the Bureau of Economic Analysis at http://www.bea-gov/industry/.
4. The "Predicted Firm Size" variable is average firm size in the industries in the metropolitan area, weighted by the employment share of each industry in the area and is used to correct for the industrial mix of the MSA. See text for a detailed description of how this variable was calculated.
5. The measure of venture capital used to calculate the "Log Venture Capital per Capita (State Level)" variable and the "Log of VC/capita Interacted with High-Skilled Info Services" variable is found at https://www.pwcmoneytree.com/MTPublic/ns/index.jsp.
6. The "Input Measure" variable captures the share of an industry's inputs that are bought from other industries. See text for a detailed description of how this variable was calculated.
7. The "Chinitz Measure" variable is used to capture the number of firms that supply an industry's needs in this metropolitan area, based on Chinitz's argument that the overall level of entrepreneurship depended on the presence of many small firms that can readily supply new start-ups. See text for a detailed description of how this variable was calculated.
8. The "Labor Mix Measure" captures the labor mix of an area. See text for a detailed description of how this variable was calculated.
9. The "Demand" variable captures the demand of other industries for a particular industry's goods. See text for a detailed description of how this variable was calculated.
10. There are two measures of consumer demand, captured with "Log of Population Interacted with Retail Trade" variable and the "Share of Population over 65 Interacted with Health Services" variable. See text for a detailed description of how these variables were calculated.
11. The coefficient and standard error on the Chinitz Measure were multiplied by 100 for readability.

In regression (2), I also include the input measure and an interaction of the venture capital measure with high-skilled manufacturing. In this case, the interaction works as predicted, as more venture capital is associated with smaller average firm sizes in high-skilled manufacturing. The input measure is associated with smaller average firm size, but the effect is small. As this variable increases by 0.05, there are 0.0015 fewer workers per firm in the industry in the metropolitan area. Still, this confirms the view that there is more entrepreneurship in places where inputs are more readily available.

The third regression includes the Chinitz measure, which captures the firm size in industries that supply inputs in the area. The Chinitz measure is quite significant statistically. If the number of firms per worker increases by 0.1 in every industry that supplied this industry, then the expected number of workers per firm in this industry would change by −0.03. The presence of many suppliers doesn't impact self-employment, but it does increase the number of independent firms.

The fourth regression includes the labor mix variable, which has a significant negative impact on average firm size. If this variable increases by 0.05, which indicates that 20 per cent of all employment moves from occupations that provide none of the workers for this industry into occupations that provide 25 per cent of the workers for this industry, then the predicted number of workers per firm changes by −0.35.

In regression (5), I include the demand-side measures. Though more demand is associated with smaller firms, the effect of this variable is quite modest. As this variable increases by 0.05, workers per firm changes by −0.002. The other demand measures – the interaction between retail trade and population and the interaction between health and the share of the population that is older – have no impact.

In regression (6), I include all of the major explanatory variables; their coefficients are relatively stable, except for the Chinitz variable, which switches signs. All four variables remain statistically significant, but the labor mix variable and the Chinitz variable are the most important measures. Overall, input measures and demand do all seem to matter, but the variables that are particularly important for small firms are multiple input suppliers and abundant workers.

Evidence from the Longitudinal Research Database

Table 5.7, my final table, is taken from Dumais, Ellison and Glaeser (1997), and contains evidence on new establishment creation in the Longitudinal Research Database (LRD). The advantage of this data is that I am able to look at the creation of new plants over time. Unfortunately, the restricted nature of this data means that I have not been able to update these results

Table 5.7 Employment growth due to births and closures

	Dependent variable: log(1 + ΔE^j_ist)					
	MSA Level			State Level		
	(1) New firm births	(2) New firm births	(3) Old firm births	(4) New firm births	(5) New firm births	(6) Old firm births
Input	0.00	0.00	0.03	0.04	0.04	0.08
	(0.0)	(0.0)	(2.8)	(5.5)	(5.6)	(7.8)
Demand	0.02	0.02	0.01	0.03	0.03	0.01
	(3.2)	(3.4)	(0.6)	(5.1)	(5.1)	(1.6)
Labor Mix	0.18	0.17	0.13	0.43	0.43	0.25
	(13.4)	(12.6)	(9.7)	(11.0)	(10.6)	(5.4)
Labor Mix*Closure Rate		0.02			0.00	
		(6.1)			(0.0)	
Integration	0.08	0.08	0.10	0.06	0.06	0.09
	(5.0)	(5.2)	(4.9)	(5.9)	(5.9)	(6.5)
Integration*College		0.01			−0.05	
		(1.2)			(−1.5)	
Technological Flows	0.00	0.00	0.04	−0.01	−0.01	0.03
	(0.3)	(0.3)	(4.9)	(−1.5)	(−1.5)	(3.3)
Adjusted R^2	0.56	0.56	0.32	0.73	0.73	0.54
Number of observations	163938	163938	163938	27234	27234	27336

Notes:

1. Data is from the Longitudinal Research Database, and includes only data from manufacturing; it represents a panel with linked establishment level data between 1972 and 1992.
2. The dependent variable is the increase in employment due to new establishments in industry i, place s, and time period t.
3. The "Input" and "Demand" variables are the same as described in the other tables. The "Labor Mix" variable is defined slightly differently. See text for a detailed description of how these variables were calculated.
4. The "Closure Rate" of firms in this industry interacted with the "Labor Mix" is used as a proxy for volatility.
5. The "Integration" variable represents the tendency of other firms in that industry to be co-owned with other firms from the other industries in the metropolitan area. See text for a detailed description of how this variable was calculated.
6. The "College" variable is a measure of the fraction of the employment in the industry that is contained in occupations that would normally require a college degree. It is interacted with the "Integration" variable to create a measure of intellectual spillovers.
7. The "Technological Flows" variable uses an input-output chart for patents and attempts to measure the intellectual connection between different industries. The source for this data is Scherer (1984). See text for a detailed description of how this variable was calculated.
8. MSA level regressions include MSA-, industry-, and year-fixed effects. State-level regressions include state-, industry-, and year-fixed effects.

Source: Dumais, Ellison and Glaeser (1997)

or change the regressions. This data includes only data from manufacturing and it represents a panel with linked establishment level data between 1972 and 1992.

My regressions here are of the form:

$$Log(1 + \Delta Emp_{ist}) = \beta_1 Input + \beta_2 Demand + \beta_3 Labor\ Mix + Other\ Controls \quad (5.4)$$

The variable $Log(1 + \Delta Emp_{ist})$ reflects the increase in employment due to new establishments in industry i, place s, and time period t. We distinguish between new firm establishments and old firm establishments. New firm establishments are those establishments that are not part of the same firm as any other establishment in the manufacturing database. Old firm establishments include those establishments that are part of the same firm as other firms in the database. The new firm employment growth is probably closer to capturing the amount of entrepreneurial growth in the area.

The input and demand measures are the same as those described above. The labor mix variable, however, is different and in this case is based on the industrial structure of the area. Labor mix is here defined as

$$Labor\ Mix_{i,MSA} = -\sum_{o}\left(\frac{Emp_{i,o,USA}}{Emp_{i,USA}} - \sum_{j\neq i}\frac{Emp_{j,s,MSA}}{Emp_{MSA} - Emp_{j,MSA}}\frac{Emp_{j,o,USA}}{Emp_{j,USA}}\right)^2$$

which is defined as the difference between the occupation pattern in the industry in the US as a whole and the average occupation pattern of the other industries in the metropolitan area.

The regression also includes a control for integration and technology flows. Integration represents the tendency of other firms in that industry to be co-owned with other firms from the other industries in the metropolitan area. The integration measure is

$$Integration_{i,MSA} = \sum_{j\neq i}\frac{Emp_{j,MSA}}{Emp_{MSA}}\frac{Co\text{-}Owned_{ji,USA}}{Emp_{i,USA}},$$

where $Co - Owned_{ji,USA}$ measures the amount of employment in plants in industry i that are in multi-establishment firms with plants in both industry i and industry j. We specifically eliminate co-ownership that is due to input–output linkages and the hope is that this measure captures more intangible reasons for connections across industries. Our measure of technology flows uses an input–output chart for patents and attempts to measure the intellectual connections between different industries, and so equals

$$Techflow_{i,MSA} = \sum_{j \neq i} \frac{Emp_{j,MSA}}{Emp_{MSA}} \frac{Citations_{ji,USA}}{Citations_{j,USA}},$$

where the citations measures give us that share of all patent citations made by innovators in industry *j* that come from industry *i*. The source for this data is Scherer (1984).

I also control for the general growth in that industry and that area; there are MSA-, industry- and year-fixed effects. All of the measures have been normalized to have mean zero and standard deviation of one. The first three regressions use metropolitan area-level data and the last three regressions use state-level data.

In the first regression, we find no positive correlations between new firm employment growth and both input suppliers. The demand measure has a weak positive effect. A one standard deviation increase in this variable is associated with a 0.02 log point increase in new firm plant birth employment. The labor mix variable is much more powerful. A one standard deviation increase in this variable is associated with a 0.18 log point increase in new firm plant birth employment. The integration measure is the second most powerful variable in the regression, after labor mix. A one standard deviation increase in this variable is associated with a 0.08 log point increase in employment growth. The technology flow variable is insignificant.

Regression (2) tests two related hypotheses. First, labor mix will be more important in more volatile industries. According to this hypothesis, the willingness of workers to take a chance on a new firm depends on the presence of many other employers with whom they could potentially work. The labor mix variable can be seen as measuring the extent of local demand for firms in industry *i*. The second hypothesis suggests that integration measures something about information spillovers across industries, and that these are more important for more skilled workers.

Regression (2) uses the closure rate of firms in this industry as a proxy for volatility. The importance of the labor mix variable is higher in those industries with a higher closure rate. The integration measure is not particularly higher for those industries with more college educated workers.

Regression (3) repeats regression (1) using employment growth due to plant birth, in cases where plants are co-owned with other plants in the LRD. The results are broadly similar, although in this case the presence of input suppliers becomes marginally more important. The importance of labor mix falls somewhat, but this variable remains the most important one in the regression. A comparison of regressions (3) and (1) suggests at least that labor mix may be more important for new plant start-ups than for existing firms starting new plants in an area.

Regressions (4)–(6) repeat regressions (1)–(3) using states rather than metropolitan areas as the units of analysis. At the state level, the importance of labor mix rises to 0.43 in regression (4). Both input and demand measures are statistically significant, but they are about one-tenth the size of the labor mix variable. Regression (5) shows that the interactions are insignificant at the state level. Regression (6) shows that labor mix is again far less important for old firm plant birth and that input suppliers have become more important.

Table 5.7 provides us with a different view of entrepreneurship by looking exclusively within manufacturing and looking at the amount of new employment in an area associated with new plant births. The results do look different from the other work. The presence of firms that use the same type of labor seems like the crucial aspect for the location of these new manufacturing plants. Input suppliers and customers matter much less. The integration measure also has some significance, but interpreting this measure is far from easy.

CONCLUSION

This chapter has documented a series of stylized facts about entrepreneurship over space. I have used average firm size and the self-employment rate as my measures of entrepreneurship. Both of these measures have their problems, but I believe that they certainly capture something about the level of entrepreneurship in an area. Moreover, both of these measures predict urban success at the metropolitan area level. The number of workers per firm is also strongly negatively associated with growth at the industry level within metropolitan areas.

There is a significant amount of heterogeneity in entrepreneurship over space, and this heterogeneity appears more strongly within individual industries than across the economy as a whole. Florida appears to be particularly entrepreneurial, while many Rust Belt[2] metropolitan areas are not. Across individuals, age and schooling both predict entrepreneurship. These demographic variables, and industry sectors, together explain about one-half of the heterogeneity in overall self-employment rates across metropolitan areas.

I find mixed evidence for the existence of a ‘culture of entrepreneurship’ in a particular metropolitan area. Self-employment rates are higher among individuals who live in metropolitan areas that are filled with particularly entrepreneurial industries. However, this effect does not hold within more narrow industrial categories. As the industry mix changes in a way that predicts one extra worker per firm, the actual number of workers per firm only increases by 0.25. As such, there is little evidence for a social multiplier where entrepreneurial industries create abundant entrepreneurs outside of their industries.

One general fact is that these entrepreneurship figures always decline with the concentration of an industry in an area. The number of self-employed workers and the number of firms per worker are higher in areas where industries are less common. This fact can be explained by many factors, including the possibility that entrepreneurs are spread relatively evenly, but in some areas they are more successful. In that case, high levels of employment would be associated with a lower number of entrepreneurs per employee.

The presence of an appropriate workforce is the most powerful predictor of new firm birth (a third measure of entrepreneurship) and small firms. Workers seem to be a crucial input into new businesses. There is no correlation between labor mix and the self-employment rate. A measure of the presence of small firms in supplying industries, as suggested by Chinitz (1961), also correlates strongly with the presence of small firms. The self-employment rate is most strongly associated with input suppliers, but that variable is more weakly connected with either of the other two measures of entrepreneurship. The presence of customers seems to be relatively unimportant in all of the regressions.

Overall, these results are, at best, suggestive. There are no forms of exogenous variation and there are many potential explanations for each one of the facts. However, they do point to the paramount importance of labor supply in driving entrepreneurship. Skilled, older people are much more likely to be entrepreneurs, and entrepreneurship increases in areas with an appropriate labor force, presumably because these people provide both workers and entrepreneurs. These results suggest that pro-entrepreneurship policies might focus particularly on attracting the right type of workers.

ACKNOWLEDGEMENTS

Kristina Tobio provided superb research assistance and oversaw a team consisting of Yün-ke Chin-Lee, Elizabeth Cook, Andrew Davis and Charles Redlick. Jason Furman provided helpful comments.

NOTES

1. https://www.pwcmoneytree.com/MTPublic/ns/index.jsp.
2. The Rust Belt consists of the areas of the Northeast and Midwest that used to be major centers of heavy industry and manufacturing but are now in decline.

REFERENCES

Blanchflower, D.G. and A. J. Oswald (1998), 'What Makes an Entrepreneur?' *Journal of Labor Economics*, 16 (1), 26–60.

Chinitz, B. (1961), 'Contrasts in Agglomeration: New York and Pittsburg', *American Economic Review*, 51 (2), 279–289.

Dumais, G., G. Ellison and E.L. Glaeser (1997), *Geographic Concentration as a Dynamic Process*, NBER Working Paper no. 6270, Cambridge, MA: NBER.

Ellison, G., E.L. Glaeser and W. Kerr (2007), *What Causes Industry Agglomeration? Evidence from Coagglomeration Patterns*, NBER Working Paper no. 13068, Cambridge, MA: NBER.

Evans, D.S. and B. Jovanovic (1989), 'An Estimated Model of Entrepreneurial Choice Under Liquidity Constraints', *Journal of Political Economy*, 97 (4), 808–827.

Glaeser, E.L., H. Kallal, J.A. Scheinkman and A. Shleifer (1992), 'Growth in Cities', *The Journal of Political Economy*, 100 (6), 1126–1152.

Miracky, W. (1994), 'The Firm Product Cycle', MIT mimeograph.

Moretti, E. (2004), 'Estimating the Social Return to Higher Education: Evidence from Longitudinal and Repeated Cross-Sectional Data', *Journal of Econometrics*, 121 (1–2), 175–212.

Porter, M.E. (1990), *The Competitive Advantage of Nations*, New York: Free Press.

Saxenian, A. (1994), *Regional Advantage: Culture and Competition in Silicon Valley and Route 128*, Cambridge, MA: Harvard University Press.

Scherer, F.M. (1984), 'Using Linked Patent Data and R&D Data to Measure Technology Flows', in Z. Griliches (ed.), *R & D, Patents and Productivity*, Chicago: University of Chicago Press.

6. Star scientists, innovation and regional and national immigration

Lynne G. Zucker and Michael R. Darby

> The world, in fact, is only beginning to see that the wealth of a nation consists more than anything else in the number of superior men that it harbors . . . Geniuses are ferments; and when they come together, as they have done in certain lands at certain times, the whole population seems to share in the higher energy which they awaken. The effects are incalculable and often not easy to trace in detail, but they are pervasive and momentous. (William James 1911, p. 363)

In the last half of the twentieth century, America was the location of choice for the best and brightest scientific minds in the world. Recently America has partially rolled up its welcome mat to foreign doctoral and postdoctoral students while a reverse brain drain has set in for senior professors. Does this matter for the US economy or is it a matter of purely academic concern – in both senses? This chapter reports evidence that a sizable fraction of the very top scientists are responsible for start-up firms across the broad range of high-technology industries whether they are in the United States or abroad. When America loses its star scientists – or star scientists in the making – it is losing not only their academic research and teaching, but new firms and jobs.

On the order of one-third of the star scientists actually become involved in commercializing their discoveries at least once in their career; so losing a few hundred star scientists will have a small effect on the number of firms started in the US over the next generation. However, the firms started with star scientists as principals have proven to be the leading firms in terms of innovation and employment growth in a number of high-technology industries, such as biotechnology, lasers and semiconductors. In America and similar economies, most economic growth is concentrated at any given time in a relatively few firms in a relatively few industries experiencing very large productivity gains or introducing new products of much greater value than their cost of production (Harberger 1998; Darby and Zucker 2003). These firms are most often but not always somewhere en route from entrepreneurial start-up to large, industry-dominant firms.[1] Losing to other countries star scientists who are likely to become star innovators is a recipe for shifting leading firms in specific new technologies abroad, leaving an imitative or no role for American firms.

This chapter is organized in four sections. The first section discusses research findings in the literature on university–industry technology transfer before focusing on our research on the role of star scientists in determining where and when firms enter the biotechnology industry, which firms are most successful, how quickly they go public, and the stock market returns for particular firms. The second section presents evidence that – at least so far as starting firms is concerned – these top scientists are star innovators across the gamut of high-tech industries. The third section presents evidence on the emergence of a reverse brain drain from the US to other countries that has reduced the number of these top scientists operating in and starting firms in the US. The final section offers conclusions and concerns for policy makers.

TOP SCIENTISTS AS STAR INNOVATORS

The importance of basic university science to successful commercialization of scientific discoveries has been confirmed in a number of research studies, especially the importance of intellectual human capital (Di Gregorio and Shane 2003). Faculty are a key resource in creating and transferring early, discovery research via commercial entrepreneurial behavior (Yarkin 2000). Jensen and Thursby (2001) confirm that active, self-interested participation of discovering professors is an essential condition for successful commercial licensing of most university inventions. Thursby and Thursby (2002) find that the sharp increase in university–industry technology transfer has not resulted so much from a shift in the nature of faculty research as from an increased willingness of faculty and administrators to license and increased interest on the part of firms.

Labor mobility of discovering scientists becomes very important in technology transfer, however, when a new discovery has both high commercial value and a combination of scarcity and tacitness that defines natural excludability, the degree to which there is a barrier to the flow of the valuable knowledge from the discoverers to other scientists (Zucker and Darby 1996b; Zucker, Darby and Brewer 1998). Those with the most information about breakthrough discoveries are the scientists actually making them, so there is initial scarcity.

To the extent that the knowledge is both scarce and tacit, as it often is in breakthrough discoveries, it constitutes intellectual human capital retained by the discovering scientists and is embodied in them. At the extreme, labor mobility is required to transfer the knowledge successfully (as found empirically by Jensen and Thursby 2001). To measure the extent of labor mobility of the stars, we use the count of 'linked' articles authored by stars with firm employees. These linked stars are most often local academic scientists-entrepreneurs who possess a significant equity or founding interest in the firm. The number of such articles serves as an indicator of the depth of the star's involvement with the firm's research effort. Nearly 70 per cent of the Institute for Scientific Information (ISI) highly cited stars, who are the focus of the next two sections of this chapter, write at least one article with at least one firm employee, with 10 per cent of all articles written by these stars linked to a firm.

In order to gain access to the knowledge of discovering scientists, firms in related areas of technology employ them. In most cases, the discovering scientists are initially employed by universities and research institutes; we are concerned with the extent to which they move at least part of their labor effort to specific firms. Some of these firms are incumbent firms which adopt the new technology (see Zucker and Darby 1996a, 1996b, 1997a, 1997b; Darby and Zucker 2001), but many of the firms are newly created around these star scientists, who often become residual owners as well as employees (Zucker, Darby and Brewer 1998). The discovering scientists often become the main resource around which firms are built or transformed (Zucker, Darby and Brewer 1998; Zucker, Darby and Armstrong 1998, 2002; Zucker and Darby 2006; Darby and Zucker 2007). Star scientists are important in the process of technology transfer because the knowledge is both scarce and tacit and because their knowledge contributes significantly to the success of firms (Zucker, Darby and Torero 2002).

Our biotechnology database and research program was built around the 327 most productive scientists in terms of genetic sequence discoveries through 1989, a period encompassing the formative years of biotechnology but ending before the advent of automated sequencers which made our selection criterion obsolete in the 1990s. These 'star' scientists are truly among the best and brightest in the world: accounting for only 0.7 per cent of the authors of articles reporting genetic sequence discoveries through 1989, they accounted for 17.3 per cent of the published articles. Great scientists – including these stars – differ from ordinary scientists in many ways, from mentoring fewer and brighter students to many more articles published, citations to those articles, and patents (Zuckerman 1967, 1977; Zucker, Darby and Armstrong 1998). Not only did these scientists play a major role in shaping the advance of the science underlying biotechnology, our research has also shown that they played an important role in determining where and when firms entered biotechnology and which of those firms were most successful.

Zucker, Darby and Brewer (1998) and Darby and Zucker (2001)

examined entry of new firms and incumbent firms into biotechnology in America and Japan respectively. We argue there that the geographic distribution of a new science-based industry can be mostly derived from the geographic distribution of the intellectual human capital embodying the breakthrough discovery upon which it is based. This occurs when the discovery – especially an 'invention of a method of discovery' (Griliches 1957) – is sufficiently costly to transfer due to its uncodified complexity or tacitness (Nelson 1959; Arrow 1962, 1974; Nelson and Winter 1982; Rosenberg 1982) that the information can effectively be used only by employing those scientists in whom it is embodied. Technological opportunity and appropriability – the principal factors that drive technical progress for industries (Klevorick *et al.* 1995; Nelson and Wolff 1997) – are also the two necessary elements that created extraordinary value for our stars' intellectual human capital during the formative period of biotechnology. The employment of stars with a firm was often as a founding principal and usually part-time near their university laboratory (Zucker, Darby and Armstrong 1998; Zucker, Darby and Torero 2002). When the new techniques have diffused widely, access to stars is less essential, but once the technology has been commercialized in specific locales, internal dynamics of agglomeration tend to keep it there (Marshall 1920; Grossman and Helpman 1991; Audretsch and Feldman 1994, 1996; Head, Ries and Swenson 1995).[2]

In both the US and Japan, where and when star scientists are active has a strongly positive and significant independent effect on where and when biotech-using firms entered into biotechnology, and this effect is always separate from, and in addition to, the effects of research support for university scientists and local general economic conditions. We do find that intellectual capital variables play a relatively more important role for entry in the US whereas it is the local economic geography variables which are more significant in Japan.

As far as we know, neither we nor any other scholars have done any comparable research for Europe for this formative period through 1989. To a large degree, this may reflect a real disconnection during this period between academic science and industry. We recall a German pharmaceutical executive complaining, as late as the early 1990s, that the only way his firm could get German scientists to do genetic engineering for it was to employ them in the United States. A series of papers by Cooke (2001, 2004 and 2005) suggests that this disconnection has since been bridged in some European metropolitan regions.

Table 6.1, adapted from Zucker and Darby (1999b), shows that Europe in fact had enough of the world's star scientists during the formative period to have been a major player in the commercial biotechnology revolution rather than playing the peripheral role that it did. Europe, plus Russia and Israel,

Table 6.1 Star bioscientists, their ties to firms and migration rates: top-10 countries, 1973–1989

Countries	Share of stars[1]	Fraction tied to firms[2]	Migration rate	
			Gross[3]	Net[4]
United States	50.2	33.3	22.2	2.9
Japan	12.6	42.3	40.4	9.6
United Kingdom	7.5	9.7	58.1	−32.3
France	6.1	0.0	20.0	4.0
Germany	5.8	0.0	50.0	8.3
Switzerland	3.6	20.0	93.3	−40.0
Australia	3.4	7.1	35.7	7.1
Canada	2.4	0.0	50.0	−30.0
Belgium	1.7	14.2	42.9	14.3
Netherlands	1.2	20.0	80.0	0.0
Top-10 countries as a group	94.7	14.9	35.4	-0.8

Notes:
1. Total stars ever publishing a genetic-sequence discovery article 1973–1989 in this country as a percentage of total stars ever publishing such an article 1973–1989 in any country. This involves some double-counting of multiple country stars. Countries in the omitted rest of world with any stars are Denmark, Finland, Israel, Italy, Sweden and the USSR.
2. Percentage of stars ever publishing a genetic-sequence discovery article 1973–1989 in the country that ever published such an article in which the star or a coauthor was affiliated with a firm in the country.
3. Gross migration rate = 100 x (immigration + emigration of stars)/(number of stars ever publishing in the country).
4. Net migration rate = 100 x (immigration - emigration of stars)/(number of stars ever publishing in the country).

Source: Adapted from Zucker and Darby (1999b), Table 1

accounted for 32 per cent of the stars, counted once per nation in which they published, compared to 62 per cent for the US and Japan. The European university–industry disconnection is underlined by the fact that the corresponding percentages for stars ever working as or with a firm employee were 9 and 90. Small net immigration into a few countries did not offset the large emigration from Britain and Switzerland to the benefit of the US and Japan. Anecdotal evidence suggests that the greater hospitality of the latter countries to academic scientist-entrepreneurs played a role in this pattern, with immigrants establishing firm ties soon after moving. We hypothesize in our third major section (below) on the reasons that the virtuous circles present in America and Japan may have been largely short-circuited in Europe.

We have found that the publication of articles by a star as, or with, a firm employee is a robust indicator of substantial involvement of that star with the firm. Substantial involvement of one or more star bioscientists was not a sufficient condition to make a firm successful, but it dramatically improved the odds relative to those firms that did not have it. For example, we consider the 38 publicly traded 1975 members of the Pharmaceutical Manufacturers Association. Of the 15 firms which had developed working arrangements with star scientists by 1990, 80 per cent (12 firms) survived until 1999. Of the 23 firms without such star participation, only 17.4 per cent (4 firms) survived to 1999 (Darby and Zucker 2001). A pharmaceutical firm not doing cutting edge biotechnology by the 1990s was either going out of business or into generics or other businesses.

In Zucker, Darby and Armstrong (1998) we analyzed the success of a census of Californian biotech firms in terms of number of products in development, number of products on the market and employment growth. We demonstrated that what appear to be 'geographically localized knowledge spillovers' (positive externalities as proposed by Jaffe 1986; Jaffe, Trajtenberg and Henderson 1993) from academic science to the research productivity of nearby firms were in fact concentrated in the relatively few firms with stars linked via co-authorship; other firms gained no advantage from locating near the leading research universities.[3] These results were obtained from Poisson regressions, which controlled for the effect of firm characteristics such as incumbency-new-entrant status, technology used and time since entry. The estimated effects are quite significant as indicated on the left side of Figure 6.1. The more star-linked articles a firm had – indicating deeper involvement of the star at the bench level – the better the firm did, whether judged by products in development, products on the market or employment. These differences are large enough to explain the difference between success and failure: a biotech firm with no star-linked articles (with all other factors set to their mean values) had an expected employment growth of 80 workers from 1984 to 1989 compared to 341 and 734 for firms with 2 and 5 articles, respectively.

We replicated these results for Japan in Zucker and Darby (2001), with the star impacts indicated on the right half of Figure 6.1. There are two notable differences from the California results: firstly, the entire profile of products on the market in Japan was much lower and flatter, as they were lagging behind California by approximately five years. Secondly, we were unable to get usable estimates of biotechnology employment for Japanese firms, which were almost exclusively large incumbent firms using the technologies in a limited sector of their businesses. As a result we substituted the number of US patents granted as a third measure of success and found results that fit the pattern of strong effects from star involvement.

There is much more evidence that the star scientists play a special role,

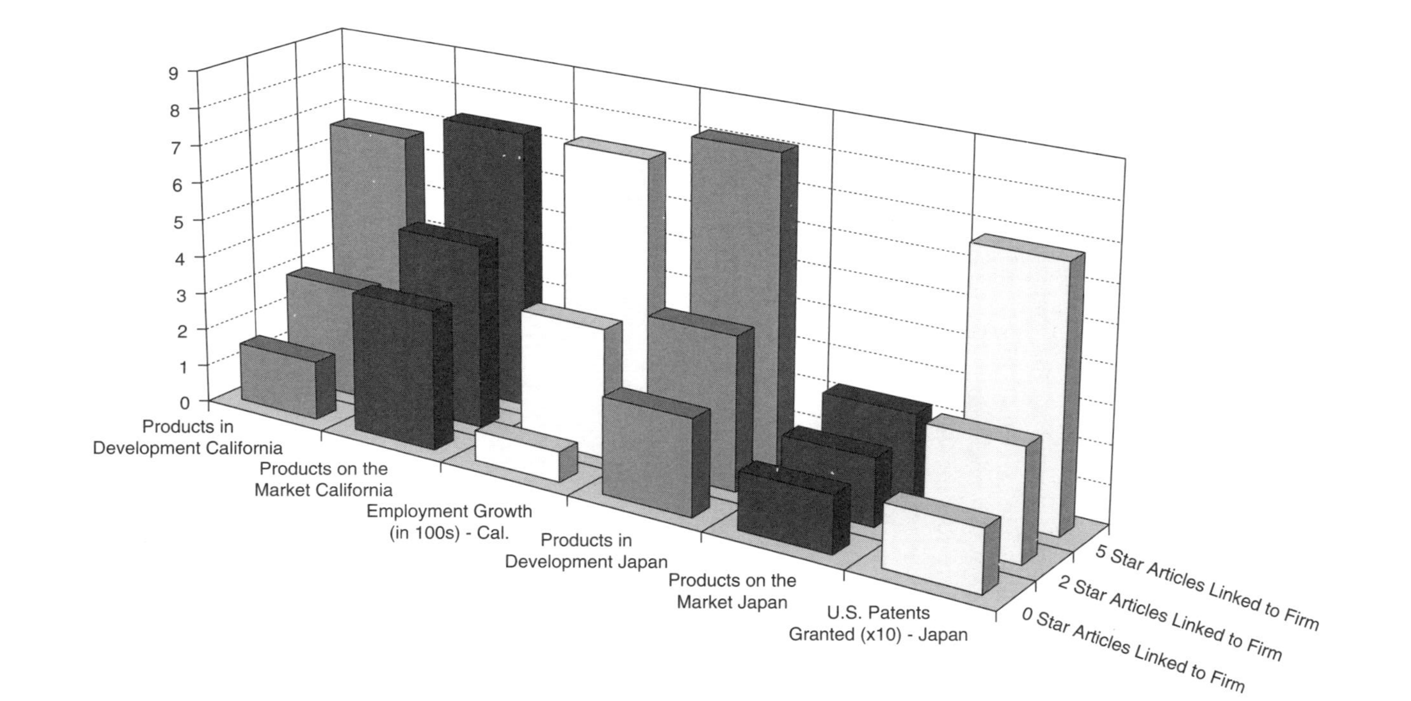

Sources: Zucker, Darby and Armstrong (1998) for California and Zucker and Darby (2001) for Japan

Figure 6.1 *Estimated effects of number of university star-firm linked articles on success of Californian and Japanese biotechnology-using firms*

independently from their potentially separable research discoveries, in shaping the formation and transformation of biotechnology-using industries. Figure 6.2 illustrates that star articles are a much stronger indicator of firm success than popular alternatives such as all-firm articles co-authored with top research university faculty members or venture capital funding. Audretsch and Stephan (1996) had analyzed the locational patterns of university scientists appearing in the prospectuses of biotechnology firms going public between March 1990 and November 1992, many of whom overlapped with our set of stars. In Darby and Zucker (2007) we show that firms with deeper star involvement do go public significantly more quickly than other biotech firms; implying that the characteristics described by Audretsch and Stephan differed systematically from the entire population of private biotech firms which might go public. Darby, Liu and Zucker (2004) show that not only does the stock market value star involvement in pricing publicly traded biotech firms, but those firms follow different high risk, high return strategies reflected in larger jumps or discontinuities in the evolution of their stock prices. Zucker and Darby (2007a) show that the stars' contributions to open science increase during their period of involvement with a firm, so that both science and commerce profit in the mutually reinforcing 'virtuous circle' alluded to previously.[4]

In short, direct involvement of the very best academic scientists in the commercialization of cutting-edge discoveries is a key determinant of which firms will win the competitive race and which will fall by the wayside. In high-technology, the race most often goes to the smartest.

TOP SCIENTISTS AND ENTRY OF HIGH-TECHNOLOGY FIRMS

We are beginning to investigate whether or not top scientists provide important top innovators across the gamut of high-technology industries, or whether this is a characteristic only of scientific areas undergoing very rapid change, like biotechnology and nanotechnology. We report here on the results of research into whether or not the presence of top scientists in a region or country generally lead to more entry there of firms in related technologies. Complete details of the statistical procedures, data and results can be found in Zucker and Darby (2006).

Data

This project is challenging because data are difficult and costly to obtain and far from perfect for investigating entrepreneurial companies, particularly

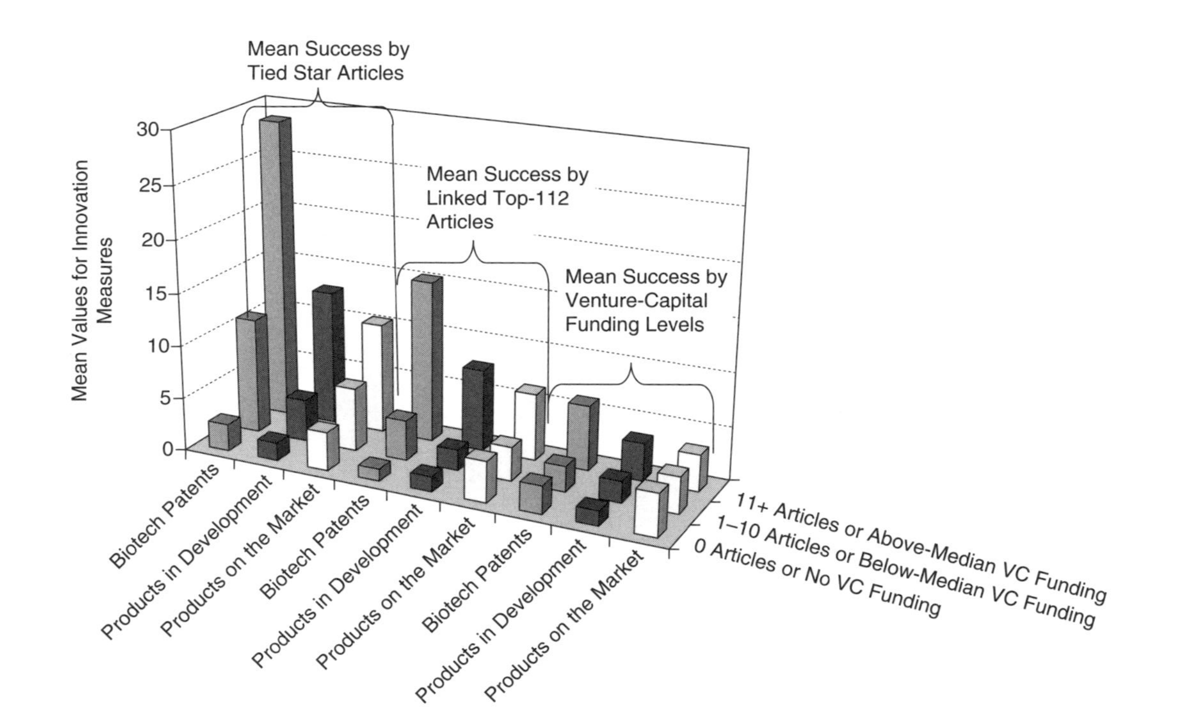

Source: Zucker, Darby and Armstrong (2002)

Figure 6.2 Success of US Biotech by ties to star scientists, links to top 112 research university faculties and venture-capital funding levels

in the formative years of a new technology, when most of the firms are not publicly traded and hence not required to make public disclosures. The entry of high-technology firms into a technology can be approximately dated from the date of their first patent application or scientific article publication. For NanoBank.org, we developed as complete as possible a list of companies using nanotechnology (Zucker and Darby 2007b; Zucker *et al.* 2007). We verified that substituting entry dates for those firms gave us essentially the same results as we obtained using the patenting-publication method of identifying firms.

We examine the pattern of firm entry for six science and technology areas (biology, chemistry and medicine; computing and information technology; semiconductors, integrated circuits and superconductors; nanoscale science and technology; other sciences; and other engineering). The five areas other than nanotechnology were developed for and detailed in analyses reported in Darby and Zucker (1999) and Zucker and Darby (1999a) that span scientific articles, patents and university doctoral programs data from the National Research Council (1995). We were unable to find finer breakdowns that did not require data in greater detail in one or more of these sources. Under National Science Foundation funding, we are developing a public digital database Nanobank.org, which permits us to extract specific articles and patents for nanotechnology from the other five areas in which they would otherwise appear. See Zucker *et al.* (2007) for a discussion of the methodology used to define nanotechnology articles and patents. Geographic units are either the 179 US functional economic regions or the 25 top science and technology countries in the world in terms of patenting and publication.[5]

Another data challenge has been identifying star scientists across the broad range of scientific and engineering disciplines. In our previous research, we identified the stars using measures of scientific productivity uniquely tailored to the particular science area and independent of their direct involvement in the commercialization of their discoveries. In order to generalize the star concept, we needed to find a criterion of scientific productivity which was comparable across fields and not dependent on whether or not the star was actually involved in commercialization. (Since we are investigating star scientists who do commercialize their inventions, we need to define top scientists independent of that involvement.)

The Institute for Scientific Information®, Inc. (ISI®) has developed the ISI Highly Cited component of the ISI Web of Science®, which is very close to what is needed. The *ISI HighlyCited.com* website (Institute for Scientific Information 2005b) offers a database of the top 250 individual researchers in terms of 20-year rolling window citation counts in each of 21 subject fields – 19 of which are science and engineering fields. Information for each highly cited author includes a curriculum vitae (usually full but sometimes abbreviated[6]), a list of publications taken from the author's curriculum vitae, and links for those publications in ISI-listed journals to the full bibliographic information indexed in the *ISI Web of Science®* (Institute for Scientific Information 1981–1997, 2005a). Altogether we thus identify 5401 star scientists, one or more of whom are credited with authorship of some 520839 articles that appear in the *ISI Web of Science®* database. The articles are used to identify where the stars are active based on those 299583 cases (52.5 per cent of the appearances of stars as authors) where their affiliation is unambiguous.[7] We have used these addresses to identify each US region or non-US country in which these star scientists were active during 1981–2004. We code the stars as active in a region from two years before their first publication there until they move to another location. During transitional phases they are coded as active for up to two years in both locations. Stars who maintain long-term affiliations in multiple countries also are coded as active in each location.

Empirical Results

Zucker and Darby (2006) illustrate the relationship between stars ever active and cumulative firm entry 1981–2004 for US regions for the largest science and technology area (biology, chemistry and medicine) and the newest (nanoscale science and technology) respectively. In each case there is a high correlation between the number of star scientists and the number of firms that have entered the corresponding area of science and technology. However, the actual number of stars is much smaller relative to the number of new firms in the nanoscale science and technology (S&T) area than in the biology, chemistry and medicine area. We believe that this difference reflects the speed with which discoveries with nanotechnology application are being commercialized versus the slowness of recognition of star scientists in this new multidisciplinary area. This latter measure is based on counts of citations to their work relative to other publications in the same pre-existing discipline as the journals in which most of an author's articles appear.

Zucker and Darby (2006) also illustrate the relationship between stars ever active and cumulative firm entry 1981–2004 for the top 25 science and technology countries in the world for the same two science and technology areas. The pattern is strikingly similar to what was seen for US regions. It would take literally hundreds of maps to cover all six science and technology areas for entry and star presence each year at the US regional level and nationally. Furthermore, maps cannot adequately account for other variables which may account for the correlation. In Zucker and Darby (2006) we have used advanced statistical methods to simultaneously take account of other measures of scientific base and economic geography. We were particularly concerned with including measures of the actual discoveries in a region (patents, highly-cited articles, other articles) to distinguish the effect of the stars personally from that of their discoveries.

The statistical results are clear: holding other measures of scientific base and economic geography constant, regions or countries with more of these top scientists present in one of the six S&T areas also exhibit a significantly higher rate of firm entry in that S&T area. The effects are quite large in magnitude, as illustrated in Figure 6.3, adapted from Zucker and Darby (2006). The left half of the figure refers to estimates based on data for US regions for each year, 1981–2004. The right half of the figure refers to estimates based on the 24 non-US countries among the top 25 S&T countries in the world. Separate estimates on the effects of star scientists on the rate of firm entry by region per year and by country per year are obtained for each of the six S&T areas which are abbreviated at the bottom of the horizontal axis. The height of the bar indicates the predicted rate of entry for a particular assumed number of stars in the region or country given that all the other determinants are at their mean values relative to the same rate if the number of stars was also equal to its mean value. The first bar in the quartet for a given S&T area gives the relative probability assuming that there is one star scientist in the S&T area and region/country in a given year. The second bar – always equal to 1 – is the relative ratio if the assumed number of stars equals the mean value. The third and fourth bars increase the number of stars above the mean by one and by two standard deviations respectively. The associated increase in the rate of firm entry is substantial – in several cases astonishingly so – for all cases except for the anomalous negative effect for Other Sciences in the top 24 non-US S&T countries. The anomalous cases, semiconductors for both samples and computing/IT for the US case, are not statistically significantly different from zero, but all the other estimates are significantly positive. If we consider the estimates – not illustrated in Figure 6.3 – for all top 25 S&T countries (including the US), then entry has a significant positive impact in every case. However, since the data may impart a US-centric bias and since the much higher number of stars in the US than in any of the other countries may pick up any institutional advantages for entrepreneurial entry, we will not consider those estimates further.

We have conducted various experiments to test the robustness of the results. One set of questions concerns our use of the date of the first patent application or scientific article publication in a region/country and S&T area to measure the entry date of high-technology firms in that place and technology area. We do it because there is generally no alternative.

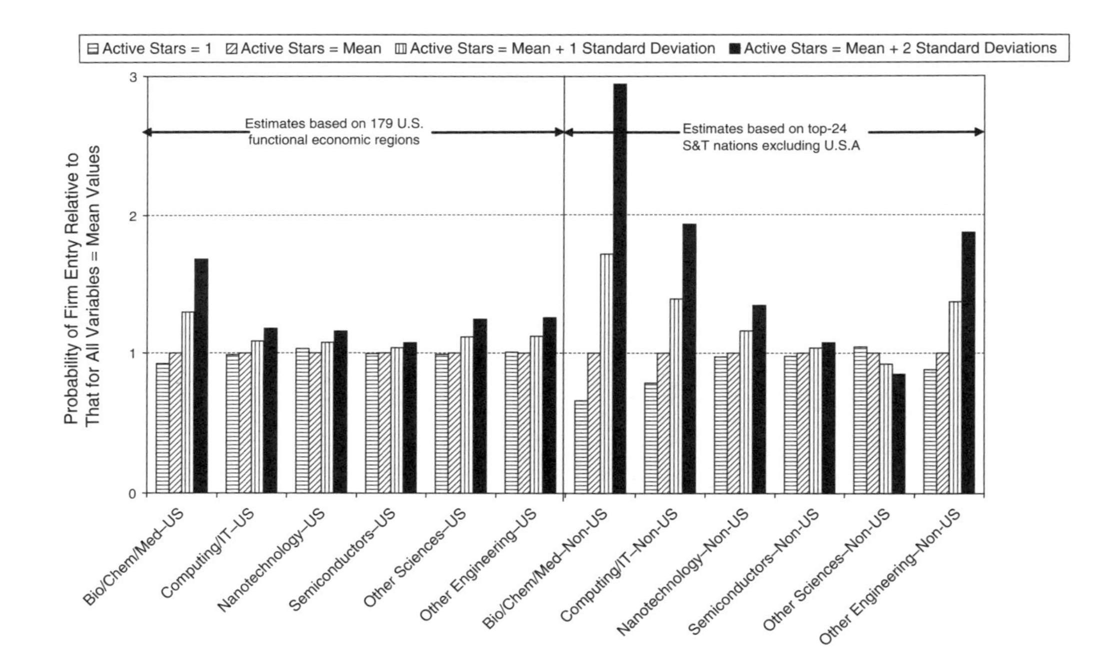

Note: All other variables = mean values.

Source: Zucker and Darby (2006)

Figure 6.3 *Star scientists and engineers increase the probability of firm entry into new technologies: relative probabilities with different numbers of active stars*

However, for NanoBank.org, we developed as complete as possible a list of companies using nanotechnology, using industry directories, web searches and other archival sources (Zucker and Darby 2007b). We verified that substituting entry dates for those firms gave us essentially the same results as we obtained using the patenting-publication method of identifying firms.

Another concern was that the ISI Highly Cited numbers were large relative to previously used techniques for identifying star scientists in particular technology areas. We restricted our list of stars to the first third reported in ISI – roughly the top 100 in each of the 19 science and engineering fields – and obtained slightly improved results, illustrated in Figure 6.4, drawn from results reported in Tables A.2 and A.4 in Zucker and Darby (2006). The headline results are very similar to those in Figure 6.3, but this is not surprising unless the impact of the remaining stars is higher than those whose information we have discarded from the statistical analysis.

These results are only a first step in demonstrating that the very best and brightest scientists frequently become involved in commercializing their discoveries, often as a founder or co-founder of an entrepreneurial firm. We believe that it is a large first step in the direction of showing that these extraordinary individuals play a role in innovation and growth across the full spectrum of high technology industries.

EMERGENCE AND MIGRATION OF TOP SCIENTISTS

Given the right institutional conditions, a significant fraction of star scientists become star innovators who drive growth and progress via creating and transforming high-technology industries, usually while continuing to make major contributions to science. These individuals are true geniuses in the original sense – not just having extraordinary intelligence and transcendent creativity but actively using it to transform their world and ours. Finding time and resources to do all that they are doing is an ongoing struggle and they rarely become involved in starting new companies or transforming existing ones very far from where they are doing the rest of their work. Therefore, the geographies of technological progress and star scientists tend to coincide. In this section we will consider where the stars begin their professional careers, change regions or locations of residence and/or enter new scientific fields.

Economic geography provides us with the useful concepts of agglomeration and diffusion, which are two sides of the same coin. Agglomeration occurs with respect to a particular measure of interest if concentration

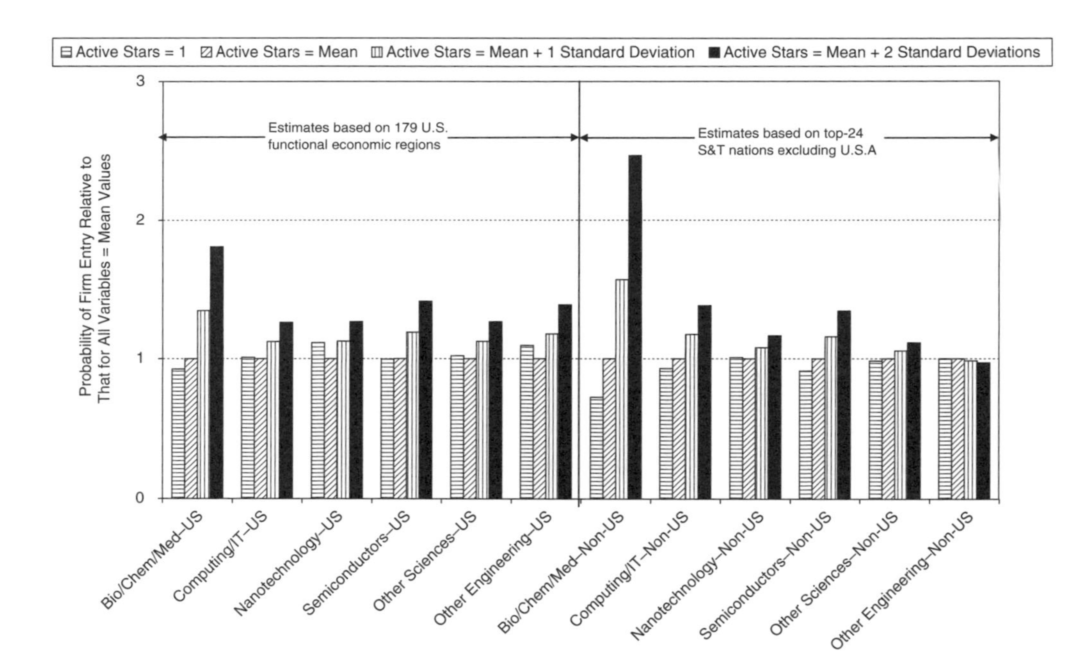

Note: All other variables = mean values.

Source: Zucker and Darby (2006)

Figure 6.4 Star scientists and engineers increase the probability of firm entry into new technologies. Stars defined as first 1838 (first 34%) in ISI HighlyCited^{SM}: relative probabilities with different numbers of active stars

is increasing over time: regions or countries with larger values of this measure have disproportionately high growth rates for the same measure while those with lower values have disproportionately low growth rates. High-technology industries, for example, tend to concentrate over time or agglomerate in a relatively few centers, and knowledge in a specialty or subspecialty tends to grow faster in centers which have achieved a 'critical mass' of scholars (Zucker *et al.* 2007). Diffusion is the mirror image of agglomeration: regions or countries with smaller values have disproportionately high growth rates for the measure being considered while those with higher values have disproportionately low growth rates. Diffusion is the goal of many economic development schemes, notably in the European Union, as well as a natural process for the spread of knowledge.

The correlation coefficient of the level and growth rate of a variable measured across regions or countries and over time is a direct index of agglomeration or diffusion. If the correlation coefficient (which ranges from −1 to 1) is positive, the variable is agglomerating, while a negative correlation coefficient shows that the variable is diffusing over time. In Table 6.2, we present these correlation coefficients for a number of variables of interest and for different sets of countries. Whether we look at US regions or any of the listed combinations of the top 25 S&T countries in the world, university article publication is diffusing, with traditionally weaker regions and countries tending to catch up with traditional scientific leaders. This suggests that more regions and countries will over time provide a fertile ground for new star scientists to emerge where before it would be very difficult. This observation is confirmed – but more weakly – by the tendency for high-impact articles (those that are very highly cited by other scientists) to diffuse, although that diffusion is statistically significant only where the US is not included in the set of countries.

The third line for each geographical comparison tells us that firm entry is in fact agglomerating across the gamut of broad high-technologies both across US regions and across the non-OECD (developing) countries among the top 25 S&T countries. On the other hand, this tendency toward concentration of broad high-technologies is not statistically significant or non-existent for the geographic comparisons, including 18 (without US) or 19 (with US) of the OECD (developed) countries. Whether or not high-technology firm entry is agglomerating seems to be determined in substantial part by whether or not star scientists are agglomerating, with that tendency being strongest across US regions and across the non-OECD countries among the top 25 S&T countries. Star scientists' entry shows strong agglomeration and tends to drive agglomeration of the number of star scientists resident in a region or country unless offset by migration (Zucker and Darby 2007c).

Table 6.2 Agglomeration or diffusion? Correlation coefficients for the levels and growth rates of articles, firm entry and star scientists and engineers

	Correlation Coefficients of Level and Growth Rate across Years and Regions/Countries by S&T Field[1]					
	Bio/Chem/Med	Computing/IT	Nanotechnology	Semiconductors	Other Sciences	Other Engineering
US Regions						
University Articles[2]	−0.07**	−0.08**	−0.09**	−0.08**	−0.04^	−0.04^
High-Impact Articles[2]	−0.02	−0.04	−0.03	−0.03	−0.03	−0.04
Firm Entry	0.09***	0.16***	0.22***	0.20***	0.17***	0.04*
Star Scientists & Engineers	0.04^	0.08**	0.19***	0.07**	0.11***	0.19***
Star Scientist Entry	0.29***	0.53***	0.85***	0.60***	0.73***	0.73***
Top-25 S&T Countries						
University Articles[2]	−0.16***	−0.18***	−0.18***	−0.21***	−0.08*	−0.16***
High-Impact Articles[2]	−0.08^	−0.06	−0.08	−0.05	−0.05	−0.05
Firm Entry	−0.04	−0.01	0.00	−0.02	−0.02	−0.04
Star Scientists & Engineers	−0.05	0.04	−0.01	0.00	0.02	0.01
Star Scientist Entry	0.01	0.12*	0.53***	0.13*	0.18**	0.28***
Top-24 Non-US S&T Countries						
University Articles[2]	−0.29***	−0.29***	−0.23***	−0.27***	−0.15***	−0.26***
High-Impact Articles[2]	−0.15***	−0.01	−0.13*	−0.09*	−0.11*	−0.09^
Firm Entry	−0.03	0.10*	0.20***	0.05	0.06	−0.05
Star Scientists & Engineers	−0.06	0.04	0.20***	0.08^	0.08	0.17**
Star Scientist Entry	0.19***	0.73***	0.93***	0.64***	0.73***	0.83***

Table 6.2 (continued)

	Correlation Coefficients of Level and Growth Rate across Years and Regions/Countries by S&T Field[1]					
	Bio/ Chem/Med	Computing/ IT	Nanotech- nology	Semi- conductors	Other Sciences	Other Engineering
Non-OECD Countries:						
University Articles[2]	−0.42***	−0.18*	−0.16^	−0.32***	−0.19*	−0.39***
High-Impact Articles[2]	−0.10	0.22**	−0.08	−0.12	−0.11	−0.12
Firm Entry	0.13	0.28**	0.45***	0.29**	0.42***	0.03
Star Scientists & Engineers	0.00	0.05	0.67***	0.31***	0.75***	0.42***
Star Scientist Entry	0.65***	0.84***	0.90***	0.83***	0.96***	0.95***
OECD Countries (Including US)						
University Articles[2]	−0.16***	−0.20***	−0.19***	−0.21***	−0.17***	−0.16***
High-Impact Articles[2]	−0.08^	−0.07	−0.09	−0.08^	−0.06	−0.05
Firm Entry	−0.05	−0.01	0.00	−0.02	−0.03	−0.04
Star Scientists & Engineers	−0.02	0.06	−0.02	0.00	−0.01	0.00
Star Scientist Entry	0.00	0.13*	0.52***	0.13*	0.17*	0.25**
OECD Countries (Excluding US)						
University Articles[2]	−0.3***	−0.32***	−0.24***	−0.26***	−0.29***	−0.24***
High-Impact Articles[2]	−0.17***	−0.03	−0.15*	−0.14**	−0.12*	−0.09^
Firm Entry	−0.03	0.08	0.09	0.07	0.04	−0.05
Star Scientists & Engineers	−0.02	0.06	0.19**	0.07	0.02	0.15*
Star Scientist Entry	0.19**	0.72**	0.94***	0.63***	0.72***	0.81***

Notes:
Significance levels: $^{\wedge}$ 0.10, * 0.05, ** 0.01, ***0.001

1. The science and engineering areas are Biology/Chemistry/Medicine; Computing and Information Technology; Semiconductors, Integrated Circuits and Superconductors; Nanoscale Science and Technology; Other Sciences; and Other Engineering. Nanoscale Science and Technology articles and patents as defined for NanoBank.org are removed from the other five areas into which they would otherwise be classified.
2. University and high-impact articles are measured as knowledge stocks computed as perpetual inventories with the input series, the current year's publication of all university or high-impact articles respectively, and the depreciation rate set at 20 per cent per year. These variables were among those used in the analysis of firm entry and accordingly articles with authors affiliated with firms were excluded in counting the input series.

Source: Zucker and Darby (2007c), Table 5 and Zucker and Darby (2006), Table 8.

Overlaying this pattern during the last quarter century, however, are movements of many US-trained foreign students who build successful careers in American academe, perhaps moving from lower to higher ranked US universities, but choose to return home when their native countries develop sufficient strength in their disciplines to both seek them out and to be attractive (Saxenian 2005). This weakens the tendency toward concentration when the US is in the country data set, but not when it is out. Since this effect is present to a somewhat similar degree in all American universities, the reverse brain drain of expatriate stars affects the average growth rate of stars in the US without weakening the positive correlation across countries.

Table 6.3 presents novel evidence on the location and migration of star scientists and engineers among the top 25 S&T countries. About 93 per cent of the world's star scientists and engineers in the world had residences in the top 25 S&T countries at the end of 2004 – 62 per cent in the US alone.[8] It should be noted that non-US scientists suspect that ISI citation measures and therefore the ISI Highly Cited are inherently biased in favor of English-speaking and particularly American scientists (and, in fact, there must be published English translations of titles and abstracts for a non-English language article to be ISI-listed). The dominant factor determining the number of stars resident in a country at the end of the period or at any time during the period is the number of professional debuts made in the country. Future stars are more likely to get their first job where they want to live and they tend to stay there. However, migration does make a difference for some countries and losing even one or two dominant firms founded by emigrants to other countries can be a significant economic event.

Table 6.3 shows clear evidence of reversal of the traditional brain drain from other countries, particularly less-developed ones, to the US and other science powerhouses like Britain and Germany. The four largest net emigrations of star scientists over the last quarter century were registered by the United Kingdom (−27 or 4.6 per cent of all stars resident in the country at any time 1981–2004), the United States (−23 or 0.6 per cent), Canada (−23 or 7.7 per cent) and Germany (−11 or 3.0 per cent). Recall that Table 6.1 showed that for biotechnology stars (defined by genetic sequence discoveries, not citations) 1973–1989, the US and Germany had inward net migration of 2.9 and 8.3 per cent respectively; so for these countries there is evidence of a reversal of direction.[9]

For the six developing countries near the bottom of Table 6.3, round-trip inward migration (where a star moves there for more than two years but later leaves) provides a significant source of brain power and innovation accounting for from 33 to 79 per cent of all star scientists ever resident

Table 6.3 Star scientists' professional debuts and migration rates: top-25 science and technology countries, 1981–2004

	Professional Debuts[2]	Outward Migration		Inward Migration		Net Inward Migration[5]	Net Stock[6]	Unique Persons[7]
		One-way[3]	Round-trip[4]	One-way[3]	Round-trip[4]			
OECD Member Countries								
Europe								
Austria	14	6	1	2	20	−4	10	36
Belgium	37	7	1	2	15	−5	32	54
Denmark	29	5	3	5	15	0	29	49
Finland	14	2	1	0	7	−2	12	20
France	135	20	19	22	114	2	137	265
Germany	222	35	17	24	123	−11	211	362
Italy	60	14	11	16	47	2	62	120
Netherlands	78	10	4	8	30	−2	76	115
Norway	12	2	1	3	13	1	13	27
Poland	6	4	3	1	15	−3	3	22
Spain	13	1	1	8	29	7	20	49
Sweden	70	12	7	5	40	−7	63	112
Switzerland	80	17	7	27	45	10	90	148
United Kingdom	424	70	31	43	122	−27	397	581
Europe[1]	*1194*	*205*	*107*	*166*	*635*	*−39*	*1155*	*1960*
APEC Member Countries								
Non-US APEC Countries								
Australia	97	15	10	25	49	10	107	170
Canada	201	51	13	28	72	−23	178	300

Table 6.3 (continued)

	Profes-sional Debuts[2]	Outward Migration		Inward Migration		Net Inward Migration[5]	Net Stock[6]	Unique Persons[7]
		One-way[3]	Round-trip[4]	One-way[3]	Round-trip[4]			
Japan	176	5	15	18	76	13	189	266
South Korea	1	0	0	4	7	4	5	12
Non-US APEC[1]	*475*	*71*	*38*	*75*	*204*	*4*	*479*	*748*
United States	3354	142	276	119	216	−23	3331	3670
APEC Countries[1]	*3829*	*213*	*314*	*194*	*420*	*−19*	*3810*	*4418*
OECD Member Countries[1]	**5023**	**418**	**421**	**360**	**1055**	**−58**	**4965**	**6378**
OECD Non-member Countries								
Brazil	1	1	0	3	15	2	3	19
China	4	1	0	11	26	10	14	39
India	10	3	1	3	14	0	10	27
Israel	57	13	5	4	28	−9	48	86
Russia/USSR	7	4	0	4	27	0	7	36
Taiwan	3	1	0	5	6	4	7	14
OECD Non-member Countries[1]	**82**	**23**	**6**	**30**	**116**	**7**	**89**	**221**
Top-25 S&T Countries[1]	**5105**	**441**	**427**	**390**	**1171**	**−51**	**5054**	**6599**
Top-24 Non-US S&T Countries[1]	**1751**	**299**	**151**	**271**	**955**	**−28**	**1723**	**2929**

Notes:

1. Totals of individual country values have not been adjusted for double counting due to within-region migration.
2. Each person who publishes or patents giving an address in the country the first year that person publishes or patents anywhere is counted as making a professional debut in the country. It is possible for one star to make a professional debut in more than one country and in a country other than the country of his or her birth or citizenship.
3. One-way immigration refers to the person stopping publishing or patenting in a country where they had been doing so and starting doing that in another country with no subsequent return to the first country. "Visits" of 2 years or less do not count for inward or outward migration.
4. Round-trip immigration refers to the person stopping publishing or patenting in a country where they had been doing so and starting doing that in another country and subsequently returning to the first country. "Visits" of 2 years or less do not count for inward or outward migration.
5. Net inward migration is one-way inward migration minus one-way outward migration. Round-trip inward and outward migration leave the stock of stars unchanged.
6. The net stock of stars is the number making professional debuts in the country plus one-way inward migration minus one-way outward migration, with no adjustment for death or retirement due to lack of information on when that occurs.
7. Unique persons is a count of the number of stars who have ever published or patented with an address in the country.

Source: Zucker and Darby (2007c) Table 6

in those countries, 1981–2004. Moreover, about 20 per cent of all inward migrant stars to these countries had not returned as of 2004, mostly due to those remaining in China and Taiwan.

At this point we read the evidence on migration of stars as cautionary for the US, but alarming for some other countries (such as Canada, Germany, Israel and the United Kingdom). We also see hope for some developing countries that inward migration (frequently of native-born, foreign-educated stars) can provide an important supplement to home-grown stars if working and living conditions are right to attract and retain them (Zucker and Darby 2007c).

CONCLUSIONS

> From the bare economic point of view the importance of geniuses is only beginning to be appreciated. How can we measure the cash-value to France of a Pasteur, to England of a Kelvin, to Germany of an Ostwald, to us here of a Burbank? One main care of every country in the future ought to be to find out who its first rate thinkers are and to help them. Cost here becomes irrelevant, the returns are sure to be so incommensurable. (William James 1911, pp. 363–364)

William James – the father of American psychology and a first-rate thinker – apparently foresaw the extraordinarily high estimates of the return current in the economics of S&T literature and perhaps the coming of the National Science Foundation, the National Institutes of Health and their sister institutions in the US and other countries. However, democratic values largely trumped the study – much less appreciation or even mention – of geniuses as a politically incorrect vestige of the 'great man theory' which should be consigned to the dustbin of history. It is only the accumulation of stubborn facts that has persuaded us that this view is fundamentally wrong so far as it comes to understanding innovation.

Innovation is mostly not about the accumulation of small changes – inching up as the Japanese would have it – but about the rare occurrence of very large improvements in how to do things or what can be done. Inching up may be better done by 100 journeyman engineers than 1 or 2 scientific geniuses but great innovations are much more likely to come from the geniuses.

The star scientists in this chapter are remarkably energetic, and when they see that one of their discoveries has substantial commercial value and the incentives (including funding more research) are right, they find a way to sell their idea to an existing firm or create a new one to commercialize it. They are opportunists in the best senses of the word: creating opportunity, seeing it where others do not and carrying it forward with a drive that gets things accomplished despite an already overfull agenda. James calls on the government to help them, but often it is enough to simply stay out of their way. They are quite used to helping themselves and smart enough to speak of team work, generally relying on small teams of extraordinary scientists or scientists in training (Zuckerman 1977).

The American system of research universities has been remarkably effective in providing a flexible home base for star innovators to work from. For decades America attracted the best and brightest from around the world to come for a doctoral education. The very best of these often never left, contributing to US growth. A century and a half ago Germany benefited from its similar role as the center of science. James included among his four exemplars of genius with obviously great cash value Wilhelm Ostwald (1853–1932), the 1909 Nobel Laureate for Chemistry for his work on catalytic reactions and Professor of Physical Chemistry at Leipzig University in Germany, 1887–1906. In the commercial realm, the Ostwald process for producing nitric acid remains a mainstay of the modern chemical industry. We should note that Ostwald, a native of Riga, Latvia, was also an exemplar of the value of brain drain to the receiving country.

Our earlier research has shown the importance of star scientists in their commercial role of star innovators creating the dominant firms in important industries driven by rapid scientific progress. Our results on firm entry suggest that this is true across the broad range of high-technology industries. The individuals at the very top of their scientific discipline are the ones most likely to fundamentally change how things are done in their science and in its commercial applications. America has profited greatly from providing a seed bed for producing and retaining most of these people for the last sixty years. There is evidence that recent policy changes such as on student visas have endangered that privileged status. It would be a very costly loss.

ACKNOWLEDGEMENTS

This research has been supported by grants from the Ewing Marion Kauffman Foundation, the National Science Foundation (grants SES-0304727 and SES-0531146) and the University of California's Industry–University Cooperative Research Program (grants PP9902, P00-04, P01-02 and P03-01). We are indebted to our research team members Emre Uyar, Jason Fong, Robert Liu, Tim Loon, Hongyan Ma and Amarita Natt. Certain data included herein are derived from the Science Citation Index Expanded, Social Sciences Citation Index, Arts & Humanities Citation Index, High Impact Papers and ISI Highly Cited of the Institute for

Scientific Information®, Inc. (ISI®), Philadelphia, Pennsylvania, USA: © Copyright Institute for Scientific Information®, Inc. 2005, 2006. All rights reserved. Certain data included herein are derived from the Zucker–Darby Science & Technology Agents of Revolution (STAR) database © Lynne G. Zucker and Michael R. Darby. All rights reserved. This chapter is a part of the NBER's research program in productivity. Any opinions expressed are those of the authors and not those of their employers or the National Bureau of Economic Research.

NOTES

1. Baumol, Litan and Schramm (2007) argue persuasively that both small entrepreneurial firms and large dominant firms play important roles in growth and prosperity. Darby and Zucker (2006) argue that the prospect of a small entrepreneurial firm's becoming a large dominant firm provides part of the incentive to bear the costs of turning a great idea into a commercial innovation in a startup firm.
2. This market-based model is an alternative explanation – and empirically superior as discussed below –for the clustering of high-tech industries around universities to achieve positive externalities (such as quicker knowledge diffusion through attending seminars), as advocated in Jaffe (1986), Dorfman (1988), Jaffe, Trajtenberg and Henderson (1993), Bania and Fogarty (1993) and Saxenian (1996). It also differs from the Crane (1969, 1972) invisible colleges view in which geography and bench-science interaction have vanishing importance.
3. These knowledge spillovers play a central role in the economics literature as causes of geographic agglomeration (local concentration) of particular industries and of endogenous growth in the 'New Growth Theory Models' (Romer 1986, 1990; Grossman and Helpman 1991; Jones 1995; Eaton and Kortum 1996, 1999) though the empirical search for their existence has proved difficult (Griliches 1992). Demonstration of statistically significant positive effects on a firm's productivity of being near great universities and other sources of scientific discovery also have been taken as fingerprints of such spillovers by Acs and Audretsch (1987, 1993), Acs, Audretsch, and Feldman (1994), and Mansfield (1995).
4. The stars' contributions to open science are measured in Zucker and Darby (2007a) by the number of articles published per year, given that the citations per article increase in the US and are insignificantly different in Japan.
5. The US Bureau of Economic Analysis defines the 179 regions as functional economic areas such that each US county is assigned to a region which includes the major metropolitan center for which commuting, shopping and newspaper readership predominates (Johnson and Kort 2004). The 25 countries are: Australia, Austria, Belgium, Brazil, Canada, China, Denmark, Finland, France, Israel, India, Italy, Japan, Germany, the Netherlands, Norway, Poland, South Korea, Spain, Sweden, Switzerland, Taiwan, the United Kingdom, the United States, and the USSR & Russia counted as the same country.
6. The curriculum vitae supplied to ISI by authors appears to be in an abbreviated (apparently National Science Foundation or National Institutes of Health) format for 41.0 per cent of these stars, with 37.8 per cent reporting exactly 10 ISI articles and 3.2 per cent reporting 5–9 ISI articles. Since the NSF and NIH formats impose strict 10-publications and 1–3 pages limits (the latter depending on the grant program), listed publications and affiliations are chosen strategically to enhance the odds of funding. Less prestigious, especially commercial, affiliations are also not infrequently omitted from full academic

curricula vitae so we chose to identify location by those listed at the time of publication of articles rather than rely on the ones reported retrospectively.

7. ISI article data do not distinguish which address (normally an organization) goes with which author except for a possible single author designated corresponding author, who then matches (at least) to the corresponding address. The cases indicated in the text are those for which the star scientist can be definitively located with an address because they are the corresponding author, the sole author, or there is only one listed corresponding or research address in a journal that reports multiple addresses on other articles in the same year. The 299 583 authorships corresponded to 276 182 different articles, with the difference (23 401) all accounted for by multiple star authors on articles with a single address.
8. A small number of the stars have residences in two countries, judging from their publications and patents, and a handful made their professional debut simultaneously in two countries, presumably reflecting the locations of their doctoral work and first job.
9. On the other hand, the United Kingdom and Canada had large outward migration rates in Table 6.1 (32.3 and 30.0 per cent, respectively) so those countries were already experiencing a brain drain. Switzerland reversed its direction favorably for that country between the two tables.

REFERENCES

Acs, Zoltan J. and David B. Audretsch (1987), 'Innovation, Market Structure, and Firm Size', *Review of Economics and Statistics*, 69 (4), 567–574.

Acs, Zoltan J. and David B. Audretsch (1993), 'Innovation and Technological Change: The New Learning', *Advances in the Study of Entrepreneurship, Innovation, and Economic Growth*, 6, 109–142.

Acs, Zoltan J., David B. Audretsch and Maryann P. Feldman (1994), 'R&D Spillovers and Innovative Activity', *Managerial and Decision Economics*, 15, 131–138.

Arrow, Kenneth J. (1962), 'Economic Welfare and the Allocation of Resources for Invention', in Richard R. Nelson (ed.), *The Rate and Direction of Inventive Activity: Economic and Social Factors*, NBER Special Conference Series vol. 13, Princeton, NJ: Princeton University Press, pp. 609–625.

Arrow, Kenneth J. (1974), *The Limits of Organization*, New York: W.W. Norton & Company.

Audretsch, David B. and Maryann P. Feldman (1994), 'The Geography of Innovation and Production', in Consorcio de la Zona Franca di Vigo (ed.), *The Location of Economic Activity: New Theories and Evidence*, London: Centre for Economic Policy Research.

Audretsch, David B. and Maryann P. Feldman (1996), 'R&D Spillovers and the Geography of Innovation and Production', *American Economic Review*, 86 (3), 630–640.

Audretsch, David B. and Paula E. Stephan (1996), 'Company-Scientist Locational Links: The Case of Biotechnology', *American Economic Review*, 86 (3), 641–652.

Bania, Neil, Randall Eberts and Michael Fogarty (1993), 'Universities and the Startup of New Companies: Can We Generalize from Route 128 and Silicon Valley?' *Review of Economics and Statistics*, 75, 761–766.

Baumol, William J., Robert E. Litan and Carl J. Schramm (2007), *Good Capitalism, Bad Capitalism, and the Economics of Growth and Prosperity*, New Haven, CT and London, UK: Yale University Press.

Bhidé, A. and H. Stevenson (1990), 'Why Be Honest if Honesty Doesn't Pay', *Harvard Business Review*, 68 (5), 121–29.
Cooke, Philip (2001), 'Regional Innovation Systems, Clusters, and the Knowledge Economy', *Industrial and Corporate Change*, 10 (4), 945–974.
Cooke, Philip (2004), *Globalisation of Bioregions: The Rise of Knowledge Capability, Receptivity & Diversity*, Regional Industrial Research Report 44, Cardiff, UK: Centre for Advanced Studies.
Cooke, Philip (2005), 'Rational Drug Design, the Knowledge Value Chain and Bioscience Megacentres', *Cambridge Journal of Economics*, 29 (3), 325–341.
Crane, Diana (1969), 'Social Structure in a Group of Scientists: A Test of the Invisible College Hypothesis', *American Sociological Review*, 34 (3), 335–352.
Crane, Diana (1972), *Invisible Colleges: Diffusion of Knowledge in Scientific Communities*, Chicago, IL: University of Chicago Press.
Darby, Michael R. and Lynne G. Zucker (1999), *California's Science Base: Size, Quality and Productivity*, Sacramento, CA: California Council on Science and Technology.
Darby, Michael R. and Lynne G. Zucker (2001), 'Change or Die: The Adoption of Biotechnology in the Japanese and U.S. Pharmaceutical Industries', *Comparative Studies of Technological Evolution*, 7, 85–125.
Darby, Michael R. and Lynne G. Zucker (2003), 'Growing by Leaps and Inches: Creative Destruction, Real Cost Reduction, and Inching Up', *Economic Inquiry*, 41 (1), 1–19.
Darby, Michael R. and Lynne G. Zucker (2006), *Innovation, Competition, and Welfare-Enhancing Monopoly*, National Bureau of Economic Research Working Paper No. 12094, Cambridge, MA: NBER.
Darby, Michael R. and Lynne G. Zucker (2007), 'Grilichesian Breakthroughs: Inventions of Methods of Inventing in Nanotechnology and Biotechnology', *Annales d'Economie et Statistique*, 79–80.
Darby, Michael R., Qiao Liu and Lynne G. Zucker (2004), 'High Stakes in High Technology: High-tech Market Values as Options', *Economic Inquiry*, 42 (3), 351–369.
Di Gregorio, Dante and Scott Shane (2003), 'Why do Some Universities Generate More Start-ups than Others?' *Research Policy*, 32 (2), 209–227.
Dorfman, Nancy S. (1988), 'Route 128: The Development of a Regional High Technology Economy', in David Lampe (ed.), *The Massachusetts Miracle: High Technology and Economic Revitalization*, Cambridge, MA: The MIT Press, pp. 240–274.
Eaton, Jonathan and Samuel Kortum (1996), 'Trade in Ideas: Patenting and Productivity in the OECD', *Journal of International Economics*, 40 (3–4), 251–278.
Eaton, Jonathan and Samuel Kortum (1999), 'International Technology Diffusion: Theory and Measurement', *International Economic Review*, 40 (3), 537–570.
Griliches, Zvi (1957), 'Hybrid Corn: An Exploration in the Economics of Technological Change', *Econometrica*, 25 (4), 501–522.
Griliches, Zvi (1992), 'The Search for R&D Spillovers', *Scandinavian Journal of Economics*, 94 (Supplement), 29–47.
Grossman, Gene M. and Elhanan Helpman (1991), *Innovation and Growth in the Global Economy*, Cambridge, MA: The MIT Press.
Harberger, Arnold C. (1998), 'A Vision of the Growth Process', *American Economic Review*, 88 (1), 1–32.
Head, Keith, John Ries and Deborah Swenson (1995), 'Agglomeration Benefits

and Location Choice: Evidence from Japanese Manufacturing Investment in the United States', *Journal of International Economics*, 38 (3–4), 223–247.
Institute for Scientific Information (1981–1997), *Science Citation Index*, machine-readable data bases, Philadelphia, US: Institute for Scientific Information.
Institute for Scientific Information (2005a), *Science Citation Index Expanded, Social Sciences Citation Index, Arts & Humanities Citation Index* and *High Impact Papers,* machine-readable data bases, Philadelphia, US: Institute for Scientific Information.
Institute for Scientific Information (2005b), *ISI HighlyCited*^{SM}, on-line machine-readable data base, Philadelphia, US: Institute for Scientific Information, http://isihighlycited.com/.
Jaffe, Adam B. (1986), 'Technological Opportunity and Spillovers of R & D: Evidence from Firms' Patents, Profits, and Market Value', *American Economic Review*, 76 (5), 984–1001.
Jaffe, Adam B., Manuel Trajtenberg and Rebecca Henderson (1993), 'Geographic Localization of Knowledge Spillovers as Evidenced by Patent Citations', *Quarterly Journal of Economics*, 63, 577–598.
James, William (1911), 'Stanford's Ideal Destiny', in his *Memories and Studies*, New York: Longmans, Green & Co., pp. 356–367.
Jensen, Richard and Marie Thursby (2001), 'Proofs and Prototypes for Sale: The Tale of University Licensing', *American Economic Review*, 91 (1), 240–259.
Johnson, Kenneth P. and John R. Kort (2004), '2004 Redefinition of the BEA Economic Areas', *Survey of Current Business*, November, pp. 68–75.
Jones, Charles I. (1995), 'R&D-Based Models of Economic Growth', *Journal of Political Economy*, 103 (4), 759–784.
Klevorick, Alvin K., Richard C. Levin, Richard R. Nelson and Sidney G. Winter (1995), 'On the Sources and Significance of Interindustry Differences in Technological Opportunities', *Research Policy*, 24 (2), 185–205.
Mansfield, Edwin (1995), 'Academic Research Underlying Industrial Innovations: Sources, Characteristics, and Financing', *Review of Economics and Statistics*, 77 (1), 55–65.
Marshall, Alfred (1920), *Principles of Economics*, 8th ed., London, UK: Macmillan.
National Research Council (1995), *Research-Doctorate Programs in the United States: Data Set*, machine-readable data base, Washington, US: National Academy Press.
Nelson, Richard R. (1959), 'The Economics of Invention: A Survey of the Literature', *Journal of Business*, 32 (2), 101–127.
Nelson, Richard R. and Sidney G. Winter (1982), *An Evolutionary Theory of Economic Change*, Cambridge, MA: Harvard University Press.
Nelson, Richard R. and Edward N. Wolff (1997), 'Factors behind Cross-Industry Differences in Technical Progress', 8 (2), 205–220.
Romer, Paul M. (1986), 'Increasing Returns and Long-Run Growth', *Journal of Political Economy*, 94 (5), 1002–1037.
Romer, Paul M. (1990), 'Endogenous Technological Change', *Journal of Political Economy*, 98 (5, Part 2 – Supplement), S71–S102.
Rosenberg, Nathan (1982), *Inside the Black Box: Technology and Economics*, Cambridge, UK: Cambridge University Press.
Saxenian, AnnaLee (1996), *Regional Advantage: Culture and Competition in Silicon Valley and Route 128*, Cambridge, MA: Harvard University Press.
Saxenian, AnnaLee (2005), 'From Brain Drain to Brain Circulation: Transnational

Communities and Regional Upgrading in India and China', *Studies in Comparative International Development*, 40 (2), 35–61.
Thursby, Jerry G. and Marie Thursby (2002), 'Who Is Selling the Ivory Tower? Sources of Growth in University Licensing', *Management Science*, 48 (1), 90–104.
Yarkin, Cherisa (2000), 'Assessing the Role of the University of California in the State's Biotechnology Economy', in John de la Mothe and Jorge Niosi (eds), *The Economic and Social Dynamics of Biotechnology,* Boston, NJ: Kluwer Academic Publishers.
Zucker, Lynne G. and Michael R. Darby (1996a), 'Costly Information: Firm Transformation, Exit, or Persistent Failure', *American Behavioral Scientist*, 39 (8), 959–974.
Zucker, Lynne G. and Michael R. Darby (1996b), 'Star Scientists and Institutional Transformation: Patterns of Invention and Innovation in the Formation of the Biotechnology Industry', *Proceedings of the National Academy of Sciences*, 93 (23), 12709–12716.
Zucker, Lynne G. and Michael R. Darby (1997a), 'Individual Action and the Demand for Institutions: Star Scientists and Institutional Transformation', *American Behavioral Scientist*, 40 (4), 502–513.
Zucker, Lynne G. and Michael R. Darby (1997b), 'Present at the Biotechnological Revolution: Transformation of Technical Identity for a Large Incumbent Pharmaceutical Firm', *Research Policy*, 26 (4–5), 429–446.
Zucker, Lynne G. and Michael R. Darby (1999a), *California's Inventive Activity: Patent Indicators of Quantity, Quality, and Organizational Origins*, Sacramento, CA: California Council on Science and Technology.
Zucker, Lynne G. and Michael R. Darby (1999b), 'Star Scientist Linkages to Firms in APEC and European Countries: Indicators of Regional Institutional Differences Affecting Competitive Advantage', *International Journal of Biotechnology*, 1 (1), 119–131.
Zucker, Lynne G. and Michael R. Darby (2001), 'Capturing Technological Opportunity Via Japan's Star Scientists: Evidence from Japanese Firms' Biotech Patents and Products', *Journal of Technology Transfer*, 26 (1–2), 37–58.
Zucker, Lynne G. and Michael R. Darby (2006), *Movement of Star Scientists and Engineers and High-Tech Firm Entry*, National Bureau of Economic Research Working Paper No. 12172, April, revised October, Cambridge, MA: NBDR.
Zucker, Lynne G. and Michael R. Darby (2007a), 'Virtuous Circles in Science and Commerce', *Papers in Regional Science*, 86 (3), 468–471.
Zucker, Lynne G. and Michael R. Darby (2007b), 'Socio-economic Impact of Nanoscale Science: Initial Results and NanoBank', in Mihail C. Roco and William S. Bainbridge (eds), *Nanotechnology: Societal Implications II: Individual Perspectives*, Dordrecht, The Netherlands: Springer.
Zucker, Lynne G. and Michael R. Darby (2007c), 'Science, Knowledge, and Firms in Developing Economies', paper presented at *Micro Evidence on Innovation in Developing Economies*, MERIT, United Nations University, Maastricht, The Netherlands, 31 May–1 June.
Zucker, Lynne G., Michael R. Darby and Jeff Armstrong (1998), 'Geographically Localized Knowledge: Spillovers or Markets?' *Economic Inquiry*, 36 (1), 65–86.
Zucker, Lynne G., Michael R. Darby and Jeff Armstrong (2002), 'Commercializing Knowledge: University Science, Knowledge Capture, and Firm Performance in Biotechnology', *Management Science*, 48 (1), 138–153.
Zucker, Lynne G., Michael R. Darby and Marilynn B. Brewer (1998), 'Intellectual

Human Capital and the Birth of U.S. Biotechnology Enterprises', *American Economic Review*, 88 (1), 290–306.

Zucker, Lynne G., Michael R. Darby, Jonathan Furner, Robert C. Liu and Hongyan Ma (2007), 'Minerva Unbound: Knowledge Stocks, Knowledge Flows and New Knowledge Production', *Research Policy*, 36 (6), 850–863.

Zucker, Lynne G., Michael R. Darby and Máximo Torero (2002), 'Labor Mobility from Academe to Commerce', *Journal of Labor Economics*, 20 (3), 629–660.

Zuckerman, Harriet (1967), 'Nobel Laureates in Science: Patterns of Productivity, Collaboration, and Authorship', *American Sociological Review*, 32 (3), 391–403.

Zuckerman, Harriet (1977), *Scientific Elite: Nobel Laureates in the United States*, New York: Free Press.

Index